Zentaro Kitagawa & Karl Riesenhuber (Eds.)

The Identity of German and Japanese Civil Law in Comparative Perspectives

Die Identität des deutschen und des japanischen Zivilrechts in vergleichender Betrachtung

Zentaro Kitagawa & Karl Riesenhuber (Eds.)

The Identity of German and Japanese Civil Law in Comparative Perspectives

Die Identität des deutschen und des japanischen Zivilrechts in vergleichender Betrachtung

W DE G RECHT

De Gruyter Recht · Berlin

Rechtswissenschaftliche Tagung „The Identity of German and Japanese Civil Laws in Comparative Perspectives" 20./21. März 2006, ausgerichtet vom International Institute for Advanced Studies (IIAS) und der Alexander-von-Humboldt Foundation sowie International Forum on the German Year in Kyoto, Japan.

♾ Gedruckt auf säurefreiem Papier,
das die US-ANSI-Norm über Haltbarkeit erfüllt.

ISBN 978-3-89949-432-7

Bibliografische Information der Deutschen Nationalbibliothek

Die Deutsche Nationalbibliothek verzeichnet diese Publikation in der Deutschen Nationalbibliografie; detaillierte bibliografische Daten sind im Internet über http://dnb.d-nb.de abrufbar.

Printed in Germany

Konvertierung/Satz: jürgen ullrich typosatz, 86720 Nördlingen
Druck und Bindung: Hubert & Co., Göttingen
Einbandgestaltung: Christopher Schneider, Berlin

Preface

The year 2006 was the German Year in Japan. For this occasion, the International Institute of Advanced Studies (IIAS) in Kyoto held two *Humboldt Kollegs* in 2005 and 2006 jointly with the *Alexander von Humbolt Stiftung* (AvH) in Bonn. The proceedings of the 2006 conference are contained in this book. It is a comparative enterprise in various respects.

First, the issue of identity is discussed, based on the early studies of *Zentaro Kitagawa* by referring to the historical process in which modern Japanese civil law theory was built upon a substantial reliance on German civil law theory, originating with the *Pandektenwissenschaft* in the 19th century. Notwithstanding that the Civil Code of Japan itself received not only German law but also French law and influences from many other civil law systems, the theory reception was based on German law. Consequently, Japanese law belonged to the German law group in East Asia. Thus, there arose the identity relationship between the two legal systems. Our question is how such identity appears today, and what it will be in the future. Will the identity of Japanese civil law be replaced by the increasingly powerful U.S. impact upon it? Will it then be converted into a historical episode or will it continue to function as the legal infrastructure of Japanese civil law? At the same time, though in a somewhat different context, the question of identity is also being raised in regard of German civil law in light of the new legal system of the EU, even though its identity will basically continue to exist.

Furthermore, the present volume enquires into foreign influences on Japanese national law, to a large extent at the legislative level but also at the judicial and academic levels. Contributions on the development of Japanese law focus on both, aspects of law and of methods. Contributions on German law discuss the influence of EU law and EC legislation on German law. This latter subject is also related back to the discussion on Japanese law when we consider the influence of the *Schuldrechtsmodernisierung* in Germany, triggered by the EC Consumer Sales Directive, on Japanese law. Finally, two contributions deal with the "outsiders' perspective" in discussing the identity of Japanese civil law from a foreign viewpoint.

The thematic thread that runs through all the contributions is the issue of identity. In a time of globalisation and legal harmonisation, the *richesse* of cultural traditions tends to suffer. On the other hand, foreign influences can have a stimulating effect on national law when the native legal tradition is able to absorb and integrate them into the legal system.

The two *Humboldt Kollegs* would not have been possible without the academic exchange memorandum between the AvH and IIAS. The AvH has not only supported the two conferences, it has also supported the publication of the present volume. We are particularly grateful to Dr. *Georg Schütte,* General Secretary of AvH, and Dr. *Heinrich Pfeiffer,* former General Secretary of AvH and IIAS Fellow, for their generous support of the project. Prior to the 2006 conference, IIAS generously supported the English translation of the four Japanese papers for the 2006 conference, and this enabled us to send them to foreign scholars not familiar with the Japanese language as material for comparative consideration. The foreign participants could in turn prepare their own reports as well as reports in response to these Japanese papers. The editors in particular wish to thank Prof. Dr. *Junjiro Kanamori,* Director of IIAS for his cooperation; the editors also wish to thank Prof. Dr. *Atsushi Omura* and Judge *Shintaro Kato* for their generous approval for us to use the four Japanese papers in the 2006 conference. Special thanks are due to Prof. Dr. *Atsushi Takada* for his wonderful organisation of the 2005 conference and to the IIAS research associates, Dr. *Akihiro Matsui,* Mr. *Yoshizumi Nakabayashi* and *Richard C. Kim,* Esq. for their effective support. Finally, the editors wish to thank Ms. *Aleksandra Mojkowka,* mag. iur., Mr. *Mariusz Motyka,* mag. iur., Ms. *Katharina Ziegler* and Mr. *Frank Rosenkranz,* assistants at Ruhr-Universität Bochum, and Ms. *Sarah Rohde*, student assistant at Ruhr-Universität Bochum, for their engaged support in the preparation of this book.

Kyoto and Bochum, July 2007

Zentaro Kitagawa
Karl Riesenhuber

Contents

Authors

Zentaro Kitagawa	Dr. iur., Dr. h.c., Professor emeritus, University of Kyoto, Director of the International Institute of Advances Studies (IIAS)
Taro Kogayu	Dr. iur., Professor at University of Tohoku
Dieter Leipold	Dr. iur., Dr. h.c., Professor at Albert-Ludwigs-Universität, Freiburg i.B.
Stephan Lorenz	Dr. iur., Professor at Ludwig-Maximilians-Universität, München
Tsuneo Matsumoto	Dr. iur., Professor at University of Hitotusbashi
Yoshio Shiomi	Dr. iur., Professor at University of Kyoto
Karl Riesenhuber	Dr. iur., M.C.J. (Austin), Professor at Ruhr-Universität, Bochum
Malcolm Smith	Late Professor at Chuo University and at the University of Melbourne

Abbreviations

a.a.O.	am angegebenen Ort
a.M.	anderer Meinung
ABl.	Amtsblatt
Abs.	Absatz
AcP	Archiv für civilistische Praxis
AGB	Allgemeine Geschäftsbedingungen
Am. J. Comp. L.	American Journal of Comparative Law
Anm.	Anmerkung
ANU	Australian National University
APSR	American Political Science Review
Art.	Artikel
Aufl.	Auflage
BGB	Bürgerliches Gesetzbuch
BGH	Bundesgerichtshof
BGHZ	Entscheidungen des Bundesgerichtshofes in Zivilsachen
BT-Drs.	Bundestags-Drucksache
CCP	Japanese Code of Civil Procedure
CEFL	Commission on European Family Law
cf	*confer*
CFR	Common Frame of Reference
Ch	chapter
CISG	Convention on Contracts for the International Sale of Goods
D. Chr.	Recueil Dalloz et Sirey de doctine de jurisprudence et de législation
d.h.	das heißt
EC	European Communities
ed, eds	editor, editors
ed.	edition
eg	*exempli gratia*
EG	1. Europäische Gemeinschaften (European Communities, s. EC); 2. EG-Vertrag, Vertrag zur Gründung der Europäischen Gemeinschaft, Konsolidierte Fassung mit den Änderungen durch den Vertrag von Amsterdam vom 2.10.1997
EGV	EG-Vertrag, Vertrag zur Gründung der Europäischen Gemeinschaft in der Fassung des Vertrags über die Europäische Union vom 7.2.1992 (Maastrichter Fassung)
et seq	*et sequentes, et sequential*
EU	European Union
EuGH	Europäischer Gerichtshof
EWG	Europäische Wirtschaftsgemeinschaft
f., ff.	folgende

Fn.	Fußnote
h. M.	herrschende Meinung
ICLQ	International and Comparative Law Quarterly
ie	*id est*
IPRax	Praxis des Internationalen Privat- und Verfahrensrechts (journal; Germany)
JZ	Juristenzeitung (journal; Germany)
L.Q.R.	Law Quarterly Review
loc. cit.	*loco citato*
m. E.	meines Erachtens
M.L.R.	Modern Law Review
MJ	Maastricht Journal of European and Comparative Law
n	note
NBL	New Business Law (journal; Japan)
NJW	Neue Juristische Wochenschrift (journal; Germany)
No, Nos	number, numbers
Nr.	Nummer
OJ	Official Journal
OLG	Oberlandesgericht
PECL	Principles of European Contract Law
PICC	Principles of International Commercial Contracts (UNIDROIT-Principles)
RabelsZ	Rabels Zeitschrift für ausländisches und internationales Privatrecht (journal; Germany)
Rn.	Randnummer
Rs.	Rechtssache
s.	see, siehe
S.	See, Siehe; Seite; Satz
Slg.	Sammlung der Rechtsprechung des Europäischen Gerichtshofes
SMG	Schuldrechtsmodernisierungsgesetz
sq	sequens
sqq	sequentes
UBC	University of British Columbia
UK	United Kingdom
ULIS	Uniform Law on the International Sale of Goods
UNICITRAL	United Nations Commission on International Trade Law
UNIDROIT	International Institute for the Unification of Private Law
UNSW	University of New South Wales
U.S.	United States of North America
usw.	und so weiter
vgl.	vergleiche
Vol.	Volume
z. B.	zum Beispiel
ZEuP	Zeitschrift für Europäisches Privatrecht (journal; Germany)

ZEV	Zeitschrift für Erbrecht und Vermögensnachfolge (journal; Germany)
ZPO	Zivilprozessordnung
ZvglRWiss	Zeitschrift für vergleichende Rechtswissenschaft (journal; Germany)

The Identity of German and Japanese Civil Law in Comparative Perspectives

Die Identität des deutschen und des japanischen Zivilrechts in vergleichender Betrachtung

Chapter 1: Introduction: The Identity of Japanese and German Civil Law

Zentaro Kitagawa

Contents

I. Viewpoint of Civil Law system

The Japanese Civil Code has already existed for more than a century since it was put into force in 1898. Although it is true that a number of amendments have been made, the question still arises as to why and how it has survived for such a long period of time. It is largely because the fundamental principles of the Japanese Civil Code still remain valid today, and what is more, the Japanese civil law system has integrated partial amendments to the Japanese Civil Code and also integrated, concurrently or separately, constructions and revisions of the provisions in response to social changes, thereby supporting and maintaining the code. In other words, the civil law system supports the civil code as a formal law, and it assures the life and modernity of the civil code even under circumstances where the provisions set forth in the civil code are insufficiently suited for the current situation. A new legal theory may be generated without any changes in the code provisions, enabling these to correspond to social changes over time. In this respect, the civil law system is double-layered as to its features. This also applies to the German Civil Code and the French Civil Code.

II. The Process toward Creation of a European Civil Code

An important problem that we presently face in comparing Japanese civil law and German civil law is the European Civil Code project. There are various difficulties standing in the way of its realization. The contemplated European Civil Code will be a symbol of a Europe that is not formed as a nation-state but is united as one. However, at the same time, there is still a long way to go before realization of the project.

The critical issue relating to the European Civil Code project in the context of the statement of issues in this symposium is, irrespective as to its feasibility, what kind of civil code a European Civil Code will become. It will not be the same as a civil code of a nation state.

A European Civil Code enacted as a result of greater European integration will be substantially different in nature from the German Civil Code or the French Civil Code. By discussing the nature of the contemplated European Civil Code, we will be able to obtain important suggestions to assist in considering how to envisage Japanese civil law and the Japanese Civil Code in the near future, and more fundamentally, what the future of its civil code should be for Japan.

III. The Position of Japanese Law in Comparative Law

Another issue that should be discussed is where Japanese law is positioned from the viewpoint of comparative law. This issue was highlighted during the period from 1960 through to the 1970s when Japan began to achieve postwar reconstruction. Among comparative law scholars in Europe and the United States of that time, Japanese law was categorized as Asian law or Western European law depending on the cases, and some regarded it as in the process of transforming from Asian law into Western European law. Despite such variations, they all applied the same standard for comparative law analysis, or in other words, they evaluated Japanese law according to the Western standard. In comparative law, Japanese law was evaluated at a distance from the Western model adopted as the evaluation standard. This evaluation method did not preclude a non-Western model but primarily applied the Western model for comparison, bringing about a representative evaluation such as that Japanese law must be included in the category of Western law rather than the category of Far-Eastern law.

In Asian countries and many other non-Western countries that have introduced the Western model, it is becoming more and more important to consider where such countries should turn to for standards for evaluating their own law. I do not intend to delve further into legal categories, legal systems, and jurisdictions across the world in this report, but nevertheless I have to make a brief comment on how Japanese comparative law scholars evaluate Japanese law. They apply a different evaluation standard from that applied by their Western counterparts. There is also a slight difference between evaluation standards used among Japanese scholars, which may result in the view that Japanese law is identical to the Western model or the opposite view that Japanese law is different from the Western model. I consider this difference to arise from the fact that Western comparative law scholars found two evaluation standards for Japanese law – norm based on positive law and norm based on tradition – and excluded the latter from the scope of legal norms, whereas their Japanese counterparts tried to establish a framework for comparison by regarding such tradition-based norm as a legal issue in the broad sense rather than denying it as a non-legal fact. This is inseparably related to the question of where we can find the identity of Japanese law.

IV. Prototype of Japanese Civil Law in Comparative Law

Let us review the historical developments of Japanese civil law. The history of Japanese civil law can be divided into three stages. At the first stage, or the 'commentaries era', efforts were made to commentate on the Japanese Civil Code that had been compiled particularly under the influence of German law and French law, by making reference also to other foreign laws. At the second stage, or the 'theory reception era' from the end of the Meiji era until around the end of the World War I, the construction of Japanese civil law was established based on the theoretical system of German civil law jurisprudence. It was at the third stage, or the 'comparative law era', that Japanese civil law scholars stopped placing excessive emphasis on German law and began to use foreign laws equally for reference.

The Japanese Civil Code is a product of the reception of aspects of various foreign civil codes, especially the German and French Civil Codes, and the prototype of Japanese civil law jurisprudence was formed by adding legal theories received from German jurisprudence onto that hybrid civil code. Through such historical developments up to the present day, Japanese civil law came to have a dual structure. In the process of this reception of legal theories, alien elements of law introduced in Japan through the reception of foreign civil codes were absorbed and merged into the structure of Japanese civil law by applying German civil law theories. From the viewpoint of comparative law, Japanese jurisprudence was cast in a mould of German jurisprudence through theory reception. In making a comparison between before and after this theory reception, textbooks, academic papers, and legal texts repeatedly used in court decisions prove out this fact. Thus, the prototype of Japanese civil law jurisprudence can be deemed to have been formed through this theory reception.

That the theoretical system of Japanese civil law was built through this process is a historical fact, irrespective of the issue of how it should be evaluated. German jurisprudence once existed as almost an absolute authority for Japanese law and Japanese jurisprudence, to a significant extent and for a considerable length of time, as a matter of fact, for some time after the end of the World War II. Research papers and textbooks written during the theory reception era clearly depict the situation at that time, where Japanese legal scholars scrambled to introduce German legal studies for the purpose of construing Japanese law rather than understanding German law. Scholarly opinion is now divided as to how Japan's reception of legal theories should be evaluated.

What should be noted now is that the prototype of Japanese civil law jurisprudence, which was formed through the theory reception of German law, has provided the concepts and institutional basis of the existing law. Therefore, how to define the scope of historical developments for evaluation is an issue of legal history, and at the same time, it is an issue for today.

V. Identity of Japanese Civil Law

We should keep questioning how Japanese civil law will develop while confirming its identity, after going through the theory reception era and making independent progress during the comparative law era. The current civil law construct encompasses Anglo-American law, French law, and German law as subjects of comparison depending on individual scholars' original views. When we pause in the midst of such somewhat apparent trends, we find ourselves facing questions such as how we have created our civil law, from what viewpoint we are to compare it with foreign laws, what the essence of our civil code is, and in which direction it will go in the future. Concerning this respect, the issue of the identity of Japanese law should be brought for discussion at this symposium.

During the theory reception era, Japanese jurisprudence was under a strong influence of legal positivism based on German conceptual jurisprudence. Reflection and criticism of such tendencies in the post-war period increased interest in law reflecting social reality. Through the progress from such trends, the independence theory evolved in Japanese civil law construction. The independence theory was developed based on internal criticism regarding the traditional dogma favoring construction based upon the German *Pandektensystem*. The independence theory is constructed using critical theory against German civil law, based on the historical study of German civil law theories as the vertical axis and the comparison between Anglo-American law and Continental Civil Law as the horizontal axis.

VI. The 2001 Reform of the German Civil Code

The German Civil Code was reformed in 2001. Through this reform, initial impossibility is no longer regarded as a ground for invalidation of contract, and the binary code provision regarding nonperformance of obligations, consisting of delay in performance and impossibility of performance, have been incorporated into an integrated code provision regarding nonperformance of obligations. Liability for defects in things is now included in the law of nonperformance. These changes suggest that the German *Pandektenwissenschaft* in the 19th century has finally moved on. This means that *Ernst Rabel's* argument, which criticized the German Civil Code while taking Roman law into consideration one hundred years ago, has come true.

However, there is one thing that still remains the same, that is the *Pandektensystem.* It still exists in the reformed civil code just like an immovable wall. The retention of the *Pandektensystem* will raise a significant question for re-construction of civil law and civil code in the future, and movements toward establishing various EU laws including a European Civil Code will encourage such questioning attitudes. We, the Japanese law scholars, should regard it as an issue that not only affects Europe but also directly relates to our practical problem of where Japanese civil law should be directed relative to the global trends of comparative law.

VII. Civil Law Model in the Near Future

German civil law will inevitably change in the midst of the movement towards unifying Europe. It is certain that *Pandektensystem* will not be able to maintain its existence as a closed and self-contained legal system as it had before. How will the German Civil Code change along with the European Civil Code project? How about Japanese civil law and the Japanese Civil Code?

Civil law will sustain its vitality as a fundamental law as long as the market economy system continues to exist. However, it will inevitably change through harmonization and globalization of private laws. The image of civil law in the near future will be that of an integrated law that retains diversity. Such civil law will serve as a fundamental law that provides for a national market economy while reflecting pluralism of social systems, and at the same time, it will also serve as a fundamental law that provides for cooperation in the global market economy.

Part 1: Foreign Influences on Japanese Civil Law

Chapter 2: Japanese Civil Law and German Law

– From the Viewpoint of Comparative Law –

Zentaro Kitagawa

Contents

I. Introduction

Between Japanese civil law and German law, there has been a history of exchange that spans more than a century. Even today, German law has a close relationship not only with Japanese civil law jurisprudence but also with Japanese jurisprudence as a whole. Particularly, the 2001 revision of the German Civil Code offers an opportunity to review the Japanese civil law jurisprudence. This article was written based on such problem awareness.

This article starts from the search for the prototype of Japanese civil law jurisprudence from the viewpoint of comparative law. Specifically, the relationship between Japanese civil law and German jurisprudence, particularly the historical development of Japanese civil law jurisprudence's relationship with *Pandektenwissenschaft* and German civil law jurisprudence as its successor, is analyzed (Part I). Next, after defining German influence, which formed the prototype of Japanese civil law jurisprudence as 'theory reception', we examine Japanese civil law jurisprudence by focusing on the two-tier structure of Japanese civil law consisting of the reception of codes and the reception of legal theory (Part II). Finally, we point out that, in order to develop legal theories for achieving independence from the prototype, it was necessary to make critical study on German civil law jurisprudence during and after Japan's reception of German legal theories, and, in this regard, we also refer to the 2001 revision of the German Civil Code (Part III).[1]

1 This Chapter aims to highlight problems in Japanese civil law jurisdiction, by focusing on comparative law, particularly on the relationship between German jurisprudence and Japanese civil law jurisdiction. First, it should be noted that, although the title of each chapter is named in general terms, exhaustive analysis of the issues represented by those titles is not the purpose of this Chapter. Accordingly, I adopted a method of electing some specific examples and examining the issues represented by the chapter's title through such examples. Here, for readers' reference, I would like to briefly introduce my works that are related to the subject of this Chapter. I started my research on civil law from analysis on the *Pandektenwissenschaft* and doctrinal history of civil law, which was a methodology commonly used in the postwar period of Japan. The achievements from such research are the above-mentioned *Keiyaku Sekinin no Kenkyu – Kouzou-Ron* [A Study of Contractual Liability: A Theory of its Structure] (Tokyo 1963); 'Songai-Baisho-Ron Josetsu – Keiyaku Sekinin ni Okeru' [A Preliminary Discussion on Damages – From the Viewpoint of Contractual Liability]

More specifically, I examine anew the prototype of Japanese jurisprudence generated through the reception of German legal theories and the theories proposed for achieving independence from the prototype as discussed in my books, *Keiyaku Sekinin no Kenkyu – Kouzou-Ron* [A Study of Contractual Liability: A Discussion on the Structure of Obligations Law] (1963), *Nihon-Hougaku no Rekishi to Riron – Minpougaku wo Chushin to shite* [History and Theories of Japanese Jurisprudence: Particularly for Civil Law Jurisprudence] (1968), and *Rezeption und Fortbildung des europäischen Zivilrechts in Japan* (1970) (hereinafter these books are referred to as *Contractual Liability*, *History and Theories* and *Rezeption und Fortbildung*). In other words, I attempt to review my past discussion on the prototype and theories of independence made about 40 years ago. Here, the expression 'the prototype' and 'theories of independence' was used for explaining my research made in those days from the viewpoint of today. The methodology adopted in this article may be useful for clarifying the significance of the 2001 revision of the German

Nos. 1 and 2, 43-1 *Hougaku Ronsou* at 1-42 and 43-3 *Hougaku Ronso* at 17–57 (1963); 'Songai Baisho no Shiteki Hensen' [Historical Development of Damages] 73-4 *Hougaku Ronso* at 1–71 (1963). Then, I had a doubt about why most studies on doctrinal history of Japanese civil law traced back to German jurisprudence as if it were taken for granted. At that time, it was common that the historical study on civil law, when it comes to the period before Meiji, traced back to the history of German civil law or German common law (*gemeines Recht*) in Europe far way from Japan, not to the law of the Edo period. During my stay in Munich University from July 1963 to February 1966, I addressed this issue squarely. Particularly in the later period of my stay, my main interest shifted to the study on Japan's reception of German jurisdiction mainly in the area of civil law, and as an academic result of it, I wrote a paper to clarify that Japanese civil law had a two-tier structure in which the reception of German legal theory was grafted onto the mixed reception of the German and French Civil Codes. I brought back this 'Munich paper' to Japan and, by supplementing supporting materials, completed it as 'Gakusetsu Keiju – Minpougaku Hatten no Ichi Sokumen' [The Reception of Legal Theories: An Aspect of the Development of the Civil Law Jurisprudence] Nos. 1–8, 194, 195, 196, 198, 204, 207, 211 and 213 *Hanrei Times* (1966–1967), which was, after some modification, published as *Nihon-Hougaku no Rekishi to Riron – Minpougaku wo Chushin to shite* [History and Theories of Japanese Jurisprudence: Particularly for Civil Law Jurisprudence] (Tokyo 1968). Afterward, the 'Munich paper' was also published as a book entitled *Rezeption und Fortbildung des europäischen Zivilrechts in Japan* (Arbeiten zur Rechtsvergleichung Bd. 45, Frankfurt a.M. 1970) in Germany, also after supplementing the supporting materials and literature.

Civil Code for the future of Japanese civil law jurisprudence, if it is conducted by considering the historical development of the relationship between Japanese and German jurisprudence from the viewpoint of comparative law.

The German Civil Code was enacted in 1896 and came into effect in 1900. In 2001, about a century after its enactment, part of obligations law was revised, and the revised Code was put into force as of January 1, 2002. Although much drastic revision was proposed initially, it was not fully realized after many twists and turns. However, the 2001 revision still can be regarded as a major revision. Before revision, the German Civil Code was an heir of *Pandektenwissenschaft* and its obligations law had a system that firstly distinguished initial impossibility of performance from subsequent impossibility and then structured rules of nonperformance of obligation or contractual liability based on subsequent impossibility. In addition, liability for defects in things was treated as a special statutory liability separated from contractual liability. Although criticism of such doctrine of impossibility of performance was proposed from the time immediately after its enactment, it took about a century before such criticism was reflected in the German Civil Code by the 2001 revision. As a result of this revision, a contract aimed at an initially impossible delivery is no longer held invalid; the importance of subsequent impossibility, which had served as a foundation for nonperformance of obligation in the Civil Code before revision, diminished performance and nonperformance is treated as liability for breach of obligations; and liability for defects in things became a part of contractual liability.

The 2001 revision of the German Civil Code raised new questions for both German jurisprudence and Japanese jurisprudence. In this regard, the first thing that strikes us is the part of the German Civil Law *changed* by the revision. The contents of this change are structurally similar to the theories which I proposed in my "Contractual Liability" for Japanese civil law. It is time to re-examine the future of Japanese civil law, which has been built on the *Pandektenwissenschaft* and subsequent German jurisprudence. When doing so, needless to say, it is important to make comparative analysis of the *changed* part, and this Chapter also mainly focuses on it. However, comparative study of the *unchanged* part of the German Civil Code, i.e., the Pandektensystem, is by no means less important to that of its *changed* part. I believe that we should examine what implication the *unchanged* part of the German Civil Code has on comparative study of law and Japanese civil law jurisprudence. If we examine both the *changed* part and *unchanged* part of the German Civil Code in the context of the globalized legal environment, I believe that we can obtain insights that will be helpful in finding the desirable future picture of the Japanese Civil Code.[2]

[2] This Chapter, whose title in Japanese was 'Nihon Minpou to Doitsu-Ho – Hikaku-Ho no Siten kara', was prepared from my keynote speech entitled 'Nihon Minpou to Doitsu-Ho – Hikaku-Ho-Shi no Shiten kara' [Japanese Civil Law and German Law: From the Viewpoint of Comparative Study on Doctrinal History] in the 2004 Seminar for Experts 'Dai Ikkai Nihon-Ho no Rekishi to Tenbou – Gaikoku-Ho no Keiju to Sono Hensen' [History and Prospect of Japanese Law – The Reception of Foreign Legal Theories and Its Development] held at Legal Research and Training Institute. The phrase 'Comparative study of legal history' is changed to 'comparative law', because this Chapter discusses not only past issues but also present and future issues (this Chapter was partly presented at the 2005 Japanese Society of History of Law as an invited report). In short, that keynote speech gave me the opportunity to reexamine the issue that I first studied as a legal scholar, almost forty years later. In that article, I attempted to analyze the development of Japanese civil law jurisprudence in a certain period of time and future tasks derived from it, by using three my previous works as a basis for doing so.
For reference, the contents of my keynote speech were as follows.
Part I. The Prototype of Japanese Civil Law Jurisprudence Viewed from the Perspective of Comparative Law
1. Liability for defects in things as an example
2. The reception of German legal theory
3. Obligations law of the *Pandektenwissenschaft* and the German Civil Code
Part II. Lessons of Comparative Study of Legal History: Critical Development of the Reception of Legal Theories
4. Structure of contractual liability
5. Historical transition of law of damages
6. The prototype of Japanese civil law jurisprudence: Its evaluation and its future development
7. Comparison of law of contracts between common law and civil law
8. Open system
9. Model contract law
Part III. Comparative Study on Doctrinal History and Future of Japanese Civil Law Jurisprudence
10. Image of the Civil Code in near future
11. Status and problems of Japanese civil law jurisprudence
12. Three models of law

II. Prototype of Japanese Civil Law Study from Viewpoint of Comparative Study of Law

1. Liability for Defects in Things

First, I wish to start my discussion by using 'liability for defects in things' as an example. One of the classic examples of cases involving liability for defects in things is as follows:

> The seller, a realty company, had delivered the land to the buyer, and the buyer finished the registration of land transfer. However, a portion of the land caved in after heavy rain, and it was found that it was due to an error in the seller's land formation work.

When a hidden defect is found in the subject matter of a contract as illustrated by the above example, the buyer is entitled to claim damages and terminate the contract. The seller's liability for defects in things is regarded as one of strict liability.[3] The idea of 'liability for defects in things' has its origins in *aedilicis action* under ancient Roman law, which was introduced separately from *ius civile* in order to protect buyers of slaves or livestock from unscrupulous merchants. The Roman law of *aedilicis action* was, through the reception, adopted by and established in European civil law as the theory of 'liability for defects in things'.[4] When European countries started the codification, this liability for defects in things theory was also incorporated in the civil codes in each country. In that era, liability for de-

This Chapter was prepared by bringing together Topics 1-4 and 6. Initially, I had planned to address all topics in the keynote speech. However, in order to meet the deadline of this special issue, I had no choice but to focus only on the historical relationship of German law and Japanese civil law. Regarding its significance for the present and the future, also, I could not discuss issues other than those relating to the 2001 revision of the German Civil Code. Fortunately, this feature issue includes *Kogayu's* report on French law, the study of which had became a major trend in Japanese civil law jurisprudence led by Professor *Eiichi Hoshino*, and *Matsumoto's* report on the common law, which has exercised great influence on Japanese jurisprudence. So, I would like to ask the readers to refer to those articles for issues I could not discuss in this Chapter.

3 For the following discussion, see Kitagawa (1968: 'History and Theories'), n 1 *supra*, 110 et seq; Kitagawa (1970: 'Rezeption und Fortbildung'), n 1 *supra*, 75–76.

4 See K. Yunoki, *Urinushi Kashi Tanpo no Kenkyu* [Study of Buyer Warranty] (Tokyo 1993) 1; Kitagawa (1963: 'Contractual Liability'), n 1 *supra*, 99.

fects in things was, reflecting its origin, separated from contractual liability for default and was treated as a seller's special strict liability that arose from sales transactions. In Germany, such orientation was further conceptually developed by the *Pandektenwissenschaft*.

In the era of the formulation of the modern system of law from the 18th century to the 19th century, commercial transactions were mainly conducted for specific things. Therefore, civil law systems in that era had structures that responded to such a transaction structure. This is the same for the *Pandektenwissenschaft* in Germany as well as the German Civil Code, which was regarded as a system that mainly focuses on specific things rather than indeterminate things.[5]

In the *Pandektenwissenschaft* in Germany and German civil law jurisprudence (which was the successor of the former), the concept prevailed that 'any performance of an obligation to deliver a specific thing should be regarded as indefectible performance, even if a defect is found in the delivered specific thing' (the 'dogma of specific things'). In other words, most German law scholars in that era believed that when a transaction is made over a specific thing, if the specific thing already has a defect at the time of conclusion of the contract, it is impossible for the seller to deliver that specific thing with no defect, and therefore the buyer cannot insist on contractual liability for default of the seller.[6] This paradoxical but theoretical reasoning was certainly an attractive point of German civil law at that time and was received by civil law jurisprudence in Japan.

Here, one may wonder what actually happened in civil law jurisprudence in Japan. I explained that by showing how *Santaro Okamatsu*, a leading civil law scholar in Japan at that time, changed his doctrine on liability for defects in things.

First, in the books *Minpo Riyuu* (Reasons for Civil Law), which were written immediately after the enactment of the Japanese Civil Code, he explained that liability for defects in things is a form of contractual liability as follows:

5 K. Ballerstedt, 'Zur Lehre vom Gattungskauf', in R. Dietz, A. Hueck & R. Reinhardt (eds), *Festschrift für Nipperdey* (Munich, Berlin 1955) 262, 263; Kitagawa (1963: 'Contractual Liability'), n 1 *supra*, 181.
6 Kitagawa (1963: 'Contractual Liability'), n 1 *supra*, 168.

> 'A seller should not be regarded as having completed his obligation only by transfer of the right to the buyer. In any case, a seller should deliver the thing with appropriate quality. Because a seller has such an obligation, the liability for defects in things as well as in rights, is only an aspect of seller's obligation that has arisen as an effect of a sales transaction.'[7]

However, he completely denied this interpretation in a subsequently published book, *Mukashitsu Songai Baisho Sekinin Ron* (Discussions on Strict Liability).

> 'It is reasonable to consider that a seller only has obligation to deliver the goods in the required condition at the time of conclusion of the contract. Of course, when such goods lack the value or quality that is ordinary regarded to, or is contractually contemplated to, reside in such goods, as mentioned above, the seller should be held to liable to such defect. However, seller's liability in such case cannot arise from a default of his contractual obligation. This is because, even if the delivered goods have a defect, sellers should be regarded as having completed performance of their obligation by delivering the goods to the buyer, the seller no longer has a right to make claim for delivery.'[8]

Both of the above citations are from *Okamatsu's* explanations on the issue of liability for defects in things. As shown above, although he once regarded it as a form of default of contractual obligation in *Minpo Riyuu* (Reasons for Civil Law), he changed his mind and insisted that liability for defects in things was not a type of nonperformance of obligations in his later book, *Mukashitsu Songai Baisho Sekinin Ron* (Discussions on Strict Liability). In other words, although he maintained his opinion that liability for defects in things was a type of nonperformance of obligation even after enactment of the Japanese Civil Code, he completely denied such an argument after having studied in Germany.

What happened to *Santaro Okamatsu* who was one of the persons cooperating in the preparation of the Civil Code? If such a phenomenon was observed only himself in the field of civil law at that time, we may conclude that the influence of German civil law jurisprudence exercised a strong influence just on him. However, this was not the case. At that time, not only *Okamatsu* but the vast majority of

7 S. Okamatasu, *'Minpo Riyuu [Ge]'* [Reasons for Civil Law [Vol. 3]] (Tokyo,1899) 52–53.
8 S. Okamatasu, *Mukashitsu Songai Baisho Sekinin Ron* [Discussions on Strict Liability] (Tokyo,1916) 587–588, 122 and 140 (cited from the book republished as *Gakujutsu Sensho III* [Part III of Academic Selection] in 1953).

civil law scholars accepted German theory on liability for defects in things and earnestly strived to develop a system for civil law construction in accordance with German jurisprudence. Such a trend was observed not only with regard to the issue of liability of defects in things but also for other areas of civil law, which brought about an overall conversion of the Japanese civil law structure. In other words, for a period of time, civil law study in Japan was under the sway of German legal theories. In the next section, I will introduce some other examples.

2. Systemization of Japanese Civil Law Jurisprudence under German Influence

A structural conversion similar to the one that occurred for the doctrine of liability for defects in things did occur also in other areas of Japanese civil law. As a result, a system of civil law constructions had arisen in Japan that was completely different from the constructions adopted at that time of enactment of the Civil Code, which, at the same time, had brought tense relations between the provisions of the Civil Code and its construction. In this section I will try to outline such conversion by using some examples.

a) Initial impossibility and subsequent impossibility

In the *Pandektenwissenschaft*, it is no exaggeration to say that discussions on impossibility for sellers to deliver constitute the backbone of the law of obligations. In Germany at that time, it was considered that impossibility of delivery was a generic concept and nonperformance of obligation was one of its species, and even that delay in performance should be understood as temporary impossibility (impossibility with regard to time of performance).[9] Although the German Civil Code did not go so far as to incorporate the latter argument in its provisions of the German Civil Code, subsequent

[9] Proponents of this dogma mentioned that delay in performance was considered as impossibility of timely performance to the extent that it passed over the timeline of performance. See F. Mommsen, *Beiträge zum Obligationenrecht – Abt. 3: Die Lehre von der mora* (Braunschweig 1855) at 27; Kitagawa (1963: 'Contractual Liability'), n 1 *supra*, 16–23.

impossibility of obligation was regarded as a main category of nonperformance of obligation. Another important component of the 'impossibility' doctrine is initial impossibility. In § 306 of the former German Civil Code, the famous thesis, 'a contract whose purpose is to deliver something that is impossible to deliver from the outset is null and void' was provided. This idea can be traced back to the concept of *impossibilium nulla est obligatio* (nobody has any obligation to the impossible) under Roman Law.[10]

By using these two concepts (initial impossibility and subsequent impossibility), the impossibility doctrine became able to cover the entire area of law of obligation and nonperformance of obligation, and to be systematically structured based on the dichotomy of these two types of impossibility. This dichotomy also enabled to distinguish nonperformance of obligation from initial impossibility, and as a result of this, discussions on nonperformance of obligation came to be limited only to nonperformance of effective obligations. In other words, the issue of nonperformance of obligation was limited to subsequent impossibility and other subsequent hindrances to perform an obligation (regarding this issue, see *infra,* III 1).

In Japan, the so-called *Boissonade* Civil Code (which was promulgated in 1890, but never enforced) also provided that initial impossibility made a contract null and void (Article 323(1)). However, this provision was omitted in the process of drafting the current Civil Code because the drafters believed that it was unnecessary to be provided by an explicit provision. In other words, the drafters of the Japanese Civil Code agreed and clearly stated that initial impossibility made a contract null and void. However, Japanese drafters neither attached much importance to this thesis nor attempted to use the concept of initial impossibility as a basis for building a system of obligations and contractual liability. The commentary on the law of obligations also did not regard this as a general thesis.[11]

10 T. Isomura, '*Impossibilium Nulla Obligatio Gensoku no Keisei to Sono Hihan Riron*' [Formation of the impossibilium nulla obligatio principle and its Critical Theories], in M. Katsumoto & K. Mura (eds), *Ishida Bunjiro Kanreki Kinen Ronbunshu* [Collected Papers for the Anniversary of Prof. Bunjiro Ishida's 60th Birthday] (Tokyo 1955) 399.

11 See Kitagawa (1968: 'History and Theories'), n 1 *supra*, 40–42.

Shortly after that, however, this rule was established as a solid legal doctrine.[12] Such conversion is a result of the definitive influence of *Pandektenwissenschaft* and German civil law jurisprudence as its successor. Under such German influences, doctrines of law of obligations and contractual liability in Japanese civil law changed greatly in both conceptual and structural terms, and discussions on impossibility of performance and delay in performance almost exclusively followed German theories.

b) Contractual liability

From the viewpoint of the comparative study of law, the discussion on contractual liability may be seen as a classical example of such reception of German legal theory. Article 415 of the Japanese Civil Code was drafted basically based on French law, but also by referring to other countries' laws. This article is a provision for setting basic rules regarding nonperformance of obligation. The draft provision first submitted to the Code Investigation Committee provided that 'if an obligator fails to effect performance in accordance with the tenor and purport of the obligation, the obligee may demand compensation for damages, provided that the obligor is responsible for cause of the failure to effect performance'. This was changed to current form for the reason that it seems unreasonable to include impossibility of performance in the expression 'failure to effect performance'. Consequently, this provision was considered to cover both delay in performance and impossibility of performance, but had a different nature from the default provision in the German Civil Code which regarded that nonperformance of obligation was limited only to those two categories (delay in performance and impossibility of performance).[13]

At the time of enactment of the Civil Code, scholars explained that 'to effect performance in accordance with the tenor and purport of the obligation' was to deliver the subject matter of the obligation at the proper time and proper place and in a manner that fitted the pur-

12 See Kitagawa (1968: 'History and Theories'), n 1 *supra*, 42–44.

13 See Kitagawa (1968: 'History and Theories'), n 1 *supra*, 38. As an article that examined default provisions from the viewpoint of Civil Code structure, see Z. Kitagawa, 'Saimufurikou no Kouzou to System' [Structure and System of Default of Obligation] 116 *Hougaku Ronsou* (Nos.1–6) at 217–257 (1980).

pose of the obligation and thereby to completely perform the obligation (liability for defects in things was considered as an example of this duty). The term of impossibility of performance was used as a mere explanatory note in this connection and impossibility of performance was not treated as an important category of contractual liability at that time. In addition, many scholars explained that impossibility of performance arisen through no fault of the obligor constituted a ground for releasing the obligor from the obligation. Furthermore, imperfect performance, which is now regarded as a category of default, was not known.[14]

Shortly after, however, this situation changed dramatically and the Civil Code came to be construed in a completely different manner. This is because civil law scholars introduced the German default provision's bipartite structure of delay in performance and impossibility of performance and the principle underlying such parallel structure (ie initial impossibility theory) into Japan and these concepts became the conceptual backbone of Japanese law of obligations. At the same time, theories on positive breach of an obligation or imperfect performance, which played the role of covering the *lacuna* of the default provisions in the German Civil Code, were also introduced and accepted in Japan. Certainly, Japan's introduction of these concepts may be understood as a form of reception of foreign legal theories, but we should not forget that Japan's situation differed somewhat from that of German civil law. In the beginning of the 20th century the German civil law doctrine went through an agonizing experience: a *lacuna* was found in the German Civil Code immediately after its enactment (from viewpoint of legal positivism of conceptual jurisprudence, such *lacunae* should not exist in the Civil Code). The theory of positive breach of obligatory rights and imperfect performance were introduced into German civil law only after intense confrontations and tension within civil law circles. On the other hand, Japanese civil law jurisprudence accepted these theories without resistance. As a result, the German-type tripartite structure theory fast became the prevailing legal theory for discussion on law of nonperformance of obligation. The fact that Article 415 provides a comprehensive category of nonperformance and therefore has no *lacuna*

14 See Kitagawa (1968: 'History and Theories'), n 1 *supra*, 38 (n 31 and 32).

such as that found in German Civil Code's provisions on nonperformance of obligation may also promote such wide acceptance of tripartite theory. This German tripartite structure theory maintained its position as the prevailing theory in Japan's civil law jurisprudence for a long period of time before and after World War II – even after World War II it maintained its prevailing position for a considerable period of time.[15] During this period, an uniform requirement vanished for nonperformance of obligation from the theory of nonperformance of obligation and contractual liability in Japan.

c) Compulsory performance

With regard to compulsory performance, the construction of Article 414 of Japanese Civil Code was changed completely from premodern interpretation of 'direct compulsion of performance' to something similar to the 'compulsory performance' concept adopted by the German Code of Civil Procedure. Firstly, it should be noted that Article 414 of the Japanese Civil Code on compulsory performance is read as meaning something other than its wording suggests. More specifically, the term 'compulsory performance' that appeared in the first and second paragraph of Article 414 has been read narrowly and construed as meaning compulsion of direct performance only. Furthermore, it has been understood that, in addition to specific performance and alternative performance, this provision allows indirect compulsion as the third form of compulsory performance. Although this construction is still adopted in Japan, it should be regarded as a modification of the Civil Code rather than an allowable interpretation of the Civil Code.

At the time of enactment of the Japanese Civil Code, however, this provision was construed in a different manner. Article 414 is a provision that has its origins in the *Boissonade* Civil Code and the French Civil Code. At that time, the term 'compulsory performance' in Article 414(1) was understood as 'direct compulsion of performance' which may include even physical restraint of the obligor. Accordingly, alternative performance provided in the second paragraph of the same article was understood literally to mean an alternative

15 See Kitagawa (1968: 'History and Theories'), n 1 *supra*, 42–45; Kitagawa (1970: 'Rezeption und Fortbildung'), n 1 *supra*, 68–71.

method for compulsion of performance that could be used where direct compulsion could not be conducted. In addition, the phrase 'where the nature of an obligation allows compulsory performance' of Article 734 of the Japanese Code of Civil Procedure (CCP) was understood to mean delivery of a non-fungible thing. Therefore, at that time, the term 'compulsory performance' used in the Civil Code was understood as direct compulsion of performance (alternative performance was not included in direct compulsion) and the same term used in the CCP as indirect compulsion of performance. Opinion was even submitted by some scholars that indirect compulsion of performance provided in the CCP should be understood as an act by the State which forced the obligor to perform the obligation.[16]

Partly because of the fact that the German Civil Code has no provision on compulsory performance and partly because of the necessity to overcome the problem that Article 414 had adopted a legal concept of 'direct compulsion of performance' which may allow physical restraint of the obligor and was inconsistent with principles of modern laws, discussions on the issue of compulsory performance had become very complicated. In such a situation, scholars eventually made up the current form of construction of Article 414 by relying on German civil law jurisprudence. In short, the current construction of Article 414 which, as mentioned above, should be called 'modification of the law' rather than mere interpretation, was brought about as a result of the incongruity between the provisions of Article 414 of the Civil Code and those of Article 734 of the CCP and such incongruity was set aside by scholars who at the time of reception of German legal theories developed their construction based on the German CCP.[17]

d) Damages

The provisions on damages in the *Boissonade* Civil Code were under the direct influence of the French civil law. In contrast, Article 416 of the current Civil Code was not drafted by completely relying on French law but by referring to legal systems of various countries.

16 See Kitagawa (1968: 'History and Theories'), n 1 *supra*, 57, 61–62.
17 See Kitagawa (1968: 'History and Theories'), n 1 *supra*, 56–58; Kitagawa (1970: 'Rezeption und Fortbildung'), n 1 *supra*, 73–74.

From viewpoint of comparative law it should be noted that the provisions on damages in the Japanese Civil Code were strongly influenced by a UK precedent.

However, during the period of the reception of German legal theories, both the legal concept of damage and the principle of compensation were changed to adopt German civil law theories. This example clearly shows how strongly German civil law jurisprudence exercised its influence on Japan's civil law. Though Article 416 of the current Civil Code adopted the specified concept of damage and restrictive damages principle, Japan introduced the German "difference theory" (*Differenztheorie*) which was a uniform concept established by the *Pandektenwissenschaft* in the 19th century and the principle of complete compensation which was supported by difference theory. These German theories on damages became the prevailing theories in Japan.

The draft provisions of Article 410 (which corresponded to current Article 416) submitted to the Code Investigation Committee provided that 'a claim for damages shall be for the compensation by the obligor of such damage as would ordinarily arise from the nonperformance of an obligation. With regard to damage that the parties had foreseen or could have foreseen from the beginning, even if such damage has arisen through special circumstances, the obligee may claim damages therefore'. These draft provisions had already introduced a theory that the scope of damages should be determined according to causation, irrespective of whether or not the damage occurred as a direct consequence of the obligor's act or omission. Also, in this draft provision the scope of damages did not depend on culpability of the obligor. Accordingly, it can be considered that the draft provisions had already departed from the French law system. However, the provisions on damages were modified three times before they finally became the current text (Article 416) and the distinction between general damages and special damages was introduced into it as a result of the influence of the UK's preceding court decision in *Hadley* v. *Baxendale* (1854).[18]

Such legislative history indicates that Article 416 was generally construed as adopting the restrictive damages principle. However, when

18 See Kitagawa (1968: 'History and Theories'), n 1 *supra*, 64–68, 73–74.

reception of German legal theories started, German doctrines such as the difference theory, the uniform concept of damage and the doctrine of adequate causation were introduced in Japan, bringing about drastic changes in the structure of Japanese civil law theory and rapidly attaining the position of the prevailing theory. In other words, Article 416 of the Civil Code, which was originally drafted based on foreign concepts that were of a different nature from German law, had been completely redyed a German colour.[19]

Article 416 has, from the viewpoint of comparative law, its origins in common law (or its ancestor, French law) and adopted neither the concept of damage based on difference theory nor the principle of complete compensation. Nevertheless, Japanese civil law jurisprudence adopted German legal theory despite its different nature. In specific individual cases, this inconsistency had caused rather strong tension between the original German theory and the Japanized German theory (ie the German theory as modified and prevalent in Japan). In any event, the law on damages represents an excellent example of German-influenced systemization of Japanese jurisprudence.

e) Cancellation

Originally, Article 541 of the Japanese Civil Code was drafted as a provision for setting the basic rules for cancellation of a contract. In other words, the phrase 'if one of the parties fails to perform his obligation' in that article was originally understood as corresponding to the phrase 'if an obligator fails to effect performance in accordance with the tenor and purport of the obligation' in Article 415. Although Article 541 did not adopt a structure based on implied condition subsequent which had been adopted in the cancellation provisions of the French Civil Code and the *Boissonade* Civil Code, the concept of right to change a legal relationship (*Gestaltungsrecht*) was not known at that time. Furthermore, it was considered that the effect of cancellation was an *in personam* effect by which the contract was treated as if it had never been entered into.

[19] See Kitagawa (1968: 'History and Theories'), n 1 *supra*, 75–80; Kitagawa (1970: 'Rezeption und Fortbildung'), n 1 *supra*, 73–75.

Such understanding of Article 541 was completely changed by the reception of German legal theories. The scope of this article was narrowed down from a general cancellation provision to a cancellation provision only for delay in performance. Furthermore, most scholars came to consider that the effect of cancellation was *in rem.* In other words: when the cancellation right, which was a kind of right to change a legal relationship, was exercised, the contract was retrospectively extinguished. In short, although the text of Article 541 has never changed, its construction was altered. As a result, however, a new *lacuna,* which could not arise under the initial construction, had arisen: Due to the abovementioned narrowing down of the scope of Article 541, although its language still covers imperfect performance, it came to be understood not to cover imperfect performance. In order to overcome such problem, some scholars adopting the prevailing theory even created a construction that either Article 541 or Article 543 should apply in such a case depending on whether the imperfectness could be cured or not.[20] Furthermore, while in Germany compensation for expectation interest was not allowed as an effect of cancellation (Articles 325 and 326 of the former BGB) the Japanese Civil Code provided that damages could be claimed even in a case of cancellation. Accordingly, the position on this issue adopted in the German Civil Code is clearly different from that adopted in the Japanese Civil Code. However, Japanese civil law jurisprudence adopted the German direct effect theory – which was then the prevailing theory in Germany – through reception of German legal theories which brought about inconsistencies between academic legal theory and the texts of the Civil Code. Since the obligation of payment of damages was expressly provided in the Civil Code and therefore could not be ignored, some civil law scholars at that time even attempted to propose that the statutory obligation of payment of damages should be considered as a rule based on policy considerations for protecting obligees. Anyway, regarding this issue, the academic theories at that time were more or less unclear. It is considered that what brought about such situation was the perceived importance of the German direct effect theory under which the existence of contract itself was legally denied and therefore expectation interest,

20 See Kitagawa (1968: 'History and Theories'), n 1 *supra*, 86.

which requires the existence of contract as its premise, could not arise.[21]

In this section, we outlined the fact that, although no revision was made to the Japanese Civil Code, a large gap was generated between the civil law theories at the time of enactment of the Civil Code and those adopted at the first quarter of the 20th century as a result of the overwhelming influence of German civil law jurisprudence. Why has such a phenomenon occurred? How can we understand it?

III. Reception of Civil Code and Reception of Legal Theories

1. Mixed Reception of Foreign Civil Codes

As is generally known, during the drafting process of the Japanese Civil Code, French law exerted an overwhelming influence on Japanese civil law through a series of lectures given by Professor *Gustave Boissonade*, an invited foreign jurist, and the preparation of the former Civil Code (*Boissonade* Civil Code). However, the former Civil Code was never enforced and in 1898 the current Civil Code was enacted and enforced instead. The latter was drafted by using as its model the draft German Civil Code which was the successor of *Pandektenwissenschaft*.

In the background to such development is the fact that the German Empire won the Franco-Prussian War in 1871 and emerged as a great power in Europe and then that Japan, an emerging nation in Asia, decided to follow the German model in terms of national strength, culture, arts, science and technology. Such pro-German orientation was

21 See Kitagawa (1968: 'History and Theories'), n 1 *supra*, 96–98; Kitagawa (1970: 'Rezeption und Fortbildung'), n 1 *supra*, 75–76. Even in Germany, it was only after Japan's reception of German legal theories that the theory of right to damages for reliance interest in case of cancellation of a contract was developed. Therefore, in Japan at the time of the reception, no scholar discussed that right to damages, which are allowed to claim simultaneously with obligation of restoration arisen from cancellation, was right to damages for reliance interest.

brought about by the political upheaval in 1881.[22] As a result of this, enforcement of the former Civil Code, which was already enacted and was scheduled to enter into force in 1893, was postponed by Law No. 8 of 1892. In the meantime, the Code Investigation Committee decided to adopt the *Pandektensystem* of the draft German Civil Code in the Japanese Civil Code and after a short period of deliberations the new Civil Code was enacted and enforced in 1898. Enforcement of the Japanese Civil Code was two years earlier than that of the German Civil Code.[23]

[22] Z. Kitagawa, 'Nichidoku Hougaku no Isseiki' [A Century of Japan and German Jurisprudence] 116 *Hougaku Ronsou* (Nos. 4-6) at 68; Z. Kitagawa, 'Ein Jahrhundert deutsch-japanische Rechtswissenschaft', in Hans G. Leser (ed), *Ein Jahrhundert deutsch-japanische Rechtswissenschaft* (Marburg 1990) 13–38.

[23] The following chronological table shows how the former Civil Code (Boissonade Civil Code) was abolished and how the current Civil Code was enacted: it shows that the former Civil Code, despite already having been enacted in 1890 and scheduled to become effective in 1893, had its enforcement postponed in 1892 (ie only one year before the scheduled enforcement) and was eventually abolished with no parts of it ever being enforced.
(i) In March 1890, Articles 1–285 of the Property and its Acquisition Part, Claim/Security Part and Evidence Part of the former Civil Code were promulgated by Law No. 28 of 1890. In October, the Human Affairs Part and Articles 286–435 of the Property and its Acquisition Part were also promulgated by Law No. 98 of 1890. All of these Parts were scheduled to become effective from January 1, 1893.
(ii) In November 1892, Law No. 8 postponed the Civil Code, Commercial Code and Law concerning Application of Laws in General until December 31, 1896.
(iii) In April 1896, Books 1–3 of the new Civil Code were promulgated as Law No. 89 of 1896, which also abolished the Part of the former Civil Code that was promulgated by Law No. 28 of 1890.
(iv) In December 23, 1896, enforcement of the remaining Part of the former Civil Code (the part promulgated by Law No. 98 of 1890) was again postponed by Law No. 94 of 1896 until June 30, 1898.
(v) In June 21, 1898, Books 4 and 5 of new Civil Code were promulgated as Law No. 9 of 1898. On that day, the remaining Part of the former Civil Code was abolished.
(vi) By Imperial Decree No. 123, All of the five Books of the new Civil Code (the current Civil Code) were enforced from July 16, 1898.
As recent literature regarding drafting of the Civil Code, see M. Katou, 'Nihon-Minpou Hyakunen-Shi' [A History of a Hundred Years of Japanese Civil Law], in M. Katou et al. (eds), *Minpou Gakusetsu Hyakunen-Shi – Nihon Minpou Shikou Hyakunen Kinen* [A History of a Hundred Years of Civil Law Theories in Japan – A Hundred Years Anniversary of Enforcement of Japanese Civil Code]

However, it should be noted that, although the current Civil Code adopted the *Pandektensystem,* French influence still remains in a considerable number of its provisions as already discussed in relation to provisions on cancellation and compulsory performance. Furthermore, as *Nobushige Hozumi*, a jurist who participated in the drafting of the Civil Code, noted that the Civil Code was a product of comparative study of laws,[24] the current Civil Code was drafted by referring not only to the German and French civil codes but also to those of other various countries. When considering the influence of those foreign civil codes, it may be said that the Japanese Civil Code was a product of the mixed reception of the German Civil Code, the French Civil Code and various other foreign civil codes.[25]

2. Discontinuity between the Civil Code and Civil Law Theories

As already discussed, *Minpo Riyuu* (Reasons for Civil Law), the three-volume book by *Santaro Okamatsu*, is an article-by-article commentary on the Civil Code and includes various related foreign laws. In this book we can find no influence of the *Pandektenwissenschaft.* The same is true for other civil law textbooks of that time. However, during the short period from the enactment of the Civil Law to around 1921 the entire picture of Japanese civil law was redrawn by German jurisprudence, a successor of the *Pandektenwissenschaft.* As a result, a definite discontinuity arose between the civil law theories prevalent at the time of enactment of the Civil Code and the legal theories that emerged through the influence of German jurisprudence and immediately dominated the entire field of Japanese civil law.

(vol. 2, Tokyo 1999); T. Maeda(ed), *Shiryo Minpouten* [Historical Materials for Research of the Civil Code] (Tokyo 2004) 1116.

24 N. Hozumi, *The New Civil Code* (Tokyo, 912) 22.

25 For French influence on the Japanese Civil Code, E. Hoshino, 'Nihon Minpouten ni Ataeta France Minpouten no Eikyo, No.1' [Influence of the French Civil Code on Japanese Civil Code, No.1] 3 *Nichifutsu Hougaku* 1 (1965), also included in *Minpou Ronshu* Vol. 1 (1970) 69; Kitagawa (1968: 'History and Theories'), n 1 *supra*, 30; Kitagawa (1970: 'Rezeption und Fortbildung'), n 1 *supra*, 34. Also see Katou, n 23 *supra*; Maeda & Harada (ed), n 24 *supra*, at 3.

In this regard, is might be useful to look back upon my past research experiences, because they were quite common to what Japanese legal researchers from the 1950's to the 1970's experienced. When I started to study civil law, I was interested in determining the historical or contemporary significance of this discontinuity. I encountered it when I started my study from examining the history of Japanese civil law theories and frequently asked myself 'why are German legal theories, not other foreign legal theories, mainly referred to in the *de lege lata* analysis of Japanese Civil Code?', 'Why do Japanese civil law theories have their roots in the *Pandektenwissenschaft*?' and 'why can German civil law theory, which was developed for construing the German Civil Code, form the basis for Japanese jurisprudence?', as briefly discussed by giving some examples in the preceding part (*supra,* II).

However, *de lege lata* analysis of Japanese civil law theories alone cannot solve these problems, even though it enables us to locate them or confirm their existence. In order to solve them, it is required to examine Japanese civil law and foreign civil laws at the same time within a common discipline. Such a necessity was strongly felt particularly during my stay and study in Germany. In order to study Japanese and German civil laws in a manner that would enables us to find correlation between them it was first required to find a common platform for doing so. As such a platform, I decided to explore the issue of 'reception of foreign law' and I began the basic study necessary for that purpose. I also studied jurisprudence methodology and comparative study of common law and civil law.[26]

In the final half of my stay in Munich I spent much time verifying hypotheses. In other words, I analyzed what happened in specific important areas of Japanese civil law. Although some constraints

26 I learnt many important matters that helped me to create the category of 'reception of foreign legal theory' and determine the roots of Japanese civil law jurisprudence, particularly from K. Larenz, *Methodenlehre der Rechtswissenschaft* (Berlin, Göttingen, Heidelberg 1960) and J. Esser, *Grundsatz und Norm in der richterlichen Fortbildung des Privatrechts* (Tübingen 1956). This two works contrast each other. The former is a book on methodology of legal study written by K. Larenz, who was my mentor in Munich and a heavyweight of traditional German civil law jurisprudence, and the latter is the monumental work of J. Esser, a leading authority in comparative study of laws.

existed with regard to availability of Japanese materials, I had the experience of researching the minutes of the Code Investigation Committee as a part of my study on the structure of contractual liability before going to Germany and the knowledge gained from that study helped a great deal.[27] During this period I gradually strengthened my belief in the hypothesis that, apart from reception of foreign codes, another type of reception of foreign law occurred in Japan. From this hypothesis I created the concept of 'theory reception'.[28]

3. What is Theory Reception?

As explained above, the reception of foreign law offered a common platform for me to re-evaluate Japanese law from the viewpoint of comparative law. Through it, I successfully found the unique relationship between German and Japanese jurisprudence. The scope of such relationship was greater than expected. After the process of re-

27 After the return to Japan, my work confirming my hypothesis on the historical development of Civil Code construction during the Meiji Period by historical materials became full-fledged. The work had been made at the time when history of Japanese modern law *(nihon kindai hoshi)*, a relatively new academic field, was not yet established. At that time, a considerable quantity of valuable literatures in the Meiji Period stored at the book stock room of the Faculty of Law Library of Kyoto University still remained unorganized. It cannot be denied that I felt some resentment about the unjustifiably great difference between treatment for legal literature of Western Countries and that for Japanese legal literature of the Meiji Period. At the same time, however, I certainly enjoyed the work of organizing that Japanese literature, which was even not allocated call numbers, by taking them one by one and classifying them. As a matter of course, I sometimes felt limits to my ability to organize literature. But, it was undoubtedly a pioneering work and those day brought intellectual excitement to me.

28 At that time, no discussion treated 'theory reception' as one of the categories of reception of foreign law. For example, see T. Sawaki, 'Hou no Keiju' [Reception of Foreign Law] 14 *Gendai-Ho* [Modern Law] 115 (1966). However, it cannot be denied that this expression started to garner attention. For example, M. Okuda, 'Nihon-Ho ni okeru Gaikoku-Ho no Sesshu: Doitsu-Ho' [Absorption of Foreign Laws into Japanese Law: In Case of German Law] 14 *Gendai-Ho* [Modern Law] 218 (1966) distinguished reception of foreign legal theory from reception of foreign code and noted that 'on the whole, it may be concluded that Japan's law system was reorganized from French-type law system to German-type one'. Also, I had already used the expression 'legal theory reception' before having started full-scale study on reception of foreign law (Kitagawa (1963: 'Contractual Liability'), n 1 *supra,* 307 (n 17) and 388–389).

ception of foreign civil codes, German legal theories sweepingly invaded into Japan and immediately dominated over Japanese jurisprudence which should be understood as another process of accepting foreign law that was something more than a mere influence of foreign legal theory. I gave it the name 'theory reception'. In other words: 'When academization *(Verwissenschaftlichung)* occurs with regard to a certain existing law, there may be cases in which lawyers (in most cases, jurists) in that country, by essentially relying on the jurisprudence of a particular foreign country, reconstruct or modify all aspects or at least various important aspects of that law in a manner that greatly deviates from the normative structure that that law originally had. I call such a phenomenon 'theory reception'.'[29]

Generally, reception of foreign law may be divided into two processes: the process of reception of foreign law(s) and the process of

29 See, Kitagawa (1968: 'History and Theories'), n 1 *supra,* 25 and 144; Kitagawa (1970: 'Rezeption und Fortbildung') n 1 *supra,* 17, 67 and 189. For 'academization (Verwissenschaftlichung)' see n 44, Chapter 3. 'During the process of theory reception, foreign legal order, which has been formed based on legal theory different from that adopted by Japanese Civil Code, broke into and gradually achieved dominance over the legal order represented by Japanese Civil Code. It can be understood that such a phenomenon occurred because the importation of German legal theory into Japanese legal order base on its positive law was achieved through its institutionalization among then Japanese jurists. As a result of this, the way of legal thinking of Japanese jurists and legal practitioners was converted into German-type one. (...) Thus, even if 'theory reception' as discussed above differs in its nature from reception of foreign codes, it still can be regarded as another form of reception of law' (Kitagawa (1968: 'History and Theories'), n 1 *supra,* 154). It goes without saying that reception of foreign legal theory occurred essentially at the dimension of logical elements of law. It did not bring about major conversion at the dimensions of factual elements or value elements (ie principles adopted for drafting the Japanese Civil Code). Because such a conversion occurred only at the dimension of logical elements of law, reception of German legal theory occurred so extensively. For the issues of reception of legal theory and law-making, see Kitagawa (1968: 'History and Theories'), n 1 *supra,* 333 (particularly 378) and Kitagawa (1970: 'Rezeption und Fortbildung'), n 1 *supra,* 385.
Yoshiyuki Noda, though not from viewpoint of reception of foreign law, commented that, from end of the Meiji Period to the Taisho Period, Japanese scholars used German jurisprudence to establish the civil law system in Japan. I agree with this observation. See Y. Noda, 'Nihon ni okeru Gaikoku-Ho no Sesshu: Josetsu' [Absorption of Foreign Laws into Japanese Law: A Preliminary Discussion] 14 *Gendai-Ho* 172 (1996).

assimilation of such law(s). Between these two processes, historical significance and role of the reception of German legal theory lies in the assimilation process which occurred subsequent to the enactment of the Japanese Civil Code. This assimilation process can be regarded as a process for developing the Japan's domestic civil law system by casting the product of the mixed-type reception of foreign codes (ie Japanese Civil Code) into a mould imported from a foreign country (ie German jurisprudence).[30] In other words, by grafting the German legal system onto the product of a mixed type reception of foreign codes, the Japanese civil law system had developed its unique two-tiered structure. This is the *prototype* of Japanese civil law jurisprudence *from the viewpoint of comparative law* and, in this sense, Japanese civil law can be regarded as a system homogenous to German civil law. In this, German jurisprudence attained its unique position as a homogenous foreign system that had directly contributed to development of *de lege lata* analysis of the Japanese Civil Code, in addition to its role in comparative study of law. *Claus-Wilhelm Canaris* stated that 'theory reception is a discovery of a unique legal issue'.[31]

Such a phenomenon occurred not only among scholars but also among legal practitioners. For a long time it was not unusual for a court to give a decision that was based on or incorporated German theory.[32] Furthermore, it was not unique to the field of civil law but

30 Kitagawa (1970: 'Rezeption und Fortbildung'), n 1 *supra,* 97 (Theorien-Rezeption als Assimilation des rezipierten Rechts); Kitagawa (1968: 'History and Theories'), n 1 *supra,* 385.

31 C.-W. Canaris, 'Theorienrezeption und Theorienstruktur', in H. Leser (ed.), *Wege zum Japanischen Recht – Festschrift für Z. Kitagawa* (Berlin 1992) 59.

32 Among judges in courts, there was also a habitual reliance on German jurisprudence. In *History and Theories,* Z. Kitagawa analyzed some examples showing such habits on page 227 *et seq.* For example, a judge who was familiar to German jurisprudence commented that German literature was more useful than constructions proposed by Japanese legal scholars (comment by Justice *Saburo Iwamatsu, id.* at 227). In addition, there was even an episode that, when an attorney asked to the judge why court decision was not still delivered despite the trial was concluded some little time ago, the judge answered 'Could you wait a little more time? I have ordered the relevant German literature but it has yet to be delivered to me.' However, although the strong German influence can certainly be observed in some individual cases, it cannot be said that it wholly changed practices in Japan's courts. In this regard, see Kitagawa (1970: 'Rezeption und

observed also in other fields of law generally. In addition, academic papers and textbooks at that time commonly used the German legal theories. Indeed, for a certain time lawyers fell over one another to introduce the latest German theories and they adopted them one after another.[33] At that time, there was even a tendency for people to think as if only the German Jurisprudence were jurisprudence and studies not based on German jurisprudence were not accepted.[34]

As discussed above, it was in 1881 that the government of Japan decided the basic policies for establishing a constitutional monarchy in Japan. More specifically, the political upheaval that occurred in that year became the turning point for Japan at which it dramatically

Fortbildung'), n 1 *supra,* 244 (the reception of German legal theory certainly exerted a great influence on the formation of legal concepts and system of the law in Japan, but this did not go as far enough as forming the law of Japan itself).

33 A leading Roman Law scholar commented that Japan is like a 'boiler gauge that has indicated a pressure change occurring in German law more quickly than it is perceived in Germany' (P. Koschaker, *Europa und das Römische Recht* (3rd ed. Munich 1958) 132, n 1). See Kitagawa (1968: 'History and Theories'), n 1 *supra,* 27.

34 The following citations may greatly surprise readers, but it was nothing other than true. 'Before World War I started, German Jurisprudence had inconceivably and overwhelmingly dominated Japanese lawyers' (a remark by *Izutaro Suehiro* in Editorial Division of Nippon-Hyoron-Sha (ed), *Nihon no Hogaku Zadankai* [Symposium on Japanese Jurisprudence] (Tokyo 1950) 81. 'At the beginning of the Taisho Period (1910s), it was considered that Japanese jurisprudence and German jurisprudence had almost no essential differences.' (I. Suehiro, 'Minpo Gakusei Jidai no Kaiko' [Memoirs of my School Days], in Tokyo Imperial Univ. (ed), *Tokyo Teikoku Daigaku Gakujutsu Taiakan* [The Academic Overall View of Tokyo Imperial University] (Tokyo 1942) 116). As a result, 'it is no exaggeration to say that German jurisprudence almost overwhelmingly controlled the way of thinking of Japan's legal scholars and that principles on legal construction had almost automatically been employed to construct the laws in Japan' (Y. Noda, 'Nihon ni okeru Gaikoku-Ho no Sesshu: Josetsu' [Absorption of Foreign Laws into Japanese Law: A Preliminary Discussion] 14 *Gendai-Ho* 172 (1996)). Among some scholars, even the mentality that aimed to transform Japanese jurisprudence into something that was identical to German jurisprudence was observed' (Kitagawa (1968: 'History and Theories'), n 1 *supra,* 27 and 259). Certainly, it may be felt as being 'bizarre' from the contemporary viewpoint that 'such phenomenon existed in the construction of law at that time' (S. Kawakami, *Mipou-Gaku Nyumon Minpou Sousoku Kougi – Joron* [Introduction to Civil Law Study: A Lecture on the General Rules of Civil Law – Preliminary Discussion] (Tokyo 2004) 127). However, it can be understood as the natural consequence of the general atmosphere in those days that is reflected in the literature cited above.

changed directions and began to imitate German-style policy. At that time, Japan was an emerging country in Asia and had great enthusiasm for developing itself into one of great powers in the world. Given that situation, we can suppose that German jurisprudence which comprised strict legal concepts and a solid legal system, might have been immensely attractive to Japan's scholars at tat time. The reception of German legal theories had occurred in such an overall trend and had rapidly cast Japanese jurisprudence into the mould of German jurisprudence. The reception of German legal theories had brought about systemization of *de lege lata* analysis of law which had played a major role in modernizing Japanese jurisprudence. Such a process should be understood not only as a historical event but also as an issue of current civil law to the extent that the reception contributed greatly to the formation of the legal concepts and legal system used for constructing and applying the current Civil Code. The legal scholars had long been required to (i) learn the German *Pandektenwissenschaft*, (ii) then understand German jurisprudence, the successor of the *Pandektenwissenschaft*, using knowledge learnt in the first stage and (iii) finally to study how the Japanese Civil Code should be construed. Such a methodology was also a product of the theory reception and subsequent conversion of the Japanese legal structure. In that period Japanese scholars devoted maximum efforts to introducing the German legal concepts and system into Japan. Similar phenomena were widely observed in various fields in the course of the modernization of Japan.[35]

[35] It should be noted that, though it appeared to have occurred as a total change, such process was in fact 'reception with some reservation' in various aspects. This is obvious also in case of the civil law. The same applies to other fields. *Karl Rathgen,* an invited foreign expert at that time, commented that 'though it looks like a total acceptance of the Western systems on the face of it, in fact, the Japan's administrative system has a unique paternalistic structure which was built by modifying the German-type administrative system in accordance with the traditional Japanese spirit'. See Z. Kitagawa, 'Nichidoku Hougaku no Isseiki' [A Century of Japan and German Jurisprudence] 116 *Hougaku Ronsou* (Nos. 4–6) at 72–73 (1990); Kitagawa (1990: 'Ein Jahrhundert'), n 22 *supra,* 28–29. This issue is related to the concept of 'Japanese spirit and Western learning' that had been widely discussed in and after the Meiji Period.

4. Reception of Foreign Legal Theories and Relation to Contemporary Civil Law Study: Historical Nature and Contemporary Significance

Until when did the reception of German legal theory continue? Unlike in the case of the reception of foreign codes, this question is difficult and answering it requires cautiousness. However, the two world wars can be regarded as turning points for putting an end to the unique relationship between Japan and German jurisprudence. Among them, the World War I seems more important. By then, Japan had completed the process of reconstructing Japanese jurisprudence through the reception of German legal theories. At that point the Japanese jurisprudence came to have a strong interest in sociological jurisprudence to know law in action and also came to have an interest in how academic discussion on construction of law functioned in the real world. As a result, case law became a subject matter of legal study. In short, new trends were brought about to Japanese jurisprudence, which had previously devoted itself to proceeding to its systemization relying on German jurisprudence. In other words, the reception of German legal theory started to become a process of the past.[36]

After the end of the reception of German legal theory, what became of the relationship between Japanese and German jurisprudence? From the viewpoint of comparative law, German jurisprudence had become a foreign law that had a structure identical to Japanese jurisprudence. In this sense, it may be coined as a prototype for modern

36 With regard to the issue when the reception of German legal theory ended, see Kitagawa (1968: 'History and Theories'), n 1 *supra,* 154–155 (Around 1922, sociological jurisprudence emerged and attracted strong interest from legal scholars and new approach to studying case law was also proposed. These trends can be understood as being a symbolic manifestation of the academic undercurrent that was critical of and countervailing against the mainstream of Japanese jurisprudence at that time, which was built on German conceptual jurisprudence [in particular, hermeneutic study of the positive law]. The most important thing regarding such trends is the fact that such innovative movement was taken seriously and accepted also by the then leading scholars as an issue that directly pertained to their area of study.); Kitagawa (1970: 'Rezeption und Fortbildung'), n 1 *supra,* 205; Z. Kitagawa, *Minpou no Taikei to Riron* [System and Theories of Civil Law] (Tokyo 1987) 3–4.

Japanese civil law. German jurisprudence as such foreign law continuously exerted a unique and strong influence on Japanese jurisprudence even after the end of the reception of German legal theory.[37] However, even though phenomena similar to those observed in the period of the reception of German legal theory were continuously observed, it should be understood as a mere aftereffect of the theory reception. The more important thing is the fact that research results that were unique to Japan and could be regarded as having a post-reception nature started to emerge.[38] There were scholars who, though relying on German civil law jurisprudence, eventually developed their own theories.[39]

37 A prime example of this can be found in the theory of liability for defects in things. T. Süss, *Wesen und Rechtsgrund der Gewährleistung für Sachmängel – Ein dogmatischer Beitrag zur Lehre von der Gewährleistung* (Leipzig 1931) reinforced the 'dogma of determinate things' and established the unique statutory liability doctrine. This unique and well-established German doctrine on liability for defects in things had had a strong influence on Japanese civil law jurisprudence.

38 Such works includes S. Wagatsuma, *Kindai-Ho ni okeru Saiken no Yuetuteki-Chii* [Dominant Position of Law of Obligations in the Modern Law] (Tokyo 1953); T. Kawashima, *Shoyuken-Ho no Riron* [Theories of Law on Property Right] (Tokyo 1949). In relation to the subject matter of this Chapter is *Otoshiro Ishizaka's* discussion on the need for the independence of Japanese Jurisprudence (*Ishizaka* is a leading scholar of the period of the reception of German legal theory). In O. Ishizaka, 'Nihon-Hougaku no Dokuritsu' [The Independence of Japanese Jurisprudence] Vol. 23 No. 17 *Shinpou* 73 (republished in O. Ishizaka, *Kaisan Minpou Kenkyu – Jou* [Newly Edited Version of Study of Civil Law I] (Tokyo 1915) 41, he wrote: 'In the reality of Japanese jurisprudence, even today, there still remains a tendency in which some scholars still construe Japanese law by applying theories borrowed from foreign laws directly to Japanese law and want none of the independence of Japanese jurisprudence. (…) This seems inevitable phenomenon in the period of reception of foreign law. However, it is time for the Japanese jurisprudence to become independent. (…) We should not apply German theory on construction of law directly to Japanese law. It should be used only as a material for comparing Japanese law and foreign law for the purpose of drawing thereupon.' This article was published in the midst of the reception of foreign legal theory (ie in 1913). It seems worthwhile to research how many scholars at that time had such awareness.

39 As an epoch-making work of such nature, we should not forget F. Oho, *Zaisan-Kanri-Ken Josetsu* [Preliminary Discussions on Right to Manage Property] (Tokyo 1954) which consists of eleven articles originally published in the period of 1933 to 1940. This work started from analysis of doctrinal history of the German jurisprudence and its doctrines for construction of law, proposed a unique

After World War II, heated debates occurred among legal scholars on the issues of how jurisprudence should maintain its scientific nature and what methodologies should be used for the interpretation of law and the analysis of case law.[40] In that period, the study of interpretation of law itself played only a backseat role, even though that may be difficult to imagine for today's reader. What played the leading role in those days' debates was strong criticism of conceptual jurisprudence (*Begriffsjurisprudenz*). Theories formed as a result of or regarded as residuals of the reception of German legal theory bore the brunt of the force of such criticism. Such criticism was often made against the German jurisprudence by calling it 'German type conceptual jurisprudence'.[41] Amid such debates, however, I had doubt about it. In the following paragraphs I wish to explain this more specifically.

As stated in the beginning of this Chapter, when I first became interested in the study of civil law jurisprudence a little while after the end of World War II, I was interested in why the doctrinal history of Japanese jurisprudence did not analyze the various legal theories discussed around the time when the Civil Code was enacted and why it

concept of 'right to manage property', verified its position in the Japanese civil law structure, thereby established the unique principles of construction of a Japanese civil law that was independent from the German theories received by Japan.

40 Certainly, there may be a necessity to examine the contemporary significance of the controversies in the immediate postwar years. Here, however, I would point out that, even at the time of such ideological controversies, I aimed, to establish a new system of legal doctrines that would be based on a problem awareness independent of the prototype for Japanese civil law rather than discussing such ideological controversies. See Kitagawa (1968: 'History and Theories'), n 1 *supra,* 2–5; Kitagawa, 'Nachkriegszeitliche amerikanische Einflüsse auf das japanische Recht – Japan als Treffpunkt zweier westlicher Rechtssysteme', in B. Dieselkamp, Z. Kitagawa, J. Kreiner et al. (eds), *Zwischen Kontinuität und Fremdbestimmung – Zum Einfluss der Besatzungsmächte auf die deutsche und japanische Rechtsordnung 1945 bis 1950 – Deutsch-japanisches Symposium in Tokyo vom 6. bis 9. April 1994* (Tübingen 1996) 384.

41 This expression may be appropriate for German jurisprudence at the time of reception of German legal theory, but is not correct any longer with regard to German jurisprudence in the post-war period. After World War II, German jurisprudence had already showed the orientation towards value jurisprudence, through criticism of conceptual jurisprudence after the World War I and the transition to interest jurisprudence in the 1930s. For an outline of such development of German jurisprudence, see K. Larenz, *Methodenlehre der Rechtswissenschaft* (5th ed. Berlin, Heidelberg, New York 1983) 19.

was directly connected to the doctrinal history of *Pandektenwissenschaft* and the German jurisprudence. During my study on individual issues regarding this I found various problems that gave me a broader perspective. In the course of this I noted a phenomenon that can be called tensions among various norms of Japanese civil law jurisprudence which were brought by the influence of German legal theories. For example, Japanese civil law had a two-tier structure consisting of various norms that was brought about by mixed reception of foreign codes and subsisted in the Japanese Civil Code, on one side, and German-type legal theories established through the reception of German legal theories, on the other side. This unique structure had generated the tension between these two types of legal norms. This posed some questions: How should post-war Japanese jurisprudence understand such a unique structure of Japanese civil law? Among the legal concepts or systems that were introduced from German civil law, how should we differentiate those already internalized in the Japanese civil law system from others and how should we treat them? In addition to these, how should Japanese jurisprudence understand the tension between civil law norms introduced from foreign countries and Japanese traditional legal norms that has existed in Japan's communities from the pre-modern era? One of my answers to these questions was as follows: As long as German civil law jurisprudence was introduced into Japanese civil law and it was assimilated into the legal concepts and system of Japanese civil law, such German elements should not be removed. However, at the same time, we should not uncritically accept them as Japanese legal construction principles. I also concluded that this was a civil law issue that is unique to Japan and that this issue should be examined not from the dimension of criticism of the conceptual jurisprudence but as a question that should be answered from the perspective of study of the construction of law. These are questions posed by the prototype of Japanese civil law (see *supra,* II) to today's as well as to tomorrow's Japanese jurisprudende.

During the period from end of World War II to the start of the post-war recovery of the Japanese economy and society, most academic papers published in the field of civil law concerned family law or law of inheritance. In the area of property law, leasehold law played the leading role. In such a situation the historical linkage that the prototype of Japanese civil law had with the *Pandektenwissenschaft* and German civil law jurisprudence was clearly brought to light. This is because Japanese civil law jurisprudence at that time still retained a considerable part of its prototype in the period of the reception of German legal theories and the prototype still reigned as the prevailing theory in Japanese civil law jurisprudence. Therefore, in order to identify it and create new Japanese civil law jurisprudence, it was required to clarify the characteristics of German jurisprudence and the *Pandektenwissenschaft* prevailing in the 19th century which had become the parental body of the prototype of Japanese civil law. Such a clarification was absolutely required for achieving the independence of Japanese civil law jurisprudence. Here, German jurisprudence, in addition to its role of a subject for comparison in comparative study of law also became a subject of the contemporary study of construction of civil law because the prototype of Japanese civil law study belonged to the same legal family as German jurisprudence.[42]

In this sense, after World War II, the Japanese study of civil law construction was forced to squarely confront the German Civil Code and German jurisprudence. In other words, Japanese civil law study was required to overcome the influence of German civil law through examination of it and to build up its own legal theories for achieving independence. It was a task for the restoration of the Japanese civil law study to get a lead for reconstructing a legal system that would be in conformity with the Japanese Civil Code. Therefore, in order to examine the prototype of Japanese civil law jurisprudence and to

[42] This issue still does not lose its relevance to Japanese civil law jurisprudence. Recently, at an international symposium, I received the following comment from a participant: 'In my opinion, Japanese positive law scholars should recognize the existence of historical imbalance in various study areas of positive law. More specifically, it seems that it is required to intensively study the problems arising from the dominance of German-type legal dogmatics over Japanese civil law study' (a remark by Eiichi Hoshino, at 'Legal Dynamics in the Global Era: Multidisciplinary Perspectives on the Transformation of Market and Law' organized by Kobe University, Center for Legal Dynamics of Advanced Market Societies (Vol. 54, No.1 *Kobe Hougaku Zasshi* 203 (2004)). This question concerns what is called 'the prototype of the Japanese civil law jurisprudence viewed from the perspective of comparative law' in this Chapter, and I share the same problem awareness as that participant in the sense that problems residing in the study of positive law in Japan should be reexamined, even if the conclusions on this matter differ between him and me (*id.* 204).

create legal theories for achieving independence from it, it was necessary to study German civil law jurisprudence and its predecessor, the *Pandektenwissenschaft* in the 19th century.[43]

IV. Theories for Attaining Independence from the Prototype of the Japanese Civil Law and Revision of the German Civil Code

1. *Pandektenwissenschaft* and Law of Obligations under the German Civil Code

German civil law jurisprudence has its origins in the *Pandektenwissenschaft* that was generated from the reception of Roman law during the late German common law (*gemeines Recht*) period and was completed in the 19th century. The *Pandektenwissenschaft* was a systemized academic positivism and represented a perfect form of 'academization of essential legal aspects of human life'[44] which had proceeded during the centuries of the reception of Roman law.[45] The system of the *Pandektenwissenschaft* aimed at exhaustively academizing every legal question that a person may encounter during his/her life by using elaborate concepts and establishing sophisticated mechanisms. Its purpose was clearly to categorize all of its subjects by using various abstract concepts such as lawful act vs. unlawful act, person vs. thing, corporeal (or tangible) thing vs. incorporeal (or intangible) thing, and right *in rem* vs. right *in personam* and to

43 On this point, M. Katou, n 23 *supra,* 41, stated that 'Nowadays, there are opinions that regard Japanese jurisprudence in the period of the reception of German legal theories as a mere imitation of a foreign jurisprudence and deny it. At that time, however, in order to fully complete the reception of Western laws, the reception of legal theories was the first thing to be done by Japanese legal scholars'. See for further thoughts on the German impacts on Japanese civil law in East Asia, Z. Kitagawa, 'Development of Comparative Law in East Asia', in M. Reimann & R. Zimmermann (ed.), The Oxford Handbook of Comparative Law, 2006, p. 239.

44 F. Wieacker, *Privatrechtsgeschichte der Neuzeit unter besonderen Berücksichtigung der deutschen Entwicklung* (Göttingen 1952), at 66, 76 and 128.

45 Ibid at 253 (As a 'legal image of academic positivism', there was 'a view on law that aimed to derive all statutes and regulations and all court decisions from various legal concepts and various legal propositions'.).

allocate these legal concepts into systematically organized legal areas, thereby building a comprehensive legal system consisting of these various legal concepts. In other words, the *Pandektenwissenschaft* was meant to be a *lacuna*-free, self-sustaining system consisting of a 'ladder of concepts' in which various abstract concepts were logically differentiated from each other. Such a system had considerable theoretical transparency and special attractiveness which promoted its succession.[46]

Such an academic positivistic legal structure was completed by the German *Pandektenwissenschaft* and reached its culmination in the enactment of the German Civil Code. One of the examples in which such characteristics have been well reflected is the law on contractual liability and nonperformance of obligation. In light of this historical background, the Japanese civil law jurisprudence can be evaluated by using the doctrinal history of the Civil Law (especially one starting from German *Pandektenwissenschaft* and reaching the subsequent German jurisprudence) as the vertical axis and comparison between the Civil Law and the Common Law as the horizontal axis.[47]

In Germany, *F. Mommsen* completed the legal structure on nonperformance of obligation in the mid-19th century.[48] With regard to

46 For generation of German conceptual jurisprudence in the 19th century, see Larenz, n 41 *supra*, 19. Here, it should be noted that, although the *Pandektensystem* has often been regarded as a self-sustaining, 'closed' system that consisted of a ladder of concepts, it has not been always true and at its initial phase, the *Pandektensystem* was rather a 'open' system. See Z. Kitagawa, 'Minpou no Taikei to Hou-Kaishaku System' [Structure of Civil Law and System of Legal Construction Principles] 134 *Hougaku Ronsou* (Nos.3&4) at 4–7 (1994); Z. Kitagawa, 'Minpouten to Hikakuho – Kenkyu Note' [The Civil Code and Comparative Law – A Note for Study] 58 *Hikakuho Kenkyu* at 85 (Note 3) (1996; this article was a part of a feature entitled 'Doitsu Minpouten no Hyakunen' [A Century of the German Civil Code]).

47 See Kitagawa (1963: 'Contractual Liability'), 6–41 (Chapter II Keiyaku Sekinin-Ho ni okeru Doitsu Minpou no Ichi [The Position of the German Civil Code from Perspective of Contractual Liability Law]). In the course of developing academic perspectives based on comparative law, I obtained many insights from Max Rheinstein, *Die Struktur des vertraglichen Schuldverhältnisses im anglo-amerikanischen Recht* (Beiträge zum ausländischen und internationalen Privatrecht – Heft 5; Berlin, Leipzig 1932).

48 F. Mommsen, *Beiträge zum Obligationenrecht – Abt. 1 Die Unmöglichkeit der Leistung in ihrem Einfluss auf obligatorische Verhältnisse* (Braunschweig

various hindrances to performance of obligation, the prevailing theory of *Pandektenwissenschaft* 'set impossibility of delivery itself as a boundary: This boundary is effective for both initial impossibility and subsequent impossibility'.[49] Such a theory gave a positive significance as an independent category of nonperformance of obligation to the concept of impossibility which had been merely a negative requirement (a ground for releasing an obligor from his/her obligation). Furthermore, the *Pandektenwissenschaft* combined it with the dogma of initial impossibility ('initial impossibility will make a contract null and void'), divided the concept of hindrance to performance into the two categories of initial impossibility and subsequent impossibility, and limited application of nonperformance of obligation only to subsequent impossibility. In other words, initial impossibility was ruled out from the discussion on nonperformance of obligation (see *supra* II 2).

After having been limited to subsequent impossibility, the nonperformance of obligation doctrine eventually distinguished impossibility in terms of time (ie delay in performance) from other impossibility of performance, and resulted in a parallel structure consisting of delay in performance and impossibility of performance. They were the objective elements of nonperformance of obligation. With regard to the subjective elements, on the other hand, negligence was uniformly applied to both of them. This dominant doctrine was adopted in the provisions regarding nonperformance of obligation of the German Civil Code.[50] According to *Ernst Rabel*,

> 'the doctrine of impossibility, which applied formulas vitalized by *Mommsen* and polished by *Windscheid*, was adopted in the German Civil Code with its stern self-evidentness (*imponierende Selbstverständlichkeit*). (...) The basic idea of this doctrine is an independent and unified legal category, which becomes a starting point of legal analysis. (...) If (the delivery is) possible, the contract will be considered effective. If the contract is effective, among the conceivable cases of nonperformance of obligation the law knows only the

1853); *Abt. 3 Die Lehre von der mora nebst Beitrag zur Lehre von der culpa* (Braunschweig1855). Regarding discussions of *Mommsen*, see Kitagawa (1963: 'Contractual Liability'), n 1 *supra*, 16–18.

49 G. Hartmann, *Die Obligation* (Erlangen 1875) 166. See also Kitagawa (1963: 'Contractual Liability'), n 1 *supra*, 22–23.

50 See Kitagawa (1963: 'Contractual Liability'), n 1 *supra*, 21–22, 27–30, 31–35. See also *supra*, II 2.

> two groups of nonperformance of obligation (ie delay in performance and impossibility of performance). There, impossibility of performance precedes in all aspects.'[51]

This doctrine of nonperformance of obligation which was infused into the German Civil Code from the *Pandektenwissenschaft* cannot be wholly understood without comprehension of its relationship with the law on liability for defects in things (see also *supra,* II 1). The concept of 'liability for defects in things' has its origins in *aedilicis action* under ancient Roman law, which had been introduced separately from *ius civile* and had been a market police to protect buyers in that era. Reflecting this historical background, in modern laws, liability for defects in things was distinguished from laws on contractual liability and nonperformance of obligation and was defined as a strict liability for initial defects of specific things. Also in the German *Pandektenwissenschaft* which was dominated by the impossibility doctrine and established a rule that limited nonperformance of obligation to cases of subsequent impossibility of delivery, liability for defects in things was strictly separated from contractual liability for default in both jurisprudential and institutional terms. The legal proposition that distinguished liability for defects in things from nonperformance of obligation is the doctrine that, with regard to an obligation to deliver a specific thing, even if the specific thing had some defects, delivery of that specific thing would be considered as an indefectible performance of the obligation ('the dogma of specific things'). This doctrine which can be called crystallization from German conceptual jurisprudence had been further advanced even after the enactment of the German Civil Code.[52]

Such legal doctrines looked as if they were a 'Great German Wall' subsisting in the German Civil Code. After about a century from its enactment, however, this great wall was finally moved by revision of the Code in 2001 (see *infra,* 3). Before discussing it I wish to discuss theories for achieving independence from the prototype.

[51] E. Rabel, *Grundzüge des Römischen Privatrechts* (2nd ed. Basel 1955) 132. See also Kitagawa (1963: 'Contractual Liability'), n 1 *supra,* 33.
[52] As a leading work in this respect, see Süss, n 37 *supra,* which is outlined in Kitagawa (1968: 'Contractual Liability'), n 1 *supra,* 142–143.

2. Theories for Achieving Independence from the Prototype of Japanese Civil Law

Even after World War II, the prototype of Japanese civil law, which was created through the theory reception of the German law, held its position as the dominant theory in Japan. As discussed above, it was necessary critically to analyze German civil law jurisprudence and its origin, the *Pandektenwissenschaft*, in order to develop a theory that would play the role of critically analyzing the then-prevailing theory (ie the prototype of Japanese civil law jurisprudence) and enable independence from it. The basic framework for examining problems in German civil law jurisprudence was already offered by *Ernst Rabel* as early as early 20th century. More specifically, *Rabel* criticized the dogma that a contract should be regarded as invalid if its purpose was to make an initially impossible delivery which had dominated over the German jurisprudence and was considered as if it were a self-evident truth and also criticized the system of nonperformance of obligation that was built based on that dogma.[53] In our case in Japan it was also required to create theories for the construction of the Civil Code. Such theories should be able to overcome and bridge the gap between the Japanese Civil Code itself and Japanese civil law jurisprudence that was established through the theory reception of the German law. In the remaining part of this Chapter, I will briefly explain my discussion about contract liability and nonperformance of obligation as such a theory.

The central part of my theory was the denial of the doctrine of initial impossibility. By doing so, we could give contract liability and nonperformance of obligation theory a unified structure that covered both initial hindrance of performance and subsequent hindrance of performance. Furthermore, I suggested that liability for defects in things should be regarded as a special contractual liability and nonperformance of obligation. When we did so, nonperformance of ob-

53 E. Rabel, *Die Haftung des Verkäufers wegen Mangels im Rechte – Erster Teil: Geschichtliche Studien über den Haftungserfolge* (Lepizig 1902); E. Rabel, 'Die Unmöglichkeit der Leistung – Eine kritische Studie zum Bürgerlichen Gesetzbuch', in F. Bernhöft et al. (eds), *Festschrift für E. Bekker* (Weimar 1907) 171–237; E. Rabel, 'Über Unmöglichkeit der Leistung und heutige Praxis' *Rheinische Zeitschrift für Zivil- und Prozessrecht* 3 (1911) at 460–490 and others.

ligation would come to cover the three categories: delay in performance, impossibility of performance and imperfect performance. As a result, initial hindrance of performance and subsequent hindrance of performance would be integrated and unified. I called it 'basic contractual liability'.[54]

To put it in more detail, in the *Pandektensystem* and the German Civil Code, contractual liability and nonperformance of obligation applied only in cases where the contract was considered effective, and was structured as a system for subsequent hindrances not covering initial impossibility (in this case, the contract was considered invalid). However, this system was defective from the outset. For example, it was considered that impossibility of performance cannot occur regarding the nonspecific things, but if a defect exists in the design quality of the nonspecific things in question it could cause initial impossibility. In addition, with regard to imperfect performance, delivery of a defective nonspecific thing was regarded as a typical example of events that would invoke contractual liability. However, in cases where imperfect performance arose due to a defect existing in the design quality of the nonspecific things, such a defect, in most cases, should be regarded as initial hindrance to performance. In short, in neither *Pandektenwissenschaft* nor the German civil law jurisprudence was the distinction between initial hindrances to performance and subsequent ones always successfully made as a doctrine for deciding contractual liability and nonperformance of obligation. Focusing on this I concluded that if we could develop a legal theory that would enable us to overcome the German dogma of initial impossibility, this may bring about a new system of contractual liability and nonperformance of obligation that would cover both initial hindrances to performance and subsequent ones. Such an

[54] Kitagawa (1963: 'Contractual Liability') at 361. 'Basic contractual liability' is a liability that has as its pivot 'an integrated system of nonperformance of obligation to deliver that will be become able to be established by making organic structural adjustment of various institutions including ones for initial impossibility, imperfect performance, liability for defects in things and *culpa in contrahendo* (negligence in the conclusion of contract)'. Afterwards, I used the expression 'nonperformance in terms of the tenor and purport of the obligation' in accordance with the expression used in the Civil Code. See Z. Kitagawa, 'Saimufurikou no Kouzou to System' [Structure and System of Default of Obligation] 116 *Hougaku Ronsou* (Nos. 1–6) (1985) at 222.

approach would also allow us to absorb part of the doctrine of *culpa in contrahendo* (negligence in the conclusion of effective contract) which appeared in German civil law jurisprudence in the early 20th century into nonperformance by regarding it as a form of initial hindrance to performance. From the viewpoint of the structure of contractual liability and nonperformance of obligation, it should be regarded as a liability for breach of obligation of delivery arising in the obligor-obligee relationship.[55]

As another theory for achieving independence of Japan's civil law from its prototype, I proposed that liability for defects in things also should be regarded as a kind of contractual liability. German civil law jurisprudence categorized liability for defects in things as a special statutory liability for initial impossibility of performance, not as a nonperformance of obligation. Even after the enactment of the German Civil Code this doctrine continued to become more advanced and was completed in about 1930.[56] However, its *prima facie* lucidity eventually isolated this German-type theory on liability for defects in things from other legal systems. The legal foundation of this special statutory liability theory was the recognition that under the obligation of a specific thing, even if the specific thing had a defect, the obligor could perform his/her obligation only by that defective specific thing. In other words, the special statutory liability theory had its basis in what was called the 'dogma of specific things' ('delivery of the defective specific things should be regarded as indefectible performance.'). Based on this dogma, liability for defects in things was treated as a special statutory liability arising after the delivery was once made. However, I thought that it was possible to find, as a part of obligation of delivery, an obligation that, in a bilateral contract for value such as a contract for sales the obligor was required to deliver

55 Contractual liability should be understood as having a multi-staged structure which includes 'supplementary contractual liability' separated from basic contractual liability. Supplementary contractual liability is comprised of breach of accessory obligations which cannot be regarded as an obligation of delivery but should be performed in order to protect the benefits of the contract, and duties of care which constitutes the exterior frame of a contract and plays the role of indirectly protecting the benefits of the contract by securing and/or maintaining the precondition for entering into contract. See Kitagawa (1963: 'Contractual Liability'), n 1 *supra,* 361.

56 For this issue, see *supra* note 52.

the specific thing of value that was worth its price. This is the core of my theory for independence and paved the way for developing a new legal theory in which liability for defects in things was categorized as a special rule of contractual liability and nonperformance of obligation.[57] This in turn would allow the law on liability for defects in things to be absorbed into contractual liability and nonperformance of obligation. These were proposed as criticism of the prevailing theories in 1960's in Japan but at the same time were new theories that would enable us to achieve independence from the prototype of Japanese civil law jurisprudence that was generated by the theory reception of German law.

These independence theories had another purpose: criticizing the *Pandektensystem* as a system for civil law. Afterwards, my efforts in this direction developed into a discussion on a more preferable system of civil law.[58] In particular, regarding the issue of nonperfor-

57 Before it, F. Oho, *Saiken Soron (Houritsugaku Zenshu)* [General Theory on Law of Obligations (Complete Works of Jurisprudence)] (Tokyo 1959) 104 (n 1), had already submitted a pioneering opinion on this issue ('Regarding liability for defects in things, particularly on a specific thing, I feel that the obligation to deliver something that has a value equivalent to the price to be received therefore in a bilateral contract for value, slipped out of the formal treatment for obligation to deliver specific thing. I think that it is possible to redefine liability for defects in a specific thing as a nonperformance of obligation, if we can be freed from the historical restraints. (...) If liability for defects in things is redefined as a nonperformance of obligation, liability for defects, including liability for defects of title, would be regarded as a representative example of imperfect performance in its nature.'). See Kitagawa (1963: 'Contractual Liability'), n 1 *supra,* at 173, 334 and particularly 365–372. As opinions that suggested treating liability for defects in things as a kind of nonperformance of obligation, K. Igarashi, 'Kashi-Tanpo to Hikaku-Ho' (1) and (2) [Liability for Defects in Things and Comparative Law (1) and (2)] 41-1 *Minshoho-Zasshi* (1959) 45 and 41-6 *Minshoho-Zasshi* (1960) 24; E. Hoshino, 'Kashitanpo no Kenkyu – Nihon' [A Study of Liability for Defects in Things – Japan] 23 *Hikakuho-Kenkyu* (1962) 3.

58 See Z. Kitagawa, *Gendai Keiyaku-Ho I (Taikei-ka no Kokoromi)* [Modern Law of Contract I (An Attempt at Its Systemization)] (Tokyo 1973) 33; Z. Kitagawa, *Minpou no Taikei to Riron* [The System and Theories of the Civil Law] (Tokyo 1987) 143; Z. Kitagawa, 'Hou Kaishaku System Josetsu – Houritsuka to Handansuru Kikai to no Yakuwari-Buntan ni tsuite' [A Preliminary Discussion on System of Legal Construction – About Role-Sharing Between Lawyers and Judgment-Making Machines] 132 *Hougaku Ronsou* (Nos. 1–3) at 1; Z. Kitagawa, 'Minpou no Taikei to Hou-Kaishaku System' [Structure of Civil Law and Sys-

mance of obligation, I attempted to bring contractual liability to the fore as a critical theory against the general theory of nonperformance of obligation in the General Provisions of Obligations.[59] It reflected the fact that the provisions contained in the General Provision of Obligatory Rights of the Japanese Civil Code were substantially provisions on contracts and they did not have enough contents that could be regarded as general rules for what is generally called statutory obligation (ie the Civil Code's provisions on unlawful acts, unjust enrichment and *negotiorum gestio*). Considering it, I attempted to analyze the issue of nonperformance of obligation from the functional viewpoint and develop doctrines to treat it from the perspective of contractual liability, and not nonperformance of obligation.[60] Such an idea, though it was originally conceived as a theory for independence, also played a greater role than expected in comparative law.[61] With regard to relationship with the 2001 revision of the German Civil Code, the issue suggested by this theory concerned its 'unchanged' part.

tem of Legal Construction Principles] 134 *Hougaku Ronsou* (Nos. 3 & 4) (1994) at 4–7.

59 *K. Tanaka's* article in M. Katou et al. (eds), *Minpou Gakusetsu Hyakunen-Shi – Nihon Minpou Shikou Hyakunen Kinen* [A History of a Hundred Years of Civil Law Theories in Japan – A Hundred Years Anniversary of Enforcement of Japanese Civil Code] (Tokyo 1999) 460 evaluated that my book 'Contractual Liability' separated contractual liability from the concept of nonperformance of obligation, by denying the general rule approaches of obligations law that treated an obligation in a manner that separated it from the cause of its occurrences and instead focused on liability arising from contractual relationship.

60 Z. Kitagawa, *Saiken Souron – Minpou Kouyou III (Dai 3-han)* [General Principles of Obligations Law – Lecture on Civil Law III (3rd edition)] (Tokyo 2004), of which the first edition was published in 1993, explains the general principles of obligation as a system of general principles of law of contract.

61 Impacts on the legislation of Chinese Law Contracts (1999) will deserve special attention: see Wang Chen, *Shakaishugishijōkeizai to Chūgoku keiyakuhō* [Socialist market economy and Chinese contract law] (1999) 199–232; Z. Kitagawa, 'Moderu Keiyaku-Ho to Chugoku no Keiyaku-Ho' [The Model Law of Contract and the Chinese Law of Contract] 120 *Hougaku Ronsou* (Nos. 4–6) (1987) at 1; Z. Kitagawa, 'Ajia ni okeru Bijinesu to Moderu Keiyaku-Ho' [Business in Asia and the Model Law of Contract], in Faculty of Law – Meiji University (ed), *Ajia ni okeru Nihon-Kigyou no Chokumen suru Houteki Sho-Mondai* [The Legal Problems Faced by Japanese Corporations in Asia] (Tokyo 1987) at 1.

3. Theories for Achieving Independence and the Revision of the German Civil Code

In the above discussion of the prototype of Japanese civil law viewed from comparative study of law and theories for achieving independence from the prototype in the 1960's, I had referred to the German Civil Code of 1900. As of today, it was revised in 2001 and the revision was already enforced in 2002. Since the revised part concerned the issue of nonperformance of obligation, the German Civil Code as revised came to have a structure that was common to the structures I proposed at that time as theories for independence and the revision can be understood to have its origins in *Rabel's* critical theory that had been developed simultaneously with the German Civil Code 1900. Before concluding, I will explain the outline of the 2001 revision and discuss its relationship with this article in the following part.[62]

By this revision, the proposition that 'an initially impossible contract is null and void' (§ 306 of the German Civil Code before the revision) was repealed. Accordingly, the initial impossibility no longer makes the contract null and void. In other words, even if the impossibility of delivery already exists at the time of conclusion of the contract, it does not prevent the contract from being valid (§ 311 a of the German Civil Code). By revising it so, the German Civil Code's nonperformance of obligation came to cover both initial and subsequent

62 For detailed discussions in Japan on the 2001 revision of the German Civil Code, see T. Oka (ed), *Keiyaku-Ho ni Okeru Gendaika no Kadai* [Challenges in Modernization of Law of Contract] (Tokyo 2002); S. Ono, *Shiho no Gendaika to Minpou* [Modernization of Justice and the Civil Code] (Tokyo 2003) 193; Y. Handa, *Doitsu Saiken-Ho Gendaika Josetsu* [A Preliminary Discussion on Modernization on German Obligations Law] (Tokyo 2004); Y. Shiomi, *Keiyaku Houri no Gendaika* [Modernization of Legal Doctrines of Contract] (Tokyo 2004) at 339. The 2001 revision was a law revision project that extended over a long period of time from the request for experts' opinion made by the German Federal Ministry of Justice in 1979 (Bundesminister der Justiz (ed), Gutachten und Vorschläge zur Überarbeitung des Schuldrechts (Köln, Bd. I, 1981; Bd. II 1981; Bd. III 1983).
Regarding the 2001 revision, detailed material for legislation and materials for understanding the revised Civil Code were published via the Internet. See, for example, http://www.jusline.de/Buergerliches_Gesetzbuch_(BGB).html, http://www.uni-koeln.de/jur-fak/lbrah/schuldrecht/schuldrecht_bmj.htm.

hindrance to performance. In addition, the original structure of contractual liability for default which consisted of the two categories of delay in performance and impossibility of performance was abolished. Instead, the comprehensive definition (breach of a duty arising under the obligation) was adopted. Furthermore, by the 2001 revision, warranty, which had been considered to be difficult to absorb into the liability for default but persistently remained in an independent form of liability was eventually absorbed into the liability for default (§§ 434, 437, 439 etc.).[63]

Work on the revision of the German Civil Code started in the late 1970's. In 1992, the report of the Obligations Law Reform Committee of the Federal Ministry of Justice was published but the recommendation of the report was never enacted.[64] The 2001 revision also experienced a complicated process before it was finally realized.[65] Certainly, the 2001 revision was an extensive revision that included integration of special laws into the Code and was therefore much discussed, but with regard to the law of nonperformance of obligation, including liability for defects in things, which is the subject of this Chapter, the contents of the revision were not so substantially changed during the process.

The prototype of Japanese civil law jurisprudence was generated through the reception of the theories of the *Pandektenwissenschaft* and its successor, German civil law jurisprudence. This had continued from the end of the 19th century to about 1920. When I started the study of civil law during the socially and politically confusing period of the 1960's, the 'Great German Wall' stood before me. In such a situation, it seemed to me a great adventure to develop theories criticizing such a great wall. In the 40 years since then, that great

63 See Handa, n 62 *supra* at 99. For a brief introduction of the 2001 revision, see also Z. Kitagawa, *Saiken Kakuron Minpou Kouyou IV* [Specific Issues of the Obligations Law – Lecture on the Civil Law IV] (3rd ed., Tokyo 2003) at 623.1; Z. Kitagawa, *Saiken Souron – Minpou Kouyou III (Dai 3-han)* [General Principles of the Obligations Law – Lecture on the Civil Law III (3rd edition)] (Tokyo 2004) at 533.12, 533.514 and 536.16.

64 Bundesminister der Justiz (ed), Abschlussbericht der Kommission zur Überarbeitung des Schuldrechts (Köln 1992).

65 Regarding the legislation process of the 2001 revision, see Handa, n 62 *supra,* at 15, Shiomi, n 62 *supra* at 342.

wall was eventually 'moved' by the 2001 revision. What is more, it was made in the direction that I challenged through the theories for criticizing the prototype of Japanese civil law. It will be very interesting to see now what response will emerge from Japanese civil law jurisprudence.[66]

As mentioned above, this revision had its origins around the 20th century in *Rabel's* theory of another legal stream that had unbrokenly existed, since Ancient Roman law, below the surface of the German *Pandektenwissenschaft* in the 19th century. After World War II the stream of legal thought developed by *Rabel* expanded together with internationalization of the world economy and came to take the dominant position in conventions on international sales of goods.[67] In other words, with the Hague Convention relating to a Uniform Law on the International Sale of Goods (ULIS) and the Convention on Contracts for the International Sale of Goods (Vienna Sales Convention, CISG) which globalized the ULIS, the German-type structure of liability for default clearly lost its influence.[68] In addition, the 2001

66 Shiomi, n 62 *supra,* 358, already discussed that: 'When we recognized the historical fact that Japanese traditional jurisprudence on the issue of obligations, which still does not lose its dominant position, had established its doctrinal structure based on the reception of German legal theories and had self-duplicated while giving sufficient consideration to the development of German civil law jurisprudence, the 'understanding' of the modernization movement in the German obligations law may have a great importance beyond that only in terms of comparative law', and made detailed analysis on what challenges were posed by the modernization of the German obligations law to the Japanese obligations law jurisprudence, through examination on the two 'modernizations' – the modernization in the legal imputation structure for nonperformance of obligation, and the modernization by integration of consumer contract law into the Civil Code (*ibid*, at 357–410).

67 Particularly important works of Ernst Rabel are *Das Recht des Warenkaufs,* Bd. I (Berlin 1957) and Bd. II (Berlin 1958).

68 The Hague Convention relating to a Uniform Law on the International Sale of Goods (ULIS) – for which the International Institute for the Unification of Private Law (UNIDROIT) started the drafting work in 1930, but the work was interrupted by the World War II – was finally adopted by the Hague Diplomatic Conference in 1964, together with the Uniform Law on the Formation of Contracts for the International Sale of Goods (CISG), and came into effect in 1972. However, when United Nations Convention on Contracts for the International Sale of Goods – which was prepared by the United Nations Commission on International Trade Law (UNICITRAL) and is also known by the following abbre-

revision of the German Civil Code can be understood as aiming at the same direction as the U.S. Uniform Commercial Code. Also important is the relationship between the development of European law and the German Civil Code. In the field of civil law, comparative law has developed globally and splendidly.

Considering this, it seems not surprising that this revision showed the tendency for the German civil law to come closer to the global trend of obligations laws (or laws of contractual liability). Certainly, the wall of the German Civil Code was moved. At the same time, however, we must find out that the foundation of the German Civil Code, the *Pandektensystem* itself was not moved (or changed). In other words, although the castle wall of the German Civil Code was moved, the castle itself was still not moved. How should Japanese civil law jurisprudence respond to the questions posed by this fact?[69]

V. Conclusion

As in the case of the German Civil Code, the Japanese Civil Code adopted the *Pandektenwissenschaft*. However, when individually examining its contents, we can find the fact that the Japanese Civil Code is in fact a fruit of the mixed reception of foreign civil codes (mainly, the German and French Civil Codes). Furthermore, after its enactment, however, the process of systemization of Japanese civil

viations: the CISG, the Vienna Sales Convention and the United Nations Sales Convention – was adopted at the Vienna Diplomatic Conference held in 1980 and came into effect in 1988; its importance has almost vanished (because the main Contracting States of the Hague Convention denounced it when they joined the CISG in accordance with the relevant provision of the Hague Convention). See K. Sono and M. Yamate, *Kokusai Baibai-Ho* [Law on International Sales] (Tokyo 1993); K. Igarashi, *Minpou to Hikaku-Ho* [Civil Law and Comparative Law] at (Tokyo 1992) 158; Z. Kitagawa, 'Minpouten to Hikakuho – Kenkyu Note' [The Civil Code and Comparative Law – A Note for Study], 58 *Hikakuho Kenkyu* (1996) at 72.

69 For this issue, see *supra* n 58, 59 and 60. For futuristic view of the Japanese Civil Code, see Z. Kitagawa, 'Minpou no Kin-Mirai Model' [Near-Future Model of the Civil Law Study], in 'Legal Dynamics in the Global Era: Multidisciplinary Perspectives on the Transformation of Market and Law' organized by Kobe University, Center for Legal Dynamics of Advanced Market Societies (Vol. 54, No.1 *Kobe Hougaku Zasshi* (2004) 161).

law jurisprudence proceeded based on legal theories of German civil law jurisprudence as a means to absorb the foreign legal elements introduced through the reception of foreign civil codes into the Japanese civil law. This process was what is called the theory reception of German law and, as a result of this, the prototype of the Japanese civil law jurisprudence was formed. This process had continued from the time immediately after enactment of the Japanese Civil Code (1898) to about 1920. Even after the theory reception of German law had ended, the influence of German legal theories did not decline and persistently remained in Japan even after World War II. However, the end of World War II certainly played a role of putting another end to the aftermath of the theory reception of German law. After such a history, German jurisprudence has now come to have a new significance for Japanese civil law – ie it has re-emerged as a foreign law that had a similar legal system to Japanese civil law.

From the perspective of comparative law, should the similarity of jurisprudence between Japan and Germany be regarded as a past event? From the viewpoint of the civil law, what is the meaning of the prototype of the Japanese civil law jurisprudence and legal theories submitted for the purpose of achieving independence thereof? Should we not examine the contemporary implication of these questions? What challenges will such an examination pose to us? At the time of globalization of laws, the unique similarity between Japanese and German jurisprudence can be regarded as an invaluable asset for comparative study of law. After the recent revision of the German Civil Code, does it raise some new questions to us? In this Chapter I introduced some of my thoughts about these questions.

For civil law scholars at the time of the theory reception of the German law and even at the time when we made efforts to achieve departure from the prototype of Japanese civil law jurisprudence, the German Civil Code and German civil law jurisprudence felt as if they were something that would be never changed – ie the 'Great German Wall'. However, this German wall was actually moved by the 2001 revision of the German Civil Code. In this Chapter I made clear or reconfirmed that it was predestined to happen. At the same time, however, the *Pandektensystem*, its foundation, is still preserved. Are there not any problems regarding it? This is an issue not only for the German Civil Code but also for the Japanese Civil Code.

It posed a new question to us: If there are many problems regarding it, what direction should Japanese civil law jurisprudence and the Japanese Civil Code aim to take? It is more than ever desirable to develop a future picture of Japanese civil law jurisprudence by examining the relationship between German civil law jurisprudence and Japanese civil law jurisprudence from the perspective of comparative law.

Chapter 3: Modernization of German Civil Law and Japanese Civil Law Interpretation

Yoshio Shiomi

Contents

I. Objective of This Article

This article addresses the issue of what significance can be found in comprehending German civil law for today's civil law interpretation in Japan.[1]

As it is generally known, many years have already passed since the debate over the relationship between German law and Japanese law in the area of civil law started in the 1970s, focusing on the origin of Japanese civil law and the role of the German civil law theories in cases where German law was not regarded as the model for Japanese law (involving the conflict between the theory of legislative intention and the theory of legal intention and the controversy over the model law-centrism or the attitude to return to the model law).[2] However, today when it has been denied that German civil law is the only model for the Japanese Civil Code and it has been recognized that the phenomenon of 'reception of legal theories' actually existed, it seems relatively rare to see such adverse circumstances of the past that required scholars who presented papers featuring German civil law to give detailed explanations about the significance of studying German law, or hear such harsh comments that criticized the efforts to develop interpretative study of Japanese civil law with the use of theories, systems, and concepts that did not exist in Japan but existed in Germany (eg 'illegality', 'ancillary obligation/custodial obligation', 'adequate causality', and 'trichotomy' of non-performance of obligation), as 'specifically German'.

1 This article, like other articles included in this issue of *Minshōhō Zasshi*, was prepared for the symposium at the Legal Training and Research Institute of Japan. Taking into consideration the questions I personally heard at the discussion and at the meeting after the symposium, and aiming to emphasize differences from the article written by *Kitagawa* that was also prepared for the symposium and is included in this issue, I made revisions and additions to my article that were reported to the symposium. This article focuses on property law in the area of civil law. The discussion in response to questions regarding the legal nature of warranty was included in this article. The discussion in response to questions regarding the meaning of Article 414 of the Civil Code is included in *Kitagawa's* article.

2 To understand the history during this period, H. Mizumoto & K. Hirai (eds), *Nihon Minpōgakushi: Tsūshi* [Overall history of Japanese civil law] (Tokyo 1997) is a useful reference. Also, see Prof. *Kitagawa's* article included in this issue of *Minshōhō Zasshi*.

Nevertheless, it cannot be overstressed that the major issue that was brought up and criticized or defended in the debate over the relationship between German law and Japanese law in the area of civil law was the study of civil law from the perspective of interpretation in a narrow sense (and in particular, such study as aiming to obtain clues for interpretation of Japanese civil law). This fact can be proven by three factors: (i) study on legal history of German civil law[3] was not criticized in the past argument; (ii) nor was study on German civil law from an ideological or philosophical perspective[4] criticized in the past argument; (iii) when German civil law was discussed within the framework of interpretation, it was often the case that scholars (both those sceptical of and those advocating the relationship between German law and Japanese law) focused on the theme of 'what influence German civil law had on Japanese civil law', without sufficiently discussing whether to deal with German law as the subject matter of comparative law or from a dogmatic perspective.[5, 6]

When we intend to specify and examine points of issues under the theme of what significance can be found in comprehending German civil law for the Japanese civil law theories, we should emphasize the significance of dealing with German civil law in civil law interpretation. In order to specify and examine issues from this viewpoint, it is naturally necessary as a premise to understand the circumstances that affect German civil law. However, as it is generally known, German civil law

3 Representative studies include the series of studies by *Tetsu Isomura* and the study on *Friedrich Carl von Savigny* by the group headed by *Shigeyoshi Harashima*.

4 There are many examples of such studies, including a series of academic works about freedom of contract and justice of contract, which have arisen from the discussion on modern contract law.

5 The issue of how the two conflicting viewpoints, the one that views German civil law from the perspective of comparative law and the other from the perspective of dogmatics, will harmonize with each other, is discussed in multiple aspects in Z. Kitagawa, *Nihon Minpōgaku No Rekishi To Riron* [History and theory of the Japanese civil law jurisprudence] (Tokyo 1968).

6 Even during this period, the studies of German civil law from the perspective of comparative law (eg K. Igarashi, *Keiyaku To Jijō Henkō* [Contract and change of circumstances] (Tokyo 1969); K. Igarashi, 'Kashitanpo to hikakuhō' [Warranty against defects and comparative law], in K. Igarashi, *Hikakuminhōgaku No Shomondai* [Issues of comparative civil law jurisprudence] (Tokyo 1976) 80 et seq) were highly evaluated.

has just gone through a large reform in the modernization of the Law of Obligations in 2001, and it is still in the process of drastic change. First of all, we should understand the 'current status' of German civil law, but this work is expected to be extremely difficult (not only for researchers who specialize in particular parts of German civil law but also for legal professionals such as judges and lawyers).[7]

This article, in the first part, gives a rough overview of the trends and tendencies in modernization (*Modernisierung*) of German civil law. The same part also points out such movements that may be important for civil law interpretation and inquires into current trends occurring in German civil law. This issue will lead to the original theme of what significance can be found in comprehending German civil law for Japanese civil law interpretation, which is discussed at the end of this article. The second part overviews what significance was found in the past argument in Japan in comprehending German civil law for the Japanese civil law interpretation. The final part provides a conclusion on what significance can be found in comprehending German civil law for Japanese civil law jurisprudence in the near future. (See also the article written by *Zentaro Kitagawa* in this volume).

II. Characteristics of Modernization (*Modernisierung*) of German Civil Law

1. Introduction

Recently there has been a rapid movement in Germany toward reconstructing the Civil Code and civil law theories under the name of modernization.[8] There are many examples of developments that show this

[7] My personal gain from the symposium was that I was made aware of the fact that judges who participated in the symposium were very interested and ambitious in the area of understanding foreign legal theories but were unable to find enough time, occupied by daily work, to pay attention to legal trends in other countries (particularly those in non-English speaking countries) in a systematic manner. For instance, they had heard that a major revision was made to the Law of Obligations but had had almost no opportunity to find out the contents and significance of the reform.

[8] 'Modernization' does not only refer to the modernization of the Law of Default of Obligations, Prescription Law, and Consumer Laws under the Law for

movement, such as the major revision in the Law of Obligations mentioned above (in particular the Law of Default of Obligations) together with that of its counterpart, the Prescription Law; the integration of the Law for the Regulation of General Trading Conditions and other various consumer-related special laws into the Civil Code the reform of the Residential Lease Law, the reform of the Tort Liability Law (including the Road Traffic Law and the Medicines Law), and the major revision in family law. Along with this, there is also a movement toward reconstructing civil law theories without reforming the Civil Code.

The characteristics of modernization of German civil law are outlined below.[9]

2. Integration of Various Consumer Laws into the Civil Code

a) *Incentive for Integration*

Through a major revision in the Law of Obligations in 2001, many consumer laws that had existed as special laws (eg the Consumer Credit Law and the substantive part of the Law for the Regulation of General Trading Conditions) were integrated into the Civil Code.[10]

the Modernization of the Law of Obligations (Schuldrechtsmodernisierungsgesetz, BT-Drs. 14/7052; usually referred to as SMG) (the Civil Code revised by SMG was put into force on January 1, 2002). This article also uses the term 'modernization' in a broader sense.

9 The reform of the Tort Liability Law is excluded from the discussion in this article because the major objectives of the reform were to respond to changes in social conditions and problems specific to modern society (reform systems and rules in response to the transformation from early-modern society to modern society) and to solve defects in the existing provisions as pointed out by many scholars. See Y. Shiomi, 'Doitsu ni okeru Songaibaishōhō kitei no kaisei to Kōtsūjikobaishōhō no kadai' [Reform of the Tort Liability Law and problems of the Traffic Accident Liability Law in Germany] *Minshōhō Zasshi* Vol. 125, No. 2 (2002) 147 et seq; Y. Shiomi, '2001nen no Doitsu ni okeru iyakuhinhigai baishōsekinin ni kansuru kitei kaisei' [Reform of the provisions on the liability for pharmaceutical accidents in Germany in 2002] *Endo Hiroshi Sensei Sanju Kinen Ronbunshū* (2002) 423 et seq.

10 The laws wholly or partially integrated into the Civil Code include: Law for the Regulation of General Trading Conditions (Gesetz zur Regelung des Rechts der Allgemeinen Geschäftsbedingungen); Mail-Order Sales Law (Fernabsatzgesetz); Consumer Credit Law (Verbraucherkreditgesetz); Law over Revocation of

Reform was also made to include in the Section of Sale of the Civil Code special rules on the sale of consumer goods which had been excluded from legislation.

The important change that preceded these reforms is that the definitions of 'consumer' (*Verbraucher*) and 'entrepreneur' (*Unternehmer*) were added as §§ 13 and 14 to the Civil Code. Section 13 provides that 'a consumer is any natural person who concludes a legal transaction for a purpose that can be included in neither his commercial nor his independent vocational activity'. Section 14 provides that 'an entrepreneur is a natural or legal entity or a legally responsible unincorporated firm, which acts, at the time of conclusion of a legal transaction, to conduct their commercial or independent vocational activity.' Upon the implementation of the Directive of the European Parliament and of the Council 20 May 1997 on the protection of consumers in respect of distance contracts into domestic legislation, partial reform was made in the Civil Code on June 27, 2000 in order to add the definitions of 'consumer' and 'entrepreneur' and guarantee consumers the right of revocation and the right to return goods.[11] Upon the implementation of the EU Directive on Distance Contracts, it was possible to establish a special law separately from the Civil Code.[12] Nevertheless, the legislators chose to implement the EU Directive into domestic legislation within the scope of provisions

Door-to-Door Sales Contracts (Gesetz über den Widerruf von Haustürgeschäften und ähnlichen Geschäften); Law over Time Rights to Residence (Gesetz über die Veräußerung von Teilzeitnutzungsrechten an Wohngebäuden). For the outline of such legal integration, see Y. Shiomi, *Keiyakuhōri No Gendaika* [Modernization of the theory of contract law] (Tokyo 2004) 393 et seq.

11 This information is available in Y. Imanishi, 'Doitsu Minpō no ichibu kaisei to Shōhishahō: Shōhisha, tekkaiken tō no kihon gainen ni kansuru Minpō kitei no shinsetsu ni tsuite' [Partial reform of German civil law and consumer laws: New provisions of civil law concerning the basic concepts of consumers, right of revocation etc.] *Kandai hōgaku Ronshū* Vol. 50, No. 5 (2000) 1104 et seq.

12 One important reform made at the same time in response to the EU Directives was to control terms of consumer contracts even where they were concluded as individual contracts not subject to the general trading conditions (i.e. introduce rules on unfair contract terms). The legislators made this reform by adding § 24(a) to the Law for the Regulation of General Trading Conditions rather than by revising the provisions of the Civil Code. This reform was made to convert the Council Directive of 5 April 1993 on unfair terms in consumer contracts, 93/13/EEC, into domestic legislation.

concerning 'persons' under the Civil Code and add the definitions mentioned above to the Civil Code.

The aim behind this choice was to implement various consumer-related EU Directives, a number of which were established into domestic legislation by taking a single action to add uniform definitions to the Civil Code. This can be said to have resulted from the 'Europeanization of private law'.

This aim was combined with the attempt to restore the Civil Code as a 'general private code' by integrating into the Civil Code various consumer-related laws that had been categorized as private laws and established as special laws separately from the Civil Code. This resulted in the reform of the Civil Code in 2001. Needless to say, the addition of the definitions of 'consumer' and 'entrepreneur' to the Civil Code formed the basis for the integration.

b) Significance of the Integration

The integration of various consumer-related special laws into the Civil Code is noteworthy in that it was successful because 'consumer' equalled 'general citizen' (*der allgemeine BGB-Bürger*)[13] and it was intended to simplify the legal structures that had become unclear due to the establishment of too many consumer-related special laws.[14] In relation to the subject matter of this article, the integration is also very significant in the following two ways.

The first relates to the fact that the integration was driven by the request for implementation of the EU Directives into domestic legislation. In modern society where it has become a practice to provide and receive consumer goods and services and make payment therefore across national borders, it is no longer appropriate to regulate consumer transactions by domestic rules of each country and transnational rules are needed. Many EU Directives established in relation

13 T. Pfeiffer, 'Der Verbraucher nach § 13 BGB', in R. Schulze & H. Schulte-Nölke (eds), *Die Schuldrechtsreform vor dem Hintergrund des Gemeinschaftsrechts* (Tübingen 2001) 133, 134. *Pfeiffer*, advocating the usefulness of the concept of 'consumers', is critical of such integration.

14 Begründung der Bundesregierung zum Entwurf eines Gesetzes zur Modernisierung des Schuldrechts, in C.-W. Canaris, *Schuldrechtsmodernisierung* (Munich 2002) 569, 591.

to consumers are aimed at regulating consumer transactions in Europe under uniform rules. Facing such circumstances there is no choice for Germany as a EU Member but to implement the EU Directives into domestic legislation with respect to transactions subject to the Directives with the exception of the parts left to the discretion of each Member State. The current modernization of German civil law can be described as reconstruction of the Civil Code in response to such 'external requests for modernization'. However there is concern that such modernization would bring about 'terms with double meanings' (*Begriffe mit Doppelbedeutung*), one arising from EU Directives and the other originating from the German Civil Code (eg 'defects of things' under sales contracts), and also bring about hybrid standards (*Hybridnormen* – eg standards for the right of revocation).[15] This concern clearly indicates problems that would occur upon the introduction of foreign laws into domestic legislation.

The second significant point relates to the fact that the legislators chose to integrate consumer-related private laws into the Civil Code by the reform in 2001 even though it was possible to respond to the EU Directives by establishing independent special laws and such measures had been taken in the past. In other words, this point focuses on why the legislators chose to integrate consumer laws into the Civil Code even though it was also possible to establish a uniform Consumer Code separately from the Civil Code[16] as well as why the integration was possible.[17]

15 H. Dörner, 'Die Integration des Verbraucherrechts in das BGB', in R. Schulze & H. Schulte-Nölke (eds), *Die Schuldrechtsreform vor dem Hintergrund des Gemeinschaftsrechts* (Tübingen 2001) 177, 182 seq.

16 To put it more clearly, there were many reasons that Germany did not choose to establish a Consumer Code; in particular, there were concerns that the establishment of a Consumer Code would cause ambiguity in terms of the scope of application (the relationship between the rules on 'consumer goods' provided in a Consumer Code and those provided in the Section on Sale under the Civil Code), and that if a Consumer Code were established to cover all legal matters, it would become either an unclear code or a superficial code indicating nothing other than the overall picture of consumer laws. J. Schmidt-Räntsch, 'Reintegration der Verbraucherschutzgesetze durch den Entwurf eines Schuldrechtsmodernisierungsgesetzes', in R. Schulze & H. Schulte-Nölke (eds), *Die Schuldrechtsreform vor dem Hintergrund des Gemeinschaftsrechts* (Tübingen 2001) 169, 172 seq.

17 T. Pfeiffer, in H.T. Soergel, J. Damrau & W. Siebert (eds), Bürgerliches Gesetzbuch (13th ed., Stuttgart 2003) § 13 paras. 17–21.

The integration of various consumer laws into the Civil Code was possible largely because most EU Directives addressing consumer issues adopted neo-liberalism as the basic ideology for consumer law. From the perspective of guaranteeing individual freedom of decision-making (right of self-determination) and protecting individuals against the violation of such freedom it is in harmony with the values and guiding principles of the early-modern civil code that is categorized as European Continental Law, to include in the civil code, while defining consumers and entrepreneurs in line with their status in the market and recognizing the fact that consumers are structurally subordinated in the market, legal techniques to restore 'contract parity' (*Vertragsparität*) for entrepreneur-consumer transactions in which lack of parity is seen in terms of information access (information disparity) and in psychological aspects or in the decision-making process (bargaining power disparity[18] – eg transparency rule, obligation to provide information or explanation), as well as legal techniques to give relief to consumers suffering from contracts that are concluded without such parity (eg right of revocation, nullification of unfair terms).[19]

The early-modern civil code under classical liberalism was established for rational persons standing at parity who were capable of making reasonable choices and decisions and the State was not expected to play a role of guaranteeing freedom of contract by actively supporting individuals in making decisions so as to provide them with an equal footing under contract (the State should intervene in freedom of contract only in exceptional cases where the agreement between the parties was defective or antistate/antisocial). On the other hand the consumer laws that have recently been integrated into the Civil Code are viewed as coming under neo-liberalism which is based on market mechanisms and individual freedom in the market. In this context the consumers' typical and structural characteristics as 'persons' are recognized while focusing on their lack of parity with entrepreneurs in terms of information access and bargaining capability. The State is required to take supportive measures to secure and

[18] In most cases, lack of parity also exists in terms of economic strength, though this is not seen for all entrepreneur-consumer transactions.

[19] K. Larenz & M. Wolf, *Allgemeiner Teil des Bürgerlichen Rechts* (9th ed. Munich 2004) 15, 33 et seq, 760; Shiomi, n 10 *supra*, 397.

promote free and fair market as well as measures to enable individuals who participate in the market to make choices and decisions of their own free will (ie it is required to develop a foundation for self-determination and secure freedom of choice and decision-making).[20] In this regard the civil code under classical liberalism and the civil code under neo-liberalism provide for different systems and rules. Nevertheless, unlike such consumer laws as those primarily intended to partially preclude freedom of contract or right of self-determination from the perspective of a welfare state and force transactions that appear to be favourable to the State, the integration of consumer laws in the sense mentioned above into the civil code would create no contradiction in civil code values or guiding principles.[21] Welfare-oriented consumer laws that are opposed to freedom of contract completely differ from independence-oriented consumer laws under neo-liberalism in terms of the relationship between freedom of contract (right of self-determination) and justice of contract.

It can be said that in Germany, in the end, the paradigm shift from welfare-oriented consumer laws to independence-oriented consumer laws (based on the information model) enabled the integration of consumer laws into the Civil Code and in consequence it changed the foundation of values of the Civil Code from classical liberalism to neo-liberalism based on market mechanisms.[22] This is another extremely important characteristic of modernization of German civil law in respect of the integration of various consumer-related special laws into the Civil Code.[23] However, it is worth considering in the

20 Information models (*Informationsmodell*) have also arisen from this viewpoint, although there is a difference in nuance among scholars as to how to specify an information model.

21 T. Pfeiffer, 'Die Integration von „Nebengesetzen" in das BGB', in W. Ernst & R. Zimmermann (eds), *Zivilrechtswissenschaft und Schuldrechtsreform* (Tübingen 2001) 481, 494 et seq.

22 This point was already discussed in H.P. Westermann, 'Verbraucherschutz', in Bundesminister der Justiz (ed), *Gutachten und Vorschläge zur Überarbeitung des Schuldrechts* (vol. 3, Köln 1983) 9 et seq. As a recent reference, see S. Grundmann, 'Verbraucherrecht, Unternehmensrecht, Privatrecht' *AcP* 202 (2002), 40 et seq which tries to interpret contract law within an information model under neo-liberalism.

23 Most papers that present and discuss the integration of consumer law into the Civil Code through modernization of the code definitely lack the viewpoint mentioned in this article. This viewpoint is only found in K. Okubo, 'Shōhishahō no

future whether or not such shift in the core structure of civil law in line with the EU rules is consistent at all with the traditional jurisprudence of German civil law and in particular basic theories such as declaration of intention and theory of legal acts.

3. Reconstruction of the Law of Default of Obligations

a) Incentive for the Reconstruction

The core of the modernization of the Law of Obligations which started to be discussed in the 1970s and resulted in the reform of the Civil Code in 2001 was the reconstruction of the Law of Default of Obligations. The objectives of the reconstruction included the following: (i) to reform rules that had become impractical given the changing state of society after the compilation of the Civil Code (in particular the Warranty Law and the Prescription Law); (ii) to codify the Judge Law (*Richterrecht*) which was developed under the Civil Code that had been put into force at the end of the 19th century and drastically changed the essential parts of the code thereby reviving law positivism (eg positive breach of a contract [*positive Vertragsverletzung*], negligence in the conclusion of a contract [*culpa in contrahendo*], defective grounds of an act [*Störung der Geschäftsgrundlage, clausula rebus sic stantibus*], warranty law introduction of relevant

taikeiteki dokuritsusei' [Systematic independence of consumer laws] *Kobe Gakuin Hōgaku* Vol. 31, No. 4 (2002) 1541 et seq, which discusses it in the course of presenting the argument of *Franz Bydlinski*, and K. Sato, 'Hito to shite no shōhisha' [Consumer as person] *Hosei Ronshū* No. 201 (2004) 459 et seq, which points out the controversy in Germany over the existence of a theoretical conflict between private autonomy, the basis of civil law, and consumer law. Other papers only follow superficial descriptions of legislative materials and aim to faithfully explain annotations on interpretative techniques. I do not deny the significance of accurate analysis of materials at all, but I cannot understand the attitude of such researchers who, despite the growing interest in the relationship between freedom of contract and justice of contract and the principles of consumer law, and probably being aware that such trends are also noticeable in Germany, merely read materials and explain interpretative methods without trying to think fundamentally or constructing a schema for legal thought; and yet when a pioneering or full-fledged study is presented in Japan regarding the issues such as the 'relationship between the Constitution and civil law', 'right of self-determination', and 'obligation to provide information', they rush to participate in the discussion while lacking the understanding of its premise.

theories of case law so as to substantively correct the relationships where only either the right to claim damages or the right to claim termination was exercisable which had been a characteristic of German law, with the aim to allow the exercise of both rights [former § 325 BGB]); (iii) to integrate the EU Directives relating to the Law of Obligations into domestic legislation (to this end it was necessary to reconstruct basic rules and systems under the Civil Code so as to maintain consistency and systematic uniformity within the Code). It should be particularly noted that during the reform process consideration was always given to harmonization with international transaction rules (the 1964 Hague Convention on International Sale of Goods in the 1970s; the 1980 United Nations Convention on International Sale of Goods; the UNIDROIT Principles of International Commercial Contracts (1994)[24] and the Principles of European Contract Law developed by the Commission on European Contract Law (1998)[25] in the 1980s and thereafter).[26]

24 At present, the 2004 version is available.

25 Only Part 1 and Part 2 were published at that time, but Part 3 has also been published to date. O. Lando & H. Beale (eds), *Principles of European Contract Law, Part I & II* (The Hague 1999); O. Lando, E. Clive, A. Prüm & R. Zimmermann (eds), *Principles of European Contract Law, Part III* (The Hague 2003). I have already obtained the right to translate these principles into Japanese with *Hisakazu Matsuoka* and *Kunihiro Nakata* (the Principles of European Contract Law is not a 'law' but a 'work' that is created by the private research group headed by *Professor Lando* and therefore it is copyrighted by the group). We will organize a joint research group and publish, in numbers, the full translations of the Principles, including the provisions, annotations, and notes, from Horitsubunkasha (the working group is currently preparing to publish a tentative translation of part of Part 3 on *Doshisha Hōgaku* as the first publication).

26 For the process during this period, see Shiomi, n 10 *supra,* 339 et seq, and references cited therein. As basic references indicating the overall picture of the reformed German Law of Obligations, see T. Oka (ed), *Keiyakuhō Ni Okeru Gendaika No Kadai* [Problems of modernization of contract law] (Tokyo 2001); Y. Handa, *Doitsu Saimuhō Gendaikahō Gaisetsu* [Overview of the German Law for the Modernization of the Law of Obligations] (Tokyo 2004). Y. Shiomi, *Saiken Sōron I (Dai Ni Han)* [General theory of claim I (second edition)] (Tokyo 2003) also conducts analysis regarding the reform. However, these references do not address the major revisions in the Tort Liability Law accompanying the reform of the Tort Law, except for the one mentioned last.

b) Significance of the Reconstruction

Setting aside for other works[27] the details of reforms of individual systems and rules which constitute the Law of Default of Obligations, through the modernization of the Law of Obligations, this section specifies the significance of the reconstruction of the Law of Default of Obligations in line with the subject matter of this article. The reconstruction of the Law of Default of Obligations through the modernization of the Law of Obligations is of considerable significance in the following three ways:

The point that should be noted first is that the reconstruction of the Civil Code was conducted in response to the 'external requests for modernization' which involved the implementation of the EU Directives into domestic legislation. Furthermore, choosing to reform the Civil Code instead of establishing an independent special law was more inevitable for the reconstruction than for the integration of consumer laws into the Civil Code that was also conducted with the aim of implementing EU Directives into domestic legislation.

In this regard, the implementation of the EU Directive on Sale of Consumer Goods[28] was of great importance. As it is generally known, in Germany warranty for sale is categorized by concepts such as 'defects in things', 'defects in right', 'wrong types of things', 'deficiency in quantity' and 'breach of collateral obligation' and the nature and contents of warranty were discussed regarding each concept. Furthermore, with respect to the nature of warranty against defects in things there was a conflict between the 'theory of contract' and the 'theory of law' (from which the conflict between the theory of legal liability and the theory of contractual liability in Japan originated). On the other hand the EU Directive on Sale of Consumer Goods has not only shifted the core concept of the seller's non-performance in sale of consumer goods from 'defects in things' to 'non-compliance with the contract' but it also basically regards the seller's liability as arising from breach of contract (non-performance of obligation). In

[27] See the relevant parts of Shiomi, n 10 *supra,* 360 et seq, and n 26 *supra.*

[28] Directive of the European Parliament and of the Council 25 May 1999 on certain aspects of the sale of consumer goods and associated guarantees, OJL 171/12.

order to secure systematic consistency in the order of domestic law upon implementing the EU Directive on Sale of Consumer Goods into domestic legislation harmonization should be achieved between the two legal frameworks in terms of the model of disturbed performance. To this end Germany chose to reconstruct the systems and rules under the Civil Code with the aim of achieving compliance with the EU Directive. More specifically, upon the modernization of the Law of Obligations while regarding the seller's liability in case of defects in right for the thing for sale or defects in the thing itself as liability for non-performance of obligation Germany chose to integrate conventional rules for warranty that could be covered by the general legal theory of non-performance of obligation (in particular, major rules on damages and termination) with the rules in the General Provisions of the Civil Code, and leave only special rules in the Section of Sale (and further establish the subsection titled 'Sale of Consumer Goods' in the Section of Sale [§§ 474 sqq] as special rules). The reform in this manner was also justified by the fact that such choice resulted in consistency with the international transaction rules mentioned above.[29]

Secondly, the reconstruction of the Law of Default of Obligations through the modernization of the Law of Obligations was also significant because as mentioned in the section discussing the incentive the reconstruction was conducted while giving consideration to consistency with international transaction rules. This point is not only evident from the 'Discussion Draft' (*Diskussionsentwurf*) published by the Federal Ministry of Justice in August 2000 but also obvious at

29 This also applies to the reform of rules for delayed performance. The 'Directive of the European Parliament and of the Council 29 June 2000 on combating late payment in commercial transactions, OJL 20/35' aims to (i) facilitate the determination of delayed performance by the debtor so as to improve payment morals; (ii) increase the effectiveness of default interest; (iii) nullify terms of contracts for payment that are extremely unfavorable to the creditor. Reform was made to § 286 (former § 284) and § 288 (former § 288) of the Civil Code by introducing these rules into domestic legislation. For the outline of the EU Directive on Late Payment and the confusion in the legislative process in Germany, see Y. Shiomi, 'EU to Doitsu ni okeru shiharai chitai seido no henkaku' [Reform of the late payment system in EU and Germany], in Y. Shiomi (ed), *Kunii Sensei Kanreki Kinen Ronbunshū, Minpōgaku No Kiseki To Tenbo* [History and future vision of study of civil law] (Tokyo 2001) 167 et seq.

a glance of the Consolidated Version of the Discussion Draft (*Konsolidierte Fassung des Diskussionsentwurfs*) published in March 2001 in response to the strong opposition to the Discussion Draft from scholars and practitioners (including the paper written by *Canaris*[30] who played a leading role in developing the Consolidated Version), as well as the Reasons (*Begründung*) for the Government Bill (*Regierungsentwurf*) published in May 2001.[31]

Consideration to consistency with international transaction rules is seen in the following two changes: (i) a complete about-face was made to reform the provision of former § 306 BGB: 'any contract intended for impossible performance shall be null', into 'the mere fact that the debtor is exempted from performance under § 275(1) to (3) and such disturbance of performance already existed at the time of the conclusion of the contract does not affect the validity of the contract'[32]; (ii) 'any cause for which the debtor is responsible' is no longer necessary to claim termination of the contract because of non-

30 C.-W. Canaris, 'Die Reform des Rechts der Leistungsstörungen' *JZ* 2001 499 et seq.

31 The following points are particularly noteworthy in this regard. (i) The 'Discussion Draft' completely denied the concept of 'impossibility' and the system focusing on 'impossibility' and aimed to shift, while making reference to international transaction rules, from the 'impossibility'-focused system to the 'non-performance'-focused system, whereas the Government Bill (and the provisions on default of obligation) has restored the concept of 'impossibility' and the system focusing on 'impossibility' (restoration of 'impossibility' as a reason for default of obligation against the claim for performance (§ 275 of the Civil Code) and restoration of the provision on the bearing of risk system, which had been integrated into the provision on termination under the Discussion Draft (§ 326 of the Civil Code). Furthermore, a clear stipulation is made that 'a contract shall not be nullified because of initial impossibility', although in a negative way (§ 311 a (1) of the Civil Code)). (ii) The framework of the 'Discussion Draft' greatly matched the requirements of the United Nations Convention on International Sale of Goods and the Principles of European Contract Law, and those involved in developing the Government Bill stress that its framework is also in harmony with United Nations Convention on International Sale of Goods and the Principles of European Contract Law, which also adopt the concept of 'impossibility'.

32 This change is in line with Article 3.2 of the UNIDROIT Principles of International Commercial Contracts (2004) and Article 4.102 of the Principles of European Contract Law.

performance of obligation (former §§ 323, 324, and 326(2)[33]) as it was required in the past under former §§ 280(2) and 286(2), though the debtor bore the burden of proof. These changes were not intended in response to the request for the codification of the Judge Law or to satisfy the concrete legislative needs to implement EU Directives. This indicates how appropriate it is to construct such systems and rules – in particular, contract law – in harmony with international trends in the course of modernizing a pre-modern civil code.[34]

Thirdly, the reconstruction of the Law of Default of Obligations through the modernization of the Law of Obligations was also of great significance in restoring the Civil Code by codifying the Judge Law (*Richterrecht*) irrespective of the introduction of external laws into domestic legislation.

Viewed from the standpoint of reception of law which relates to the subject matter of this article how the restoration of the Civil Code through the codification of the Judge Law should be characterized is clearly indicated in the following statements of *Zimmermann* who criticized the Discussion Draft as a hasty attempt.

According to *Zimmermann*, immediately after the establishment of the German Civil Code at the end of the 19th century interpretation was developed from the code itself within the 'closed framework' comprising rules established under the code upon codification. This caused rapid departure from the Pandekten jurisprudence (*Pandektenwissenschaft*) of the 19th century and on the other hand also brought about a new type of jurisprudence that was separate from European tradition and comparative law. Aiming to eliminate the

33 This change is in line with Article 49 of the United Nations Convention on International Sale of Goods, Article 7.3.1 of the UNIDROIT Principles of International Commercial Contracts (2004), and Article 9.301 of the Principles of European Contract Law.

34 Useful references about the recent trends in European common private law include Shiomi, n 10 *supra,* 290 et seq; H. Kötz (translated by Yoshio Shiomi, Kunihiro Nakata, and Hisakazu Matsuoka), *Yōroppa Keiyakuhō I* [European contract law I] (Kyoto 1999); Y. Kawasumi, Y. Shiomi, K. Nakata & H. Matsuoka (eds), *Yōroppa Shihō No Dōko To Kadai* [Trends and problems of European private law] (Tokyo 2003); J. Basedow (translated by Yoshinobu Handa et al), *Yōroppa Tōitsu Keiyakuhō E No Michi* [Road to uniform European contract law] (Tokyo 2004).

trace of conceptual law positivism immediately after the compilation of the code courts developed the Judge Law. In order to compile a law that meets the needs of the times legislation should not derive from the idea that eliminating material defects in the old provisions is the legislator's justifiable mission but it should be based on deep thinking while taking into consideration the achievements to date after years of academic effort and court practice.[35]

4. Revision of the Provisions of the Lease Law and Integration Thereof into the Civil Code

a) *Incentive for the Revision of the Provisions and the Integration thereof into the Civil Code*

In March 2001, shortly before the enactment of the Law for the Modernization of the Law of Obligations the Law for the Reform of the Lease Law[36] (*Gesetz zur Neugliederung, Vereinfachung und Reform des Mietrechts, 'Mietrechtsreformgesetz'*) was enacted and put into force on September 1, 2001.

Considering the fact that the Lease Law at that time (including the provisions on lease under the Civil Code and many special laws on lease; hereinafter the same) was obsolete in terms of language and substance and not adapted to the needs of lifestyle in modern society or capable of meeting current needs in the building/housing market and that it was unclear and difficult to understand due to a number of legal reforms and special laws, the reform law was intended to make an overall reform of the Lease Law and integrate various special laws on leases into the Civil Code. This had the objective of 'protecting the weak, supporting lessors, promoting investment in the building/housing market and environmental conservation'.

35 R. Zimmermann, 'Schuldrechtsmodernisierung?' *JZ* 2001 171, 173 et seq, 181.

36 The bill and reason therefore is available as BT-Drs. 14/4553. As a Japanese reference that gives brief explanation, S. Fujii, 'Doitsu Ni Okeru Chintaishakuhō Kaisei Gaisetsu' [Overview of the reform of the Lease Law in Germany] *Ryukoku Hōgaku* Vol. 34, No. 4 (2002) 473 et seq. Translation of the provisions of the Lease Law appears in series in Vol. 34, No. 4 and thereafter.

b) Significance of the Revision of the Provisions and the Integration thereof into the Civil Code

The reform of the Lease Law brought an end to a long-standing legislative issue in Germany.[37] Needless to say, the core of the reform was revision of the contents of the lease provisions that were obsolete. It should also be noted that in connection with the 'codification' or reconstruction of the Civil Code the reform can be characterized by the integration of the revised provisions into the Civil Code so as to make the Lease Law more understandable (*verständlich*) and clear (*übersichtlich*).

Attention should be paid to the fact that, as it is generally known in Japan the German Lease Law is an area of law that has been modified from the perspective of protecting the weak party from private autonomy and freedom of contract based on the principles of a social or welfare state. Systems and rules for precluding freedom of contract for a justifiable purpose of protecting the weak – here, freedom of contract would conflict with justice of contract – were established in the form of a special law separated from the Civil Code with the aim to avoid inconsistency in evaluation that would arise from introducing such systems and rules into the pre-modern civil code based on private autonomy and freedom of contract.

However, the integration of various special laws into the Civil Code which was aimed to make the Lease Law more understandable (*verständlich*) and clear (*übersichtlich*) actually caused a number of rules based on different principles and values to coexist in the Civil Code. Moreover, the idea of restoring freedom of contract under the Real Estate Lease Law (along with the introduction of market mechanisms) which was discussed upon the introduction of term leaseholds in Japan did not surface at the time of the 2001 reform, at least at the level of the government or the parliament.

[37] The 2001 reform arose from the request of the Federal Parliament in 1994 for the Federal Government to make the Lease Law more 'understandable' and 'clear'. The reform law of 2001 is usually referred to as the 'Law for the Reform of the Lease Law', though it effectively aimed to 'modernize' the Lease Law, largely because of such circumstances of that time.

Rather, this reform not only maintained the policy of 'protecting the weak party' (eg protecting the lessee from notice to terminate)[38] and strengthening it[39] but also established systems and rules that reflected requests for 'environment conservation'[40] and integrated a series of provisions into the Civil Code. For instance, the revised Civil Code provides for the fundamental rule as a unilateral mandatory provision that the lessee may require consent from the lessor for making necessary architectural changes or installing other facilities to enable the disabled to use or access the leased object (§ 554a). Under the revised Civil Code, the period of time during which the lessee should give notice of termination is reduced to three months (§ 573c). This also results from consideration to a growing number of elderly people living alone who were required under the conventional provision to give 12 months' notice to terminate the lease contract if it lasted for ten years or more and therefore would have no choice but to pay rent for two places simultaneously if they had to urgently move to homes for the elderly or nursing homes. Furthermore, the revised Civil Code also gives consideration to and protects the interests of unmarried couples (*Lebensgemeinschaft*) or those continuously living under the same roof (eg elderly persons who share a rented house/apartment) by ensuring that in the event of death of the lessee, the surviving partner or resident is allowed to enter or to be the successor to the lease contract (*Eintritts- und Fortsetzungsrecht* – § 563). These provisions are included in the Civil Code.

38 B. Grundmann, 'Die Mietrechtsreform' *NJW* 2001 2497, 2502. This paper regards protection of the lessee from notice of termination as the core of the Social Lease Law (*soziales Mietrecht*). Even this law was integrated into the Civil Code.

39 Upon the 2001 reform, in addition to the conventional reasons regarding the necessity to protect the real estate lessee, emphasis was also placed on the necessity of special protection for the elderly and the disabled as well as for families living in houses/apartments rented at a low price in areas where housing is highly concentrated.

40 § 559 of the Civil Code adopts the provision of Article 3 of the Law for the Regulation of Rent that if the lessor has taken architectural measures, which increase the usage value of the leased object sustainably, improve general housing conditions continuously or conserve energy or water sustainably (modernization or *Modernisierung*), the lessor may increase the annual rent by 11 percent of the costs spent for such measures.

This reform can be evaluated as having integrated the Residential Lease Law, a social law, into the Civil Code in light of the importance of habitation which is the core of people's living, thereby partially achieving the 'transformation of the Civil Code into a social law'.[41] This is even in contrast with the integration of special laws into the Civil Code in the area of consumer laws mentioned above which involved the shift in the basic philosophy of the Civil Code from classical liberalism to neo-liberalism. Furthermore, it is possible to justify the integration of consumer laws into the Civil Code for the reason that 'consumers' equalled 'general citizens', whereas even such justification is impossible for the integration of the Residential Lease Law.

The 'Modernization of civil law' in 2001 thus caused two legal areas to coexist in the German Civil Code: (i) the area justified under neo-liberalism which is regarded as an extension of the pre-modern civil code that guarantees individual freedom of decision-making, and aims to correct disparity in information access and bargaining power while maintaining orthodoxy; (ii) the area justified based on the principles of a social or welfare state that significantly restricts individual freedom of decision-making and protects the weak party (by unilateral mandatory provisions). A similar situation is also seen in respect of the Constitution in which fundamental rights as civil rights and fundamental rights as social rights form a single constitutional order. Nevertheless, in order to understand the significance of the 'transformation of the Civil Code into a social law' in the area of the Residential Lease Law in Germany examination should be made while taking into consideration the relationship between the constitutional order and the private law order and full-fledged studies by scholars and researchers in this field are greatly expected.[42]

41 H.R. Horst, *Praxis des Mietrechts – Wohnraum- und Geschäftsraummiete* (Munich 2003) 4 et seq.

42 In Japan, as a legal theory to protect residential interests of tenants in the course of regarding the House Lease Law as a social law in contrast with a civil law, 'right of residence' was studied as a kind of 'social right' in the past (R. Suzuki, *Shinban Kyojūken Ron* [New study of right of residence] (Tokyo 1981) 63 et seq). In the 1990s, the movement of describing the system and policy under the Land and House Lease Law from the perspective of freedom of contract based on market mechanisms gained strength. Recently, another movement has been seen aiming for the reconstruction of the 'right of residence' by focusing

III. The Role of German Law for Japanese Civil Law Jurisprudence

1. Introduction

The role and significance of German law in past civil law interpretation in Japan have already been discussed in detail in a lot of studies on legal methodology that have accumulated since the 1970s. This is one of the main themes discussed by *Kitagawa* in his article in this volume.

Setting aside the discussion on this theme for *Kitagawa's* article this section only points out the following. (i) In the history of civil law interpretation in Japan, the members of the drafting committee of the existing Japanese Civil Code (particularly *Nobushige Hozumi* and *Masaakira Tomii*) were conscious of German law. (ii) However, the existing Japanese Civil Code is a result of comparative law,[43] and German civil law was not the only model system (French civil law

the value of residential interests as personal rights. It intends to protect residential interests as a 'basic housing right' in connection with urban policy or housing policy. This trend finds the basis of residential interests or living interests in a right of residence or right of living that is regarded as a kind of 'personal civil right' rather than in a right of residence that is considered in the context of social law as an adjustment to private autonomy, a conventional principle of civil law. Residential interests or living interests in this sense are understood as a free or basic right, which is intended for freedom of expressing personality (M. Kaino, 'Jūtaku kihonken no hōgainen' [Legal concept of basic housing right], in K. Hayakawa (ed), *Kōza Gendai Jūkyo 1* [Study of modern residence 1] (Tokyo 1996) 37 et seq; S. Hirowatari, 'Nippon no Shakuchi Shakka Hōsei no tokushoku to sono dōkō' [Characteristics and trends of the System of the Land and House Lease Law in Japan], in T. Inaba (ed), *Shin Shakuchi Shakka Hō Kōza 1 Kan* [New study of the Land and House Lease Law Vol. 1] (Tokyo 1998) 21 et seq; S. Okamoto, 'Kyojūken no saikōchiku' [Reconstruction of right of residence], in H. Matsuo et al (eds), *Shakuchi Shakka Hō No Shintenkai* [New development of the Land and House Lease Law] (Tokyo 2004) 1 et seq). There is also an influential view that further promotes this trend and advocates 'right to living space' from a welfare state perspective (S. Hirowatari, 'Jūkyo Chintaishaku Hō no ichi to seisakuteki kinō' [Position and policy function of the Residential Lease Law] *Hōritsu Jihō* Vol. 70, No. 2 (1998) 10 et seq; K. Yoshida, 'Jūkyohōgaku mondai no chōkanzu (1)–(3)' [Picture of issues of study of residential law] *Minji Kenshū* No. 549 (2003) 10 et seq, No. 550, 2 et seq, and No. 551, 3 et seq.

43 N. Hozumi, *The New Japanese Civil Code* (Tokyo 1912) 22.

had a strong influence on the existing Japanese Civil Code, though it did not influence the whole part thereof). (iii) After the enforcement of the existing Japanese Civil Code, during the period from the end of the Meiji era through to the Taisho era, a phenomenon later referred to as the 'reception of legal theories' occurred bringing about a 'double structure' in Japanese civil law. (iv) Subsequently, as the phenomenon of 'reception of legal theories' was studied and the research on the legislative process and purpose of the Japanese Civil Code was developed since the 1970s methodological questions have been raised and concerned the development of interpretation of systems and concepts that were not derived from German law. (v) This trend led to model law-centrism, while bringing about changes to a methodological stance for using German law in civil law interpretation.

2. Reception of Legal Theories and German Law

'Reception of legal theories' cannot be avoided in the course of studying the relationship between Japanese civil law and German civil law at present and in the future. This subsection reviews the circumstances under which 'reception of legal theories' occurred in Japanese civil law jurisprudence and the details of this phenomenon.[44]

'Reception of legal theories' does not merely mean introducing foreign law or jurisprudence or being influenced by either of the two. As analyzed by *Zentaro Kitagawa*, 'reception of legal theories' is dif-

44 This is a summary of many studies that have already been published in Japan and frequently cited, and it is not particularly important in this article. Reference was made to the following: Z. Kitagawa, *Nihon Hōgaku No Rekishi To Riron* [History and theory of Japanese jurisprudence] (Tokyo 1968); E. Hoshino, papers contained in *Minpō Ronshū Dai 5 Kan* [Collected papers on civil law, Vol. 5] (Tokyo 1986); E. Hoshino, 'Nihon minpōgakushi 1' [History of Japanese civil law jurisprudence] *Hōgaku Kyōshitsu* Vol. 8 (1981) 39 et seq; N. Segawa, 'Ume, Tomii no minpō kaishaku hōhōron to hōshisō' [Methodological theory of interpretation of civil law and legal thought of Ume and Tomii] *Hokudai Hōgaku Ronshū* Vol. 41, No. 5–6 (1991) 2469 et seq; N. Tsuji, 'Ishizaka Otoshiro no minpōgaku to Doitsu minpō riron no dōnyū' [Study of civil law by Otoshiro Ishizaka and introduction of German civil law theories], in H. Mizumoto & K. Hirai (eds), *Nihon Minpōgakushi: Tsūshi* [Overall history of Japanese civil law] (Tokyo 1997) 105 et seq; M. Kato, 'Nihon minpō hyakunenshi' [One hundred years of Japanese civil law] (Tokyo 1999) 2 et seq.

ferent from a phenomenon that 'foreign legal theories have influence on the understanding of Japanese civil law'. It means that 'the whole part or essential part of an existing law of a country is reconstructed or remodelled by legal professionals of the country, based on the legal theories of a particular foreign country, beyond the normative structure of the existing law'.[45] Therefore the statement that 'Japanese civil law jurisprudence is influenced by German civil law jurisprudence' is completely different from the statement that 'Japanese civil law jurisprudence received German civil law jurisprudence'.

In Japan 'reception of German civil law theories' is usually described as referring to the trend in the development of civil law jurisprudence during the period from 1907 (Meiji era) to 1921 (Taisho era). As generally accepted, this trend arose from an objection to the jurisprudence that merely focused on legal terms or the tendency to shape reality according to the interpretation of the terms of statute law. Under such circumstances strong calls started to be heard for the necessity to achieve an 'evolution of law' as a mean to correct legal interpretation that was not well adapted to current reality and to maintain and improve society.

At that time there were two possible directions for achieving this goal through civil law interpretation. One direction was to aim for social jurisprudence or legal realism. *Izutaro Suehiro*, who severely criticized the cultural phenomenon of 'reception' of German civil law theories and put an end to it, basically followed this direction. However, Japanese civil jurisprudence at the end of the Meiji era followed the other direction of aiming for 'evolution of law' through the introduction of civil law theories from abroad. The fact that the Japanese Civil Code was developed as a fruit of comparative law by making reference to laws of more than twenty countries or regions also steered jurisprudence in Japan in this direction.

Furthermore on that occasion a reference was mainly made to German law instead of French law. There was one reason that the Japanese Code of Civil Procedure (which was established after the Civil Code) was under the influence of German law and Japanese Civil Law jurisprudence discussed therefore also the material Civil Law

45 Definition by Kitagawa, n 5 *supra*, 25.

under a strong influence of German jurisprudence. But there was another reason for the influence of German jurisprudence on Japanese Civil Law jurisprudence, as follows: at that time French jurisprudence degenerated into 'mere annotation study' or 'subjective doctrinarism' whereas German jurisprudence was excellent in its logical methods, legal concepts, systematic construction. As a result they were worth turning to methodologically for interpretation of civil law in Japan. Furthermore, German jurisprudence was good at operating logic to demonstrate statute law so it was in harmony with progressive state law positivism that was popular at that time. Against this background, the phenomenon called reception of legal theories occurred and took the civil law jurisprudence world by storm during the period from the end of the Meiji era through to the Taisho era.

However, it should not be overlooked that it was considered impossible at that time to introduce German jurisprudence in its entirety without modification. Neither should it be overlooked that it was considered difficult to transplant the spirit of German jurisprudence into Japan given a different historical environment. Rather, the greatest characteristic of reception of legal theories is that a definite emphasis was placed on the policy (systematic idea) of studying legal principle and essence by logical methods which was referred to as 'logical interpretation' at that time. Analysis from this viewpoint was successful in overcoming interpretation that merely focused on legal terms. However, at the same time it was impossible sufficiently to achieve the goal of adjusting legal interpretation to the social reality. It only succeeded in supplementing legal defects with the German law theories.

Another important characteristic of reception of legal theories is that the criticism of excessive emphasis on the interpretation of terms led to disrespect for the structure that was contemplated under the Japanese Civil Code. It was during this period of reception of legal theories that an attempt was made to construct a system by logical methods beyond the structure of the Japanese Civil Code and interpretation was developed based on such a system.

As mentioned above, reception of legal theories was promoted by the criticism that the interpretation of civil law at that time did not meet current social reality. It is very interesting in retrospect that this criticism drove the leading civil law interpretation away from the theory of legislative intention. In other words, the idea that in order to meet the needs of social reality interpretation should be allowed without restriction or constraint by legislative intention (within the bounds of logical interpretation according to the purpose of the law), led civil law scholars to adopt the theory of legal intention. As a result the necessity of efforts to explore legislative materials and search for model laws as well as the theory of legislative intention were left out of consciousness. Thus, such a phenomenon occurred in Japan, even though 'logical interpretation' as described above is not directly related to the adoption of the theory of legal intention.

3. Attitude to Return to the Model Law and German Law

In Japan criticism was made in the 1970s arising from the studies by *Zentaro Kitagawa* and *Eiichi Hoshino* of the view that regarded the Japanese Civil Code as originating from German law[46] and it was recognized as a common understanding that 'reception of legal theories' had existed in Japanese civil law jurisprudence during the period from the end of the Meiji era through to the Taisho era. The expression 'specifically German' mentioned above started to appear during this period.

From this period until today, study has been promoted, based on this understanding and in light of the 'double structure of Japanese civil law' in order to review systems and concepts advocated by existing civil law scholars and those adopted in the Civil Code established in the Meiji era from the perspective of which countries or regions they originate from, how they are regarded in the country or region of origin, to what extent they are universal, and what their cultural, historical or social background is.

During the period from the 1970s until today, remarkable studies have been made on Japanese civil law interpretation in connection

46 To learn about the understanding of the relationship between Japanese law and German law prior to the studies by *Kitagawa* and *Hoshino*, see M. Okuda, 'Nihon ni okeru gaikokuhō no sesshu: Doitsu hō' [Introduction of foreign law to Japan: German law], in M. Ito (ed), *Gaikokuhō To Nihonhō* [Foreign law and Japanese law] (Tokyo 1966) 218 et seq.

with German civil law. Such studies do not regard German law as the model for Japanese law but rather adopt other viewpoints, such as the study connecting interpretation with the principle or ideology of civil law, the study focusing on clarification of the legal logic for framing systems and rules or on system construction, and the study of legal history specializing in historical perception of law. On the other hand, the tendency that was criticized by *Kitagawa* 'explicitly or implicitly adopting, without modification, theories of the recent German literature, instead of simply presenting such literature, and publishing such theories as original theories'[47] seems to still exist.

4. Current Situation: Reasons for the Strong Influence of German Civil Law

Even today, when the reception of legal theories is advocated and the necessity of going back to carry out research based on model laws or inquiring into legislative materials is strongly argued for studying the theories of German civil law is still of great significance for Japanese civil law interpretation.

The reason for such significance that is often pointed out is the preciseness of the German civil law theories. This viewpoint is frequently used in papers titled '(...) in Germany'. However, most of such papers give no explanation as to why such preciseness is the reason for the significance of German law.[48] On the other hand, the attitude of making reference to German law from the perspective of

47 Z. Kitagawa, 'Minpō: Zaisanhō' [Civil law: property law], *Jurist* No. 400 (1968) 46. This tendency is seen not only in such studies that attempt interpretation in connection with German law, but also in studies on legal theories of other countries such as France, the U.K., and the U.S. Although it is no more than my personal impression, from what I have heard about recent efforts in selecting articles to be discussed at study meetings or recent reports presented at the conference of the Private Law Association, I feel that today when the number of scholars has increased, literature information is accessible almost in real time, and achievements are required to be made in a short period of time due to various reasons, the tendency that *Kitagawa* feared has rather intensified since *Kitagawa* and *Hoshino* first pointed it out.

48 In order to explain that preciseness cannot be the only reason, it is sufficient to recall the convoluted discussion on the Tort Liability Law in German civil law before modernization.

comparative law is relatively less dominant in the study of German civil law in Japan, probably because methods of comparative law have not yet been sufficiently established in the field of civil law interpretation in Japan and it has become difficult due to 'reception of legal theories' to understand German law objectively and externally by using methods of comparative law.

Rather, apart from the influence of papers only aimed to present literature, systems, and case law in Germany, the following decisive reasons seem to underpin the current situation where German civil law theories still have a considerable influence on interpretation of Japanese civil law.

The first reason is that the theory of legal intention is firmly supported in Japanese civil law interpretation. An extreme example can be described as follows. Legislative materials are useful as historical references or evidence for understanding the 'purpose or value of the law' and therefore they are worth studying, but at the same time historical perception is not sufficient to justify legal determinations made by applying individual norms. Studying the model law of a particular system or rule is worthy but not decisive for the same reason. The result of comparative jurisprudence is useful as references or clues for interpretation but is not decisive. The decisive factor for civil law interpretation is what can be read from legal texts. It should be noted that 'law' or 'legal texts' in this case refer to 'civil law' that has been established through reception of German civil law theories, rather than 'civil law' that can be drawn from the Civil Code compiled in the Meiji era. Therefore *Zentraro Kitagawa* says in his article in this book that in Japan there is the double structure of civil law.

The second factor is that dogmatic interpretation is still firmly supported in the field of civil law interpretation in Japan. This characteristic is reflected in the denial of free jurisprudence [*Freirechtsschule*] or interest jurisprudence [*Interessenjurisprudenz*], negative evaluation of the balancing of interests, the positioning of the science of legal interpretation separately from neighbouring sciences, and the strong orientation toward rules and systems. In particular, as more attention is paid to 'structure' rather than the 'balancing' in civil law interpretation the inclination towards German law seems to increase (without any logical necessity).

The third factor is that the basic studies accumulated about the principles and ideology of German civil law have a considerable influence on studies in Japan that arise from the same interest. Many examples of such studies can be mentioned, including those focusing on the relationship between the Constitution and the Civil Code, civil law and social law, private autonomy/self-determination and justice of contract, information provision models, viewpoints for interpretation of contracts, the binding force of agreements and the legal theory of changes in circumstances, the nature of unjust enrichment by typology, and controversy over personal rights in general.[49]

These factors are not only observed in relation to German civil law (therefore, there are many problems in denying academic results gained from such analysis, by expressing them as being 'specifically German'). Nevertheless, among individual Japanese civil law jurists who also study German law while paying attention to German tradition or orthodoxy, German civil law in the past and at present seems to be recognized and highly evaluated as having sufficient theoretical significance to satisfy the factors mentioned above.

5. The Relationship between Japanese Civil Law Interpretation and German Law

a) Continued from the Previous Section

The relationship between Japanese civil law interpretation and German law started when reference was made to German law (the first and second drafts and the civil codes of Saxony, Bavariy and Prussia) as a basis for legal comparison upon establishing the existing Japanese Civil Code. After going through the phenomenon of reception of legal theories during the period starting at the end of the Meiji era

49 In Sakae Wagazuma, *Minpō Kōgi* [Lecture on civil law] (Tokyo 1932), the overwhelming majority of situations in which German law is intensively discussed, except for those in which it supplements defects in the Japanese Civil Code, goes beyond the level of mere fragmentary interpretation of individual existing systems and indicates a basic theory that is directly related to the principle or ideology.

it has followed an unusual process to date in which the handling of German law was criticized from the perspective of methodology for civil law interpretation and the significance of German civil law theories in Japan were relativized in the course of studying legislative materials.

On the other hand, in Germany along with the changing social reality and trends in internationalization, a rapid movement has been seen toward adjusting the pre-modern civil code to social reality which is represented by the modernization of the Law of Obligations.

Under such circumstances, what significance can be found in German civil law to help in civil law interpretation in Japan? This issue should be examined from two perspectives: what suggestions can be obtained from the reform movement toward 'modernization of civil law (civil code)' in Germany in respect of the same situation in Japan and what influence will the civil law theories as introduced, improved or reformed through modernization have on Japanese civil law interpretation?

From either perspective, it is needless to say that if we try to comprehend the relationship between Japanese civil law and German civil law we must acquire accurate knowledge of the development and trends in German law per se and gain a proper understanding of the current status of German law. In particular the following three points should be noted. The first, needless to say, is that in light of the reforms of many systems and rules under the Civil Code in 2002 and thereafter it is inappropriate to accept information on the pre-reform state of law as it is (for instance, some people still believe that the Law for the Regulation of General Trading Conditions exists separately from the Civil Code). Taking just the field of the law of obligations as an example, we can find considerable changes in relevant laws – or core parts thereof – like the Law of Disturbance of Performance, the Warranty Law, the Prescription Law, the Law of Sale, the Service Contract Law, the Lease Law, the Tort Law, the Road Traffic Law and the Copyright Law. The second point is, contrary to the first one, that comparison should be made, if possible, by using Japanese papers that are aimed to present German civil law after reforms. Regarding modernization of German civil law academic arguments have been presented from various viewpoints and a number of commentaries and research papers have been published after reforms. The tone and contents of research papers depend on the status of the authors in Germany and the viewpoint that they adopted in writing the papers.[50]

b) Modernization of German Civil Law as a Legal Reform Movement, and Japanese Civil Law

If we examine the relationship between Japanese civil law and German civil law from the viewpoint of what suggestions can be obtained from 'modernization of civil law (civil code)' in Germany as a legal reform movement in respect of the same situation in Japan, we can obtain important suggestions from the analysis mentioned above.

The first suggestion is that there was a strong desire to reconstruct the Civil Code as a general private code. The movements in the

50 Regarding the Law of Default of Obligation, it goes without saying that attention should be paid to the expert opinion of *Ulrich Huber* in 1981, the draft by the committee of the Federal Ministry of Justice in 1992, the 'Discussion Draft', 'Consolidated Version of the Discussion Draft', and 'Government Bill' mentioned above, and the development process of the existing provisions of the code. In addition, a series of papers and statements by *Canaris* who played a leading role at the final stage of reforming the Law of Default of Obligation is especially important, and the textbook and papers by his follower, *Stephan Lorenz*, are also useful for comprehending the significance of systems and rules of the reformed civil code. Papers by *Jürgen Schmidt-Räntsch* who participated in the drafting process at the Ministry of Justice should also be read alongside these scholars. The reforms are also examined from the perspective of comparison or harmonization with international rules by some scholars including *Peter Schlechtriem* and *Hein Kötz*. On the other hand, we cannot ignore a series of papers by *Ulrich Huber* who was always critical of the reform of the Law of Obligations (including those written before the current modernization of the Law of Obligations). Another scholar who was always critical of the reform of the Law of Obligations is *Barbara Dauner-Lieb*. Also, R. Schulze & H. Schulte-Nölke (eds), *Die Schuldrechtsreform vor dem Hintergrund des Gemeinschaftsrechts* (Tübingen 2001), and W. Ernst & R. Zimmermann (eds), *Zivilrechtswissenschaft und Schuldrechtsreform* (Tübingen 2001) must be read as collected papers at the time of discussion and drafting. If Japanese scholars present these papers without explaining how such German papers are evaluated in Germany (and then if legal researchers and practitioners who are not engaged in studying German literature read such Japanese papers and mistakenly believe that these papers show the current situation in Germany), it would be very dangerous.

modernization process found the significance of the Civil Code in the fact that it was a basic code containing basic rules for private life matters. On the other hand, the Civil Code that contains such basic rules is underpinned by the basic principle or ideology of how the State should deal with private life matters. Such basic principles or ideology are of great importance for the interpretation of law, the supplementation of *lacunae* and for the encouragement of legislation. However, even though there were strong calls for the reconstruction of the Civil Code along with changes of society and times, it is still necessary to examine the appropriateness of the reconstruction in light of the basic principle or ideology of the Civil Code, the necessity to change the basic principle or ideology of the pre-modern civil code through modernization and the possibility of forming a new order of law based on another principle or ideology while maintaining the basic principle or ideology of the pre-modern civil code. The achievements and problems of the modernization of German civil law involving the integration of various consumer laws and the Lease Law into the Civil Code are worth examining critically (never negatively) in Japan where modernization of pre-modern law is argued for not only in the field of civil law but also in other legal fields. In particular, it is worthy to make efforts to examine and duly appreciate the significance of the German civil law jurisprudence developed with accumulated principles and ideas and the discussion of modernization of German civil law and such efforts cannot be easily denied as 'specifically German'. This is a part of the preparatory process for forming a foundation to reconstruct the interpretative theory of Japanese civil law and reform the existing Civil Code in a desirable direction.

The second suggestion is that 'modernization' of civil law in Germany was carried out along with internationalization of such systems and rules that were subject to modernization in many important fields of transaction law. Even though the current 'modernization' in Germany was launched with the objective of implementing the EU Directives (in particular the EU Directive on Sale of Consumer Goods) into domestic legislation such circumstances cannot be put aside as being specific to Germany, an EU Member. The process up to the modernization of the Law of Obligations also indicates that in addition to the implementation of the EU Directives, consideration was always also given to harmonization with the United Nations Convention on

International Sale of Goods, the UNIDROIT Principles of International Commercial Contracts, and the Principles of European Contract Law and efforts were made to ensure relevance with these international rules even at the final stage of sophistication of German civil law under conventional dogmatic. Under the circumstances where international systems and rules have been established or efforts are being made to this end, it may also be appropriate in Japan to attempt comparison between domestic systems and rules and international systems and rules within the framework of civil law interpretation.

c) Modernization of German Civil Law in Terms of the Contents of Reform and Japanese Civil Law

The 'Modernization of civil law (civil code)' in Germany as a legal reform movement should, when examined in terms of the contents of reform, also be of great significance in creating an ideal form of Japanese civil law at present and in the future. Ironically it raises serious issues regarding pro-German views on civil law that have introduced through reception of legal theories German civil law jurisprudence into Japanese civil law interpretation, thereby constructing and justifying individual interpretations.

Firstly, as a result of modernization of German civil law, Germany has adopted theories that in many cases are different from the 'Japanese civil law theories constructed through reception of legal theories'. For example, regarding warranty against defects of things, the delivery of specific (determinate) things with defects is regarded as 'breach of obligation' (*Pflichtverletzung*) and it is in principle subject to general rules on default of obligation (rules in the General Provisions under the Law of Obligations), with only special rules included in the Section of Law of Sale. In other words, the theory called 'theory of contractual liability' in Japan (or 'theory of contract' (*Vertragstheorie*) in Germany) has been adopted explicitly, with opposition to this theory rarely heard in the reform process. Also, the theory of contracts for work and materials (*Werklieferungsvertrag*) in Japan has been developed based on the theory that was received form Germany (§ 651 BGB), but as a result of the recent reform of the Law of Obligations, Germany has introduced a rule for product and supply contracts that is a little different from the conventional rule.

Secondly, through modernization of German civil law many new systems and rules have been adopted that are different from the traditional ones. For instance, the trichotomic system has been transformed by including the types of imperfect performance and positive breach of claim in the civil code and to cover all types of non-performance under the concept of 'breach of obligation' while maintaining the concept of 'impossibility' in respect of the right to claim performance and the bearing of risk. Furthermore it has been allowed to claim both termination and damages, the dogma of initial impossibility has been cast away and the scope of loss covered by the claim for compensation for non-pecuniary damage has been expanded.

Under such circumstances, what direction should be followed in the future by Japanese civil law interpretation, which has been developed based on such theories thus cast away in Germany? If any views that became dominant among Japanese scholars through the reception of German civil law jurisprudence are now denied of their German 'orthodoxy' what stance will be taken in the future by scholars who have supported such views? If such views are not internationally accepted – truly 'specifically German' – how will scholars who support such views 'justify' their stance? What position will be taken by the scholars who have argued the 'theory of legal liability' or the dogma of 'initial impossibility' based on German law? Will they remain in sublime isolation or attempt the same implementation as that in Germany? In this regard, the Japanese civil law interpretation after reception of legal theories is expected to prove itself.

However I would like to point out that whichever direction may be followed the modernization of German civil law means a possible form of modernization but it cannot be regarded as applicable to everything or universally. It may be subject to criticism that the Civil Code per se has become an aggregate of norms that are based on multiple principles or values. If these points were misunderstood the Japanese civil law jurisprudence would introduce German law far more superficially than reception of legal theories in the past, for the mere reason that 'Germany carried out modernization in this way'.

IV. Conclusion

If there is anything that we should learn from modernization of German civil law, it is the aspiration for modernization, a discussion on basic principles toward modernization, the modernization process, and aggressiveness in the reforms themselves. We should regard the output of modernization objectively as achievements specific to Germany while taking into consideration the basic principles behind modernization, and study it from the perspective of comparative law in relation to legal dogmatic and in light of international trends.

If studied from the perspective of comparative law individual systems and rules under the modernized German civil law and the basic principles behind them were of any significance in modern society, it would not be the right behaviour for civil law interpretation to cast them away for the reason that 'German law is not the model for Japanese law' or 'such systems and rules are specifically German' (some achievements in reception of legal theories in the past can be 'justified' in this respect). If we could find, as a result of comparison with German law or other foreign law any systems or rules that were needed in modern society from a dogmatic perspective and such systems or rules were not in consistency with those under the existing Japanese Civil Code it would be the existing Japanese Civil Code that must be reformed.

A civil code is a basic code under the constitutional order which provides for private life matters, and in order to make it applicable to modern civil society as a 'general private code' discussion may be necessary with the possibility of legal reforms in mind, while maintaining harmony with the constitutional order. In the discussion toward 'literary modernization' and 'substantive modernization' of Japanese civil law, it will be of great significance to know, learn and examine the modernization of German civil law.

Chapter 4: French Law Research in the Study of Civil Law in Japan*

Taro Kogayu

Contents

I. Introduction

I was asked to report on the relationship between Japanese civil law and French law at the study group meeting entitled "History and Outlook of Japanese Civil Law: Focusing on the Relationship with Foreign Laws."

It seems most appropriate to have *Atsushi Omura* talk about this theme; but to my surprise, it was *Omura* himself who suggested that I report on the subject. Although I accepted the offer, it is an extremely great challenge for me to talk on such a theme in front of the participating judges, as well as *Omura*, *Yoshio Shiomi*, and *Tsuneo Matsumoto*. The theme itself is very extensive, but my report will in-

* This report is an amended version of the author's report at a professional study meeting (May 10, 2004) of the Judicial Research and Training Institute. Since the content of the report was greatly dependent on the fact that it was an oral report at a study group meeting mainly attended by judges, the author intentionally maintained the colloquial expressions in publishing it in this book.

evitably have to deal with the content that matches my abilities and the time given. I ask for your understanding in advance.

There are several topics that I could talk about regarding the given subject.[1] Today, I will attempt an examination from the viewpoint of the relationship between the study of civil law in Japan and French law.

When looking at the history of the study of civil law in Japan from the perspective of its relationship with French law, the situation seems to have changed dramatically since the appearance of a paper ("Influence of French Civil Law on the Japanese Civil Code"[2]) by *Eiichi Hoshino* in 1965. Before then, the study of civil law in Japan generally had little relevance with French law. Of course, there were exceptions. For example, there was the research by *Sakae Wagatsuma* at one time,[3] and occasional appearances of other very impor-

1 The first paper that should be referred to regarding the relationship with French law is Y. Noda, 'Nihon ni okeru gaikokuhō no sesshu (josetsu) (Furansu)' [Ingestion of foreign laws in Japan (introduction) (France)] in J. Aomi, N. Ashibe, M. Ito et al (eds), *Gaikokuhō To Nihonhō (Iwanami Kōza, Gendaihō 14)* 1966 [Foreign laws and Japanese law (Iwanami lecture, modern law 14)] (Tokyo 1966) 161 et seq. Also see A. Omura, *Minpō Sōron* [Outline of civil law] (Tokyo 2001), 93–96.

2 E. Hoshino, *Minpōronshū Dai 1 Kan* [Collection of theories on civil law, vol. 1] (Tokyo 1970; first published in 1965), 69 et seq.

3 S. Wagatsuma, 'Sakui mataha fusakui wo mokuteki to suru saiken no kyōsei shikkō' ['Enforcement of claims intended for acts or omissions'], in S. Wagatsuma, *Minpō Kenkyū (6): Saiken Sōron* [Study on civil law (6): outline of claims] (Tokyo 1968; first published in 1932) 81 et seq, traced the history of the problem indicated in the title, which can be traced back to French law, via old Civil Code. It derived a composition that 'the realistic means for enforcement of performance and its limits must be established at the point of balance between the respect of the personality of the obligor and protection of the claim' (later-mentioned *Minpō Kōgi IV* [Civil law lecture IV] 58). Then, based on this, it established the theory of 'supplementary nature of indirect enforcement', which is that indirect enforcement is only allowed for obligations that cannot be made subject to direct enforcement or substitute execution, because it would not suit the ideal of respecting the personality of the obligor, in *Saiken Sōron (Minpō Kōgi IV)* [Outline of claims (civil law lecture IV)] (Tokyo 1930) 61–63 (the citation from the 15th print, 1951 version), and achieved a great success. The large impact of the *Wagatsuma* paper and his lectures is demonstrated in Osamu Morita's *Kyōsei Rikō No Hōgakuteki Kōzō* [Structure of performance by enforcement from the legal study perspective] (Tokyo 1995) 296–300. S. Wagatsuma,

tant studies on French law concerning the basic principles of civil law,[4] such as the changes in the principle of liability arising from negligence in civil liability. Nonetheless, French law received little attention in general.

However, after the appearance of *Hoshino's* paper, the relationship with French law rapidly increased in both quality and quantity. Since it would be quite interesting to observe the qualitatively and quantitatively increased relationship with French law, today I will focus on the relationship between the study of civil law in Japan and French law in and after 1965, when *Hoshino's* paper was published.

Meanwhile, this is not an academic conference, but a meeting attended by participating judges. As you are engaged in practical legal affairs, you may not be very familiar with the research results of the study of civil law in Japan that specifically focuses on French law. Accordingly, I will first briefly introduce some research results in the field of Japanese civil law that refer to French law. Although my report may be a little sketchy, it should give you an idea of how the study of civil law in Japan relates to French law (II). Then, based on this understanding, I would like to examine how the overall Japanese civil law study, rather than individual academic theories, relates to French law, and the reasons for studying French law; but instead of

'Teitōken to jūbutsu no kankei ni tsuite' [Relationship between mortgages and accessories], in S.Wagatsuma, *Minpō Kenkyū IV (Tanpo Bukken)* [Study of civil law IV (collateral)] (Tokyo 1967; first published in 1933) 27 et seq, also reflected the study results that have referenced French law in the theory of interpretation, and left a large impact on later generations. These studies have been published from 1932 to 1933.

4 See A. Omura, '20 seiki ga minpō ni ataeta eikyō (1)' [The influences of the 20th century on civil law (1)] *Hōgaku Kyōkai Zasshi* vol. 120 no. 1 (2003) 202, which states that *Eiichi Makino's* theory of abuse of right, *Naojiro Sugiyama's* theory of contract of adhesion, *Yoshiyuki Noda's* theory of civil liability and *Keiichi Yamamoto's* theory of property right and theory of corporation all follow the juristic measures to respond to the rapid social changes in France in the 19th century and they were themes of 'French law study in Japan' up to a certain time. Apart from the *Makino's* theory, the latter three theories were conducted as French law research by researchers of French law (in very gross terms) and seem to have a slightly different quality from the French law research conducted by civil law scholars that is introduced in II in that it does not include straightforward arguments directed to the study of civil law in Japan (though the differences are only relative).

simply delivering what comes to mind I would like to hear what you think (III). I will introduce several academic theories today, but there will naturally be the question of why the number of theories introduced is so limited and why certain theories are not addressed. I would like you to understand that the academic theories introduced are only a small handful of theories that seemed to be of interest in light of today's theme, and that the selection does not necessarily coincide with the degree of importance of the theories.

II. Relationship to French Law: Specific Examples

1. The Hoshino paper

Before I introduce the details of individual studies, I would like to confirm the message of the *Hoshino* paper once again. The *Hoshino* paper overturned the "tradition" in which Japanese civil law shared characteristics of German civil law, with an extremely empirical approach. By examining the text of the General Provisions of the Japanese Civil Code article by article, and sedulously clarifying the parts that are of French style along with those of German and other styles, *Hoshino* made the public realize that, against all expectations to the contrary, Japanese civil law shares characteristics with French law. This paper seemed to carry the message that, in studying Japanese civil law, more emphasis should be placed on the study of French law which has a genealogical linkage.

Considering the tradition of the field of civil law in Japan, which had placed weight on German law, *Hoshino's* paper must have had an impact much larger than what we imagine today. It is because, after the appearance of the Hoshino paper, *Masamichi Okuda*, who is an expert on German law research, immediately wrote a review[5] on the paper and also fully cited *Hoshino's* point of view in another paper.[6]

5 M. Okuda, 'Minpōgaku no ayumi' [Historical progress of civil law] *Hōritsu Jihō* vol. 38 no. 3 (1966) 110.

6 M. Okuda, 'Nihon ni okeru gaikokuhō no sesshu: Doitsuhō' [Ingestion of foreign laws in Japan: German law], in J. Aomi, N. Ashibe, M. Ito et al (eds), *Gaikokuhō To Nihonhō (Iwanami Kōza: Gendaihō 14)* [Foreign laws and Japanese law (Iwanami lecture: modern law 14)] (Tokyo 1966). On p. 218, it states

In addition, in 1968, *Wagatsuma* wrote about *Hoshino's* paper in an admiring tone in the preface of a collection of his works.[7] I believe

'the civil law still contains strong characteristics of French law, and property law contains influences by French law and German law to the same extent' and on p. 223, after introducing the *Hoshino* paper, it says 'therefore, it can be concluded that civil law, while having the nature of French law, is clad in a garment of German law'. Furthermore, on p. 250, it reads as follows: 'The study of civil law interpretation in the Meiji period, which was inclined toward the study of German law, governed the study of civil law in Japan for generations to come. This is the reason that the systems, which originally have a background based on French law, were interpreted in the style of German law, and naturally, investigation of the legislators' intentions – and the related research on the process of establishing civil law – were neglected in that procedure. Recently, work has finally begun to correct the conventional inappropriate inclination toward German law (omitted), to clarify the historical genealogy of Japanese civil law, investigate the history of the respective systems and provisions, and to sedulously trace both whether the systems or provisions derive from French law or German law and the process through which they came to be settled as Japanese civil law based on materials in the Meiji period. This work is done in Professor Eiichi Hoshino's 'Nihon minpōten ni ataeta Furansu minpō no eikyō (1)' [Influence of French civil law on the Japanese Civil Code (1)]. Since this work is basic work that is indispensable for the study of civil law interpretation, it is rather strange that it has never been conducted until now in the academic circles.'.

7 'When Japanese civil law interpretation theory came to be structured solely after the concept and system of German Civil Code due to the efforts of Professor Kawana, Professor Ishizaka, Professor Mitsuma and Professor Hatoyama, some provisions that were carried into the Japanese Civil Code from French civil law through the old Civil Code were cast aside as impurities that obstruct transparency of the concept and system of civil law. However, it would be presumptuous to simply consider this to be a misunderstanding or lack of understanding by the legislators. These 'impurities' must have been respectively given their reasonable statuses in the minds of the legislators. If so, the concept and system that cover them would deserve to be called the true concept and system of the Japanese Civil Code. This is what I thought in response to a suggestion by Professor *Izutaro Suehiro*. As an attempt to study this topic, I wrote 'Sakui mataha fusakui wo mokuteki to suru saiken no kyōsei shikkō' [Enforcement of claims intended for acts or omissions]. Later, I noticed some problems in this domain, but have not had the opportunity to study them. In short, the problem can be reduced to the fact that it is necessary to conduct a full-fledged study on French laws and regulations as well as systems and to derive not only legislation theory, but also interpretation theory so as to contribute to understanding the Japanese systems appropriately. When I look at the recent academic circles from such a perspective, the achievements of Professor *Akira Mikazuki* and Professor *Eiichi Hoshino* catch my eye. I do not mean to say that my above idea has served as a motive to some extent in these achievements. Nevertheless, I would like to note

that *Hoshino's* message is basically recognized as a common asset for the academic circles of civil law in Japan today. In response to this message, the academic theories of Japanese civil law came to be actively directed toward French law research from the mid-1960s.

One way of introducing individual academic theories would be to introduce them in chronological order. However, I will introduce them by roughly dividing them into three groups from the viewpoint of the relationship with French law. For the sake of convenience, the groups will be referred to as "direct linkage type", "reverse illumination type" and "conceptual source type."

2. Direct linkage type?

French law → Japanese law

(1) First group is 'direct linkage type'. I need to state in advance that I made up the names of the three groups myself, and they are not necessarily generally used terms. The direct linkage type refers to research done with the idea that specific provisions or systems of Japanese civil law should be interpreted in the same way as under French law if they originally derived from French law; or even if there is no genealogical relationship, what applies to French law should also be applied to Japanese law. The following academic theories of *Masao Ikeda*, *Toyohiro Nomura* and *Makinori Goto* could be regarded as studies with such a tendency.

The reason for putting a question mark at the end of the name of the group is that the approach of applying French law to Japanese law in the direct linkage type is subject to criticism. Indeed, *Ikeda's* research triggered the opinion that the direct linkage type should not be adopted in interpreting current law. However, *Ikeda* himself says that his theory is not the direct linkage type. Therefore, the question mark expresses reservations that the following explanation may not neces-

that I am watching, with infinite delight, young scholars doing what I thought I should do and what I wanted to accomplish, from broader and more in-depth standpoints.' *Minpō Kenkyū V: Saiken Sōron* [Civil law research V: outline of claims] (Tokyo 1968), Preface, 3.

sarily be a precise introduction; in other words, it indicates a question in terms of certainty.

(2) First, I will explain *Ikeda's* research on transfer of claims.[8] A collection of his works was published in 1993, but his underlying studies have been published since around the mid-1970s. His idea is that research on French law would be essential since the root of Articles 467 and 468 of the Japanese Civil Code, which are provisions on transfer of claims, can be traced back to French law through the old Civil Code and *Boissonade's* draft. This idea inherits *Hoshino's* message.

However, *Ikeda's* research not only clarified the genealogic relationship as well as the details of the old Civil Code and French law, but it contained a strong point of view in terms of interpretation. Specifically, it suggested that Articles 467 and 468 of the Civil Code be interpreted in a French style because they originated from French law. At this point, I can imagine *Ikeda* saying 'Absolutely not!' More specifically, *Ikeda* placed emphasis on *Boissonade* who created a draft of the old Civil Code, rather than French law, so his idea was misunderstood or understood to have directly linked *Boissonade's* ideas with the interpretation of the current law. For example, in the case of Article 467, a common interpretation would be to consider the first paragraph as the principle and the second paragraph as an exception. However, *Ikeda* indicated an interpretation that would regard the second paragraph as the principle and the first paragraph as an exception based on the history, particularly from a study of the draft of the old Civil Code and stated that the reverse order in the article was an 'oversight in legislation'.[9]

With regard to the interpretation, the criticism is directed to the part concerning direct linkage with French law, or *Boissonade*, which could be called the theory of *Boissonade's* intention.[10] However, no

8 M. Ikeda, *Saiken Jōto No Kenkyū* [Research on transfer of claims] (Tokyo 1993; enlarged ed. 1997).

9 Ibid 97.

10 With regard to the dispute over the method in the *Ikeda* paper (including information on related documents), see A. Omura, 'Tekusuto ron kara mita Furansuhō kenkyū' [French law research from the perspective of the text theory], in A. Omura (ed), *Hōgen/Kaishaku/Minpōgaku* [Source of law/interpretation/study

one denies that *Ikeda's* research has an extremely high value as a base that elucidates the original meaning of Articles 467 and 468 by tracing this genealogic relationship. I think this would be a sufficient introduction for today's report.

(3) Next, I will introduce *Nomura's* research (mistake in declaration of intention).[11] This is research on the requirements for invalidating a declaration of intention due to a mistake in Article 95 of the Civil Code, which was published in 1975. The subtitle of the paper was 'requirements theory referring to French law'. However, *Nomura's* paper has no description suggesting that Article 95 of the Civil Code is genealogically linked with French law. The reasons mentioned for referring to French law are the fact that study on French law is hardly conducted with respect to mistakes and that the discussions on mistakes in France would provide a good reference in interpreting Japanese law.[12] The professor shows almost no interest in the theoretical structure of mistakes but he pursues the practical determination standards for whether or not a declaration of intention can be invalidated due to a mistake, which appear in court cases under French law. He is critical against an approach that discusses whether or not there is any fault in the intention.

Lastly, he concluded that the various factors that decide whether or not a declaration of intention can be invalidated, which were extracted by referring to court cases under French law, mostly coincided with those of court cases in Japan, and structured a theory on the requirements accordingly. The significant point as a study on mistakes was that it presented practical determination standards on

on civil law] (Tokyo 1995) 399 et seq and M. Adachi, 'Ikeda/Adachi ronsō no sōkatsu to hansei: shimei saiken jōto ni okeru saimusha no igi wo tomenu shōdaku no riron kōsei' [Summary of and reflection on the Ikeda/Adachi dispute: theoretical structure of consent that does not give heed to the debtor's objection in transfer of a nominative claim] *Hōgaku Shirin* vol. 98 no. 3 (2001) 215 et seq. The following understood the *Ikeda* theory as a subjective interpretation theory, and defended it: K. Igarashi, '(Shōkai to hihyō) Ikeda Masao *Saiken Jōto No Kenkyū*' [(Introduction and criticism) Ikeda Masao *Saiken Jōto No Kenkyū*], *Hōgaku Kenkyū* vol. 66 no. 11 (1993) 143.

11 T. Nomura, 'Ishi hyōji no sakugo: Furansuhō wo sankō ni shita yōkenron' [Mistake in declaration of intention: requirements theory referring to French law] *Hōgaku Kyōkai Zasshi* vol. 92 no. 10 (1975) 1340 et seq (serialized).

12 Nomura, n 11 *supra*, 1368.

whether or not invalidation of a declaration of intention would be affirmed, particularly factors including the situation of the opponent of the declarant and the damage incurred by the declarant due to the mistake, based on Japanese and French court cases.[13]

(4) As the last research point in 'direct linkage type?' I will introduce *Goto's* research on the obligation to provide information.[14] Today, the obligation to provide information has become a popular issue in concluding a contract. This greatly owes to his paper.

Goto's paper refers to the value judgment concerning a specific issue under French law, similar to *Nomura's* paper. Nevertheless, *Goto* seems to have attempted to gain hints from French law even more directly than *Nomura*. Specifically speaking, *Goto's* intention seems to be to identify a value judgment or policy to legally rectify the gap in the volume of information between the parties to a contract in French law and to use it as a guideline for interpreting Japanese law.[15]

As the reason for referring to French law, *Goto* mentions that the Civil Code provisions on declaration of intention resemble such provisions under French law,[16] but the basic reason seems to be that the discussions in France made progress and were likely to provide some hints.

These academic theories, particularly the studies by *Nomura* and *Goto*, are different from the later-mentioned reverse illumination type and the conceptual source type in terms of their approach to French law in that they referenced the value judgment or policy concerning a specific issue under French law in a relatively direct manner.[17]

13 Nomura, n 11 *supra, Hōgaku Kyōkai Zasshi* (7/end) vol. 93 no. 6 (1976) 933.

14 M. Goto, 'Furansu keiyakuhō ni okeru sagi/sakugo to jōhō teikyō gimu' [Frauds/mistakes under French contract law and obligation to provide information], in M. Goto (ed), *Shōhisha Keiyaku No Hōriron* [Legal theory on consumer contracts] (Tokyo 2002; first published in 1990) 2 et seq.

15 Goto, n 14 *supra*, 71.

16 Text in the first publication (M. Goto, 'Furansu keiyakuhō ni okeru sagi/sakugo to jōhō teikyō gimu (1)' [Frauds/mistakes under French contract law and obligation to provide information (1)], vol. 102 no. 2 [1990] 62). This part was however deleted in Goto, n 14 *supra*.

17 Sometimes, the reason for referencing French law is said to be that the court cases and academic theories in France provide useful reference as 'experimental

3. Reverse illumination type

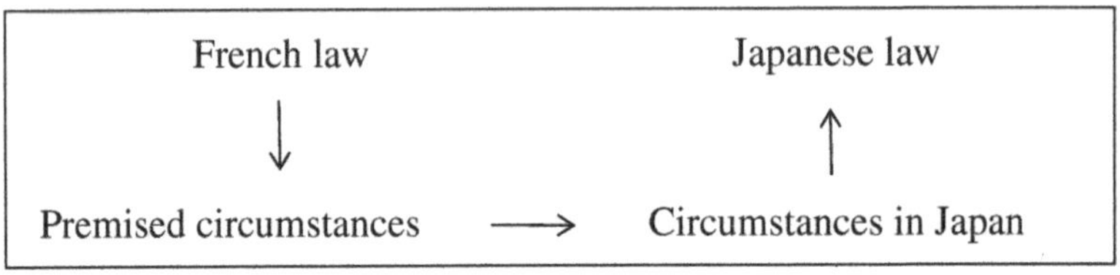

(1) Next group is the 'reverse illumination type'. While the direct linkage type directly applied French law to Japanese law, the reverse illumination type first identifies the circumstances premised by systems or provisions under French law, then examines whether or not there are such circumstances in Japan and, if there are, whether there are differences in the premised circumstances, and it illuminates Japanese law from the other side, that is, from the French law side. I would like to call such type of research the reverse illumination type. To elaborate, in this type of academic theory the first step would be to select a French system or provision that is genealogically associated with a Japanese system or provision, and subject it to the research. An easy example is to conduct research on French conveyance law to study Article 177 of the Japanese Civil Code. In this process, attention is often directed to the circumstances, the type of case and trade practices premised by that system or provision. In the next step, Japanese law is illuminated from the perspective of French law based on the understanding of French law. This 'reverse illumination' enhances the understanding of Japanese law and generates hints for interpretation. Recently, attempts for reverse illumination have also been made by studying theories of French law that have no

material under the same conditions'. The reason that French law is referenced in K. Yoshida, *Saiken Shingairon Saikō* [Review of the theory on violation of claims] (Tokyo 1991) would be that, because Japan and France have the same conditions in that tort laws have the same structure and the conveyance systems are the same, the experience of French law would be useful as experimental data particularly for the issue of violation of claims in the form of double real estate transactions (idem, 428). Also, the indication in M. Nozawa, *Keiyaku Jōto No Kenkyū* [Research on transfer of contracts] (Tokyo 2002) 3 that Japan and France are the same in that neither of them has provisions on assumption of obligation and transfer of contracts, while they have provisions on transfer of obligations, must be based on a similar understanding.

genealogical relationship as their basis. Let us look at the specific studies.

(2) First, I would like to introduce *Takehisa Awaji's* research on joint and several obligation.[18] The book was published in 1975, but the paper on which it is based was published in 1967, which is immediately after the publication of *Hoshino's* paper. This research can be taken to inherit the viewpoint of the *Hoshino* paper in that it points in the direction of French law research after indicating that Japanese provisions on joint and several obligation have a genealogical linkage with French law instead of German law,[19] but it does not cite *Hoshino's* paper.

Awaji's research questions the substantive relationship premised by the collective legal treatment of the joint and several obligation, that is, the grounds for the absolute effects on the entirety irrelevant to the individually borne parts. The paper reveals by study of Roman law and French law that the typical substantive relationships premised are the relationship of joint business or the relationship of living together among the obligors. Incidentally, he states that the grounds for the absolute effects that take effect within the scope of the individually borne parts premise a case where there is a mutual guarantee relationship.[20]

When Japanese law is 'reverse illuminated' from this point, it is indicated that Japanese law has provided a collective legal treatment irrespective of the existence of the assumed substantive relationship. This finding leads to the interpretative point of view that it would not be reasonable to provide the collective legal treatment when there is no typical substantive relationship premised by it.[21]

(3) Next, I will introduce *Nobuhisa Segawa's* research on law on the annexation of real estate.[22] The book was published in 1981, but the paper on which it is based was published from 1977 to 1978. Al-

18 T. Awaji, *Rentai Saimu No Kenkyū* [Research on joint and several obligations] (Tokyo 1975).
19 Awaji, n 18 *supra*, 69.
20 Awaji, n 18 *supra*, 158–162.
21 T. Awaji, *Saimu Sōron* [Outline of claims] (Tokyo 2002) 345, 346, 349.
22 N. Segawa, *Fudōsan Fugōhō No Kenkyū* [Research on the law on annexation of real estate] (Tokyo 1981).

though the theme indicated in the title of this book is law on the annexation of real estate, it is actually a book on the methodologies of interpreting civil law, or, a guide to civil law research. It is an in-depth study on many issues that are interesting particularly in light of today's theme, the relationship of Japanese civil law with foreign laws.

Segawa's research not only refers to French law as a foreign law but it also refers to German law to a similar extent. Thus, it is slightly different from the academic theories introduced so far in this respect. Furthermore, *Segawa* does not say that the Japanese law on annexation of real estate has directly derived from French law.

As the reason for referring to French law, *Segawa* mentioned that French law had a strong influence on Japan along with German law.[23] Therefore, the French law subject to the research is not the modern French law but the law at the time that it was adopted by Japan. Accordingly, in a broad sense, *Segawa's* research seems to be directed to French law due to the genealogical relationship.

Segawa constantly pays attention to the types of disputes that are assumed by the annexation law, be it French law, German law or Japanese law. He criticizes previous Japanese academic theories as having randomly borrowed legal concepts by detaching them from concrete disputes that were assumed or other backgrounds.[24] I would like to omit the introduction of *Segawa's* interpretation theory because it will force me to go into too much detail. However, because there is a strong inclination to observe French and German annexation laws along with the premised dispute types and other social backgrounds and to also review the circumstances premised by Japanese annexation law, I think the research can be categorized as the reverse illumination type.

(4) Next, I will introduce *Yoshihisa Nomi's* research on liquidated fines/damages and their regulations.[25] The legal treatment for a court

23 Segawa, n 22 *supra*, 49.

24 Segawa, n 22 *supra*, 214–219.

25 Y. Nomi, 'Iyakukin/songai baishōgaku no yotei to sono kisei' [Liquidated fines/damages and their regulations] *Hōgaku Kyōkai Zasshi* vol. 102, no. 2 (1985) 294 et seq (serialized).

to reduce the sum of the liquidated damages if it is excessively large seems extremely familiar and natural for Japanese lawyers. *Nomi* refers to German law and French law, but he does not provide a grand explanation on the reason for it. He points out that an almost identical provision as Article 420 of the Japanese Civil Code can be found in French law, but he does not necessarily emphasize that the Japanese law originated from French law. Rather, he seems to have chosen German law and French law in order to conduct a balanced comparative law study.[26]

Nomi's French law research[27] reveals that reduction of the sum of liquidated damages by a court had been resolutely denied in France for a long time even if the sum was excessively large. His paper sedulously finds that reduction of the sum of liquidated damages by a court was only recognized after a law was enacted in 1975 to authorize judges to make the reduction.

This suggests that, in French law, there is a strong sense of aversion to a court's intervention in the content of a contract between the parties, including liquidated damages. One of the reasons is said to be the strong dominance of the principle of the autonomy of will. At the same time, however, while the strength of the principle of the autonomy of will is emphasized in relation with judicial courts, the situation differs in relation with the Parliament or laws enacted by the Parliament. In other words, we can observe a characteristic in which a judge can regulate the content of a contract as long as he/she is authorized to do so by law, but cannot regulate it if he/she is not clearly authorized by law. This also highlights the characteristics of Japanese law. I think the significance of the French law research in this context does not converge to practical interpretation theory as in the direct linkage type but it rather illuminates the characteristics of Japanese law.

(5) *Kaoru Kamata's* research on transfer of property rights is also interesting from the viewpoint of not only interpretation theory, but also illumination of the characteristics of Japanese law.[28] *Kamata*

26 Nomi, n 25 *supra, Hōgaku Kyōkai Zasshi* vol. 103, no. 6 (1986) 998.

27 Nomi, n 25 *supra, Hōgaku Kyōkai Zasshi* vol. 102, no. 10 (1985) 1781 et seq.

28 K. Kamata, 'Furansu ni okeru fudōsan torihiki to kōshōnin no yakuwari: "Furansuhō shugi" no rikai no tameni' [Real estate transactions and the role of

points toward French law research on the premise that Japanese conveyance law was adopted from French law. In Japan, there is an understanding that a transfer of property rights can take place merely by an oral agreement between the parties to sell or buy, but this seems somewhat strange. In France, there may be unimaginable preconditions that support the presence of the theory of will. Based on this problem awareness, *Kamata* takes a look at the history and the actual situation of real estate transactions in France. What he found was that the real estate transaction practices in France were supported by notary practice. In France, the parties to a real estate transaction first prepare a private contract between them and conclude a preliminary contract. This is only preliminary and not a formal contract. They conclude the formal contract at a notary public's office. In France, when a sales contract is concluded and the debts and credits are finalized the ownership is deemed to become transferred as a natural course but the parties go to a notary public's office to conclude a contract on this transfer. The impression of the registration is to file the notary deed with the registry.

When we face such a situation of transactions in France, we can understand that the ownership is not transferred merely by an oral agreement between the parties to sell or buy, that the theory of will in France premises the abovementioned transaction practice and that there is a system where the will to make the contract effective is only established after going through a very strict process. This naturally elucidates the characteristics of Japanese law in contrast to French law, as well as has an impact on the theory of interpretation of Japanese law with respect to issues including the time of establishment of a contract and the time of transfer of the ownership. Roughly speaking, it is expected that the time of establishment of a contract will be recognized to be at a later point of time, so the theory to recognize the transfer of ownership at the time of establishment of the contract would not be so unreasonable in the future.[29]

notary public in France: for understanding the "principle of referring to French law"] *Waseda Hōgaku* vol. 56, no. 1 31 et seq, no. 1 et seq (1980) (incomplete).

29 K. Kamata, *Minpō Nōto: Bukkenhō (1) Dai 2 Han* [Civil law notebook: property rights (1) 2nd ed.] (Tokyo 2001) 19–20.

(6) The 'reverse illumination type' of research introduced above, including that of *Segawa* and *Nomi*, pointed in the direction of French law research premising that French law has a genealogical relationship with Japanese law, at least to some extent, as the reason for referencing French law. However, some of the studies that should be categorized as the 'reverse illumination type' seem to point toward French law without giving any reasons. *Hiroyasu Nakata's* research on framework agreements[30] may be one example of works that indicate such a new tendency.

A framework agreement does not have a fixed definition, but let me roughly explain it to the extent necessary for today's report. Supposing there is a basic agreement on a business relationship and individual agreements concluded based on that agreement in a continuous business relationship, a framework agreement would be the former agreement that would serve as the basis. The individual agreements based on it are called adaptation agreements. In France, discussions on the concept of this framework agreement seem to be making remarkable progress recently.

Nakata does not import the concept of framework agreement, but he investigates the background of the intense discussions on framework agreements in France and derives the differences in concept with Japanese contract law. The framework agreement is subject to diverse views; starting with the concept itself. Nonetheless, the concept of the framework agreement has continued to be used. The paper hints at the reasons for it. *Nakata's* answer to this question is that a contract in France is solid, with little room to make later adjustments once it is established and the rights and obligations take effect. Although there have been some changes in the situation recently, at least to date there has been little possibility for the fair and equitable principle to be applied or the principle of change of circumstances to be affirmed. So in order to maintain flexibility for later adjustments in the agreement, discussions inevitably developed on a two-step system in which overall matters are decided by the framework agreement and the details are dealt with by adaptation agreements later.[31]

30 H. Nakata, *Keizokuteki Torihiki No Kenkyū* [Research on continuous transactions] (Tokyo 2003; first published in 2000) 32 et seq.
31 Nakata, n 30 *supra*, 51–52.

The reverse illumination type is distinctive in that the results of French law research illuminate the characteristics of Japanese law and the major achievement of this group seems to be in the interesting factors of Japanese law that have been illuminated, rather than interpretation theories.

4. Conceptual source type

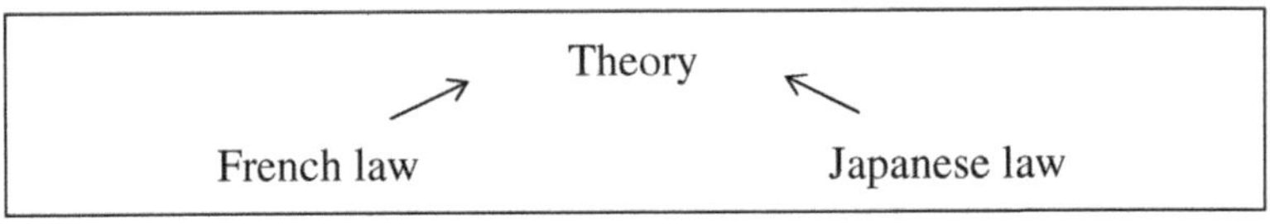

(1) Lastly, I will introduce the 'conceptual source type'. Studies that fall within this group use French law as a material, but one of their characteristics is that they do not explain the necessity for selecting French law. The genealogic linkage is sometimes mentioned but it does not seem to carry weight. In the academic theories categorized under this group, French law is only used as an indirect conceptual source. Another characteristic of conceptual source type research is that, even if it seems to write mostly about French law superficially, it is discussing problems of Japanese law in effect. I will introduce two relatively recent studies.

(2) First, I will explain *Hiroki Morita's* research on the significance of the distinction between obligation of result and obligation of means.[32] The most interesting point in *Morita's* research was that he presented a 'theory' to find fault with regard to default of obligation, not in lack of due care or negligence in the obligor's performance, but in the fact that the obligor failed to perform the obligation promised at the time that the contract was being concluded.[33] If the fault is construed in this manner, the distinction between an obligation of result and an obligation of means would be

32 H. Morita, 'Kekka saimu/shudan saimu no kubetsu no igi ni tsuite' [Significance of the distinction between obligation of result and obligation of means], in H. Morita, *Keiyaku Sekinin No Kiseki Kōzō* [Structure of faults in contract liabilities] (Tokyo 2002; first published in 1993) 1 et seq.
33 Morita, n 32 *supra*, 55.

reduced to an issue of the content and scope of the obligation in the contract, in other words, an issue of interpretation of the contract. An obligation in the case where the party promised definitely to achieve the result in a contract is an obligation of result. If the result is not achieved, it will be a fault in itself. When the party did not promise definitely to achieve the result, but promised to make specific efforts, the obligation is an obligation of means. If the party does not fail to make the promised efforts, no fault will be found.[34]

Morita's theory has been derived through French law research, but the paper treats it as being nothing special at the French textbook level and does not particularly emphasize it. It seems appropriate to see this theory as having been presented by *Morita* as an original interpretation of French law. Rather than a Japanese person freely talking about French matter that is not even heard of in France, he effectively summarized and presented one possible interpretation method as a means for understanding French law. This may be hard to imagine when we consider it in the abstract, but it is a very sophisticated, persuasive paper.

Since this paper states that the understanding of faults based on theories such as *Morita's* would be compliant with the structure of the default law in the Civil Code,[35] it does not neglect the genealogical relationship. In the paper, however, the French law is likely to have served as the conceptual source for structuring the theory on faults rather than being referenced due to the presence of a genealogical linkage.

(3) Next, I will introduce *Atsushi Omura's* study on typical contracts. It is published as a book called *Tenkei Keiyaku To Seishitu Kettei* [Typical contracts and characterization].[36] Since this book contains various messages, it is difficult to decide which one to extract. The fact that *Omura* is here today makes it even more difficult. Broadly speaking, it is a study in which *Omura* indicates his own views on law and humankind by using French law and discussions on typical

34 Morita, n 32 *supra*, 55–56.

35 Morita, n 32 *supra*, 55.

36 A. Omura, *Tenkeiteki Keiyaku To Seishitsu Kettei* [Typical contracts and characterization] (Tokyo 1997; first published in 1993–1995).

contracts as materials. The earlier-used expression, 'French law is only used as an indirect conceptual source', was originally used by *Omura*.[37]

More specifically, human abilities are limited, so they cannot act by gathering and analyzing all information. Thus, a tool will be required to reduce the burden of information processing. Such tool for the parties concluding a contract and judges who interpret contracts is typical. The typical contract types, which have been developed through experience and history, encompass the contract details that have been considered by people to be reasonable and they are regarded as a tool not for constraining contractual activity, but for supporting it.[38]

Another interesting point is that it pays attention to the process of interpretation and application of law as well as the distinction between the two. It isolates the issue of application or characterization from the issue of interpretation. It somewhat emphasizes that legal norms only take effect if they are invoked when the requirements are met. There seems to be a slight distance from the theory of weighing interests by assuming the outcome of the application of law. The research provides one perspective for looking at law by highlighting the process of characterization.

The reverse illumination type of research is of course extremely creative, but it first places importance on the objective awareness of French law. In contrast, the conceptual source type of research seems to place importance on the researcher's own interpretation rather than objective awareness of French law and literally uses French materials as a conceptual source.

III. Reasons for Studying French Law

1. Inevitability and coincidence of studying French law

(1) In the previous section, I introduced some Japanese studies on civil law that refer to French law. I would like to review the reasons given in these academic theories for studying French law.

37 Omura, n 36 *supra*, 16.
38 Omura, n 36 *supra*, 351–352.

Chronologically, many of the earliest theories introduced today give some pretext or explanation for referring to French law research. A representative reason given is that it is indispensable to study French law since Japanese civil law is genealogically related to it. This reason is mentioned in *Ikeda's* research, *Awaji's* research, *Segawa's* research and *Kamata's* research. The pretext for referring to French law seems to have been sought for a long time, including a reasoning that, even if no genealogical linkage existed, there is a need to supplement the lack of comparative law study on a certain issue, in other words, French law should be studied because French law research has been insufficient in regard to the issue, as is mentioned in *Nomura's* research.

(2) However, some recent studies, including *Nakata's* research, *Morita's* research and *Omura's* research, do not emphasize the inevitability of French law research. They only happened to allude to French law. At least, when we look at the individual papers, they do not mention the essential reason for alluding to French law.

Generally speaking, an underlying factor for the emergence of such research is the spread of awareness that French law research has matured, or that there is significance in making French law the subject of study irrespective of individual genealogical relationships because Japanese civil law traditionally developed based on Western European laws.

I should probably add that there is an increasing awareness that genealogical linkage itself is not necessarily clear-cut. For example, Article 709 of the Japanese Civil Code is said to be a French style provision,[39] but a view denying this is also prevalent,[40] so it is difficult to seek the inevitable reason for referring to French law in genealogical linkage alone. Since the respective provisions in the Japanese Civil Code have been created by referring to the civil law of various countries, many of them cannot be simply distinguished as

39 See Y. Hirai, *Saiken Kakuron II: Fuhō Kōi* [Particulars on claims II: tort] (Tokyo 1992) 12–13.

40 T. Maeda, *Fuhō Kōi Kisekiron* [Theory on faults in torts] (Tokyo 1978) Preface, 2.

French or German in style.[41] In addition, when the subject of research in Japanese law does not converge to a specific provision or system, it would be fundamentally impossible to point toward French law based on genealogical linkage.

Nevertheless, a more important factor would be the change in research style. While research on genealogically related French law will clarify the original significance of provisions or systems of civil law, *Morita's* research on the obligation of result and obligation of means in particular takes a style that forms a more abstract theory with a sideways glance at French law. This type of research seems to be producing interesting outcomes.

In fact, I feel that, being questioned on the reason for studying French law in itself reflects the uniqueness of French law research. It must be rare for a paper on German law research in the domain of civil law to mention why the research is on German law. However, when the research is on French law, the researcher would be constantly questioned on why the research is on French law, so French law researchers have always had to offer a pretext, though that has not necessarily been the case recently. It may be that the reason for referring to French law has come to be sought in the content of the law rather than formalistic aspects such as the genealogical relationship.

2. What is French style?

(1) To make this report more substantial, I would now like to change the angle slightly and consider what Japanese civil law study sees in French law. Research in civil law study often extracts something of a French style and uses it for analyzing Japanese law. The question is: what do researchers regard as being French style? It may be possible to imagine the reason why the study of civil law refers to French law from such analysis.

41 Also see the following paper, which indicates the risk of emphasizing genealogy: T. Isomura, 'Doitsu to Furansu no minpōten/minpōgaku: ichi kaishaku gakusha no shiten kara' [Civil Code and the study of civil law in Germany and France: from a viewpoint of a hermeneutic scholar] *Hōritsu Jihō* vol. 71, no. 4 (1999) 53.

Things that are of French style are defined at various levels. For example, at the technical level, the concept of countering third parties is an extremely French concept. In addition, the concept of collectively regarding the requirements for tort as *faute* instead of clearly distinguishing between illegality and culpability is also French in style. Both concepts would probably appear to be slightly hazy for Japanese lawyers who refer to the achievements of the study of German law as well. French lawyers seem to be very keen on discussing logic, and favour discussing concepts, but somehow they do not result in creating theories like those of German lawyers.

At the level of generalities, on the other hand, there is lucidness;[42] more specifically, French lawyers often notably emphasize the principle of autonomy of will or try to explain various phenomena by principle–like concepts such as will or contract.[43]

Though rather subjective, the following part mentions some interesting French aspects that are at the in-between level of the two. They are in the order of the view on contract, the view on law, and the view on society. The question is: what kinds of aspects are considered to be French in style?

(2) First is the view on contract. In this context, the view on contract does not mean the issue of the differences in mentality between Japan and France, but it means the view on contract at a more technical level, as is found in the studies I introduced today. The explanation is again not elaborate but rather general.

The view on contract can be readily estimated from the research of *Nomi*, *Kamata* and *Nakata*, but I would like to introduce it briefly. In France, emphasis is placed on the autonomy of will. However, the autonomy of will does not exist by itself. There are various underlying conditions that support the autonomy of will. The notary practice men-

42 I. Kitamura, 'Furansu ni okeru hō no meisekisa ni tsuite' [Lucidness of law in France] *Hōsō Jihō* vol. 48, no. 11 (1996) 1 et seq.
43 T. Yamaguchi, 'Furansuhō ni okeru ishi jichiron to sono gendaiteki henyō' [The theory of autonomy of will under French law and its modern transformation], in: *Hōgaku Kyōkai Hyakushūne Kinen Ronbunshū Dai San Kan* [Collected papers to commemorate the 100 anniversary of the Jurisprudence Association] (Tokyo 1983) Vol. 3, 244 et seq.

tioned by *Kamata* is one of the important conditions. When a contract for sale of real estate is established, a significant effect – transfer of ownership – takes effect. A contract is supposedly established by the consent of both parties, but when parties actually intend to conclude a contract for sale of real estate, they usually need to draft a private contract and conclude a formal contract at a notary public's office after making all the necessary arrangements. From the viewpoint of the will theory, the parties to the contract are induced carefully to consider the meaning of their own acts in the course of this process. It is also said that an agreement must accompany support of cause. This is stipulated in a provision of the Civil Code. This can also be considered as a condition that supports the autonomy of will. How the concept of cause should be understood is controversial, but there is certainly an underlying idea that abstract and formal will is insufficient for causing the binding force of a contract to take effect. In addition to these circumstances, the emphasis, or, overemphasis of documentary evidence by court is also relevant. It may be well known in judicial practice, but French judges only refer to the documents in order to understand the content of a contract, in most cases. Setting aside the reasons for this situation, people who are going to conclude an important contract would inevitably try to create a detailed contractual document on the premise of such a situation. In this manner, the will for establishing a contract seems to be supported and reinforced to a great extent by peripheral systems. In Japan, on the other hand, although establishment of a contract for sale of real estate would naturally be determined carefully, the establishment of a contract would be affirmed relatively easily with the will of the parties suddenly emerging.[44]

Under French law, once a contract is established by such reinforced will, the following can be said according to the famous expression in the Civil Code: 'agreements lawfully entered into take the place of the law for those who have made them'.[45] Since a contract is con-

44 Y. Imamura, 'Fudōsan torihiki ni okeru ishishugi no rikai' [Understanding of the will theory in real estate transactions], in N. Iijima et al. (ed), *Shimin Hōgaku No Kadai To Tenbō* [Challenges and outlook of ius civile] (Tokyo 2000) 247 et seq.

45 Article 1134, paragraph 1 of the Civil Code (Japanese translation in the Japanese version of this report is from: Research and Statistics Division, Judicial System and Research Department, Minister's Secretariat, Ministry of Justice

cluded by the noble will of the parties, other people cannot intervene with it easily. Specifically, it was clearly indicated in *Nomi's* research on liquidated damages that a court cannot easily regulate the content of a contract decided by the parties even if it was slightly unreasonable. *Nakata's* research on framework agreements is also related to this area. It confirmed that, at least under the French concept to date, a contract that has once been established and taken effect does not allow a court later to adjust the rights and obligations flexibly to make them comply with the changes in situation, and the contract is strongly bound to the framework of rights and obligation that was firmly decided between the parties in the first place. In France, the principle of change of circumstances is not affirmed by judicial courts. Let me add that this concept of respecting the agreement between the parties is something relevant to judicial courts. For example, the principle of change of circumstances is not affirmed by judicial courts, but it is affirmed by administrative courts.[46] In addition, a judicial court judge cannot regulate the content of a contract by himself/herself in principle, but the content of a contract is very frequently regulated by law. Thus, there is a tremendous difference between regulation of contracts by legislators or administrators and that by court judges.

(3) Next, I will discuss the view on law. There seems to be a certain characteristic in the view on law in research that refers to French law. It is observed in *Omura's* research on contract law. However, I would like to add that a similar characteristic is also observed in *Noriko Mizuno's* research on family law,[47] although the subject of research seems to be completely different.

(ed), *Furansu Minpōten: Bukken/Saiken Kankei* [French Civil Code: concerning real rights and claims] (Tokyo 1982) 67).

46 K. Igarashi, *Keiyaku To Jijō Henkō* [Contract and change in circumstances] (Tokyo 1969) 36 et seq.

47 N. Mizuno, 'Jitsu oyako kankei to ketsuen shugi ni kansuru ichi kōsatsu: Furansuhō wo chūshin ni' [Consideration on real parental relationship and the principle of attaching importance on blood relationship: focusing on French law], in: H. Eiichi Koki Shukuga: *Nihon Minpōgaku No Keisei To Kadai (Ge)* [Celebration for the 70th birthday of Professor Eiichi Hoshino, *Nihon Minpōgaku No Keisei To Kadai: Ge* [Formation and challenges of the theory of civil law in Japan: vol. 2] (Tokyo 1996) 1131 et seq.

Omura's theory[48] can probably be construed as follows, though it will be quite a stretch to match the content of today's report. The ground for the rights and obligations under a contract to take effect is not the will of the parties. A view to consider that certain rights and obligations take effect under law because the parties have such will or because the parties wished for them confuses a fact with a norm. The rights and obligations under a contract are only approved under legal order if there is a norm to recognize the effect of the rights and obligations desired by the parties when there is the will of the parties. The legal effect of the will only arises by law or the power of a norm, so the will and law are different, and the fact and the norm are different. As a result, the legal order can be divided between a domain where the content of a contract is decided by will and a domain where it is not. My explanation may be a little daring.

Apart from contract law, a similar characteristic is observed for family law. With regard to paternal relationships, *Mizuno* suggests that we should perceive from France that a paternal relationship at the genetic level and a legal paternity relationship are different. Just as there is a complete difference between what the parties wished for; that is, the bare content of the will and the legal effect granted to the will that was legally operated in a domain recognized by legal order, in the world of contract law, a parental relationship also differs between that at the genetic level and the legal relationship. In other words, a legal paternal relationship is approved as a result of applying systems such as the legitimacy presumption system and the recognition system, or the norms available in these systems. Under some of these norms, a legal paternal relationship may not be affirmed even if there is a blood relationship or a paternal relationship at the genetic level, based on various considerations. A typical example is the statute of limitation for taking legal proceedings to deny legitimacy. The legal effects arise as a result of applying rules or as a result of a system.

I am, in fact, not so convinced of how much consensus there is on regarding this view on law as being French in style. Nonetheless, I had

48 Omura, n 36 *supra*; A. Omura, 'Furansuhō ni okeru keiyaku to seido' [Contracts and systems under French law], in A. Omura (ed), *Keiyakuhō Kara Shōhishahō He* [From contract law to consumer law] (Tokyo 1999; first published in 1998) 238 et seq.

a similar impression when looking at French theory on corporations. A concept that was conventionally observed in the theory of unincorporated association in Japan, which is immediately to grant a juristic personality since there is an entity as a corporation, is hardly observed, and there seems to be a solid premise that juristic personality is granted only on the base of the legal order. It is said that a juristic personality is not granted deservingly, but granted on the base of the determination by legal order, even for natural persons.[49]

French style characteristics are considered to be this view on contract or view on law. However, they may only be characteristics in the eyes of Japanese observers, and the characteristics may seem different from different perspectives. In addition, these characteristics may not be specific to French law, but may share some common aspects at least with other Western European laws such as German law. Although these are major characteristics in the relationship with Japan, they must still be insufficient to be regarded as the characteristics of French law in contrast to the rest of Western European laws.

(4) If we are to look further for characteristics specific to French law, it would be the French view on society, which is perceived when making French law the subject of research. Since this topic deviates far from the realm of civil law, the explanation will be completely a layman's view, but we are near the end, so I ask for your patience.

Recently, in particular, when French law is taken up for research, it is often expected to play the role of relating the value judgment in Japanese legislation or interpretation. For example, *Mizuno's* research on family law introduced above criticizes the legitimacy presumption system and the system of denial of legitimacy as possibly hollowing out with presumption of legitimacy being rebutted one after another by actions for denial of legitimacy as well as actions for negative confirmation of kinship. This is from the viewpoint that the legitimacy presumption system and the system of denial of legitimacy are for protecting the interests of the child. In this research, French family law is used. Another example is that in the field of medical law the slightly paternalistic relationship between doctors

[49] G. Cornu, *Droit civil, Introduction/Les personnes/Les biens* (4th ed., Paris 1990) n 783 and 458.

and patients in France may be introduced in order to achieve a tone of placing emphasis on the self-determination of patients. As a more obvious example, it should be mentioned that there is an underlying French concept when trying to control a contract in the name of contract justice so as to counter excessive emphasis on the liberty of a contract. *Omura's* research is a good example. Outside the domain of civil law, a book entitled *Rōdōshakai No Henyō To Saisei* [Transformation and revival of labour society][50] written by *Yuichiro Mizumachi* who studies labour law also tries to derive a solution for countering the principle to place economy above anything else and the principle to consider market as being justice from French labour law or research on labour problems in France.

In the background of French law used in this context, there seems to be a certain common social image. I do not know how much this is being discussed in a well-defined manner, but if I were to boldly schematize it, it is as if contraposing the United States on one hand and

United States	France (alliance with Germany?)
Freedom Atomistic individualism Deregulation Emphasis on freedom of enterprises *Economy* is important	Freedom, equality, fraternity Individualism+community? Moderate regulation Certain consideration to consumers and workers Economy is important *too*

France on the other. The factors that characterize US society include freedom, atomistic individualism, deregulation and emphasis on freedom of enterprises; and *economy* is important. On the other hand, the factors that characterize French society include, not only freedom but also equality and fraternity, not only individuals but also community, not deregulation but moderate regulation, freedom of enterprises' economic activities as well as due consideration to consumers and work-

50 Y. Mizumachi, *Rōdō Shakai No Henyō To Saisei: Furansu Rōdō Hōsei No Rekishi To Rironh* [Transformation and revival of labor society: history and theory of the system of French labour law] (Tokyo 2001).

ers, and economy is not the only important thing but it *too* is important. It may mean that some people try to see a model society in this imaginary French society, which is no longer a reality but an ideal.[51]

I have pursued what is French style in this section. In the context that France still counters the United States when contraposing the United States and France, France appears as if it was in alliance with Germany. Therefore, I was unable sufficiently to examine the outstanding characteristics of France in its relationship with Germany today.

IV. Concluding Remarks

Let me conclude. In fact, this is a rather difficult process. Since I see no need to summarize my discussions in part III, I would like to make few remarks in closing with also an implication to raise an issue for the later discussions. The issue is the possibility that the academic theories on civil law in Japan are bound by France and French civil law. When a researcher refers to French law, the French law is premised on French views on things, particularly a view on society. Since the Civil Code was created by and is being nurtured by French society, the above-mentioned French values and ideas may be built into civil law to a considerable extent. Even for the reverse illumination type and the conceptual source type, which seemingly observe French law philosophically and are unbound by French law, the situation may be the same as long as they try to mirror French law.

Therefore, if I further expand the subject, once a researcher defines himself/herself as a civil law scholar, his/her political stance may become confined within the framework of civil law. In other words, once researchers call themselves researchers, libertarian civil law scholars may not appear so easily. Therefore, setting aside how true it is, there is a possibility that French law research in the study of civil law in Japan may be bound by France in that sense. So it may be interesting to make an observation from such a perspective. With this, I would like to conclude my somewhat fragmentary report.

[51] See A. Omura & Y. Mizumachi, '[Taidan] Furansuhō heno shisen' [(Table talk) view toward French law] *Shosai No Mado* vol. 518 (2002) 2 et seq (serialized).

Chapter 5: Anglo-American Law Research in the Study of Civil Law in Japan

Tsuneo Matsumoto

Contents

I. Introduction: Characteristics of Anglo-American Law Research in Civil Law

I have been asked to report on the relationship between Anglo-American law and Japanese civil law, particularly the impact of U.S. law on civil law and the study of civil law in Japan.[1]

The report by *Taro Kogayu* (*Kogayu* report) on the influence of French law on the study of civil law in Japan and the report by *Yoshio Shiomi* (*Shiomi* report) on the influence of German law on the study of civil law in Japan not only described the current status of the study of civil law in France and in Germany, respectively, they also highlight the difference in awareness between a person who mainly studies French civil law in Japan and a person who mainly studies German civil law in Japan. At the beginning of the *Shiomi* report, it is pointed out that the large influence that the study of civil law in Germany has on Japanese law is attributable to the dominance of the objective interpretation principle. The objective interpretation principle, which has taken root in the study of civil law in Japan, seems to be the ground for justifying research of Japanese civil law from a German civil law approach, with the logic for this position being that research of German civil law is not merely one domain of comparative law, but a person engaged in research of German civil law study could, in itself (*an sich*), also be affirmed as a researcher of Japanese civil law. This provides the strongest position for a researcher.

In contrast, a person who studies French civil law in Japan must first rationalize why the research is on French law, as in the *Kogayu* report. Only then can the researcher begin to justify his/her own theory of interpretation; for example, explaining the intention of the drafters of Japanese civil law, and indicating that it originated from French law. This can be considered as a kind of justification for itself (*für sich*).

Now to pose a question, are civil law scholars who study Anglo-American law in general or U.S. law in particular sublating (*aufhe-*

1 I have studied an issue similar to this report in my previous paper, 'Minpōgaku ni okeru Amerikahō no isō' [The phase of U.S. law research in the study of civil law] *Hōritsu Jihō* vol. 56 no. 1 (1984) 32. Readers are advised to refer to it along with this report. This report is a summary of the report I made at a symposium (10 May 2004) with some additional notes for explanation.

ben) the entirety (if a term of dialectic philosophy were to be used)? This is not the case. Instead, it is as if they are standing at the edge of the pond of Japanese civil law study and throwing stones in; and these 'stones' are extremely stimulating. Research from a U.S. law perspective or research that uses U.S. law as the basic material seems to be contributing the most to stimulating the discussions on the study of civil law in Japan.

It has been indicated that the code investigation committee (Hōten Chōsakai), which compiled the current Civil Code, also referred to U.K. case law, and that some parts were actually adopted from its study.[2] Conversely, no part of the Civil Code has ever been directly adopted from U.S. law. Nonetheless, research on U.S. law has had a certain level of influence on the study of civil law in Japan. Obviously, one of the main reasons for this is the overwhelming influence of the United States on Japanese society after World War II, and there is also the circumstance that the Japanese economy must inevitably adapt to Americanization in the name of globalization. However, it can be pointed out that the lack of direct adoption has made it easier for U.S. law to drive a paradigm shift of the study of civil law itself. Indeed, as mentioned later, in this report U.S. law has had an impact not only on superficial aspects of the study but also on its in-depth aspects.

U.S. law is considered to have had an influence on Japanese civil law in two ways. One is a direct influence, and the other is an indirect influence through Germany, which could be considered a kind of 'hidden U.S. law'.[3] Many German civil law scholars write their habilitation theses by comparatively studying U.S. law, and interpretation

2 It has been pointed out since the past that Article 416 of the Civil Code concerning scope of demand of compensation for damages has its origin in a U.K. court judgment, Hadley v. Baxendale, 9 EX. 341, 156 E.R. 145 (1854). See Z. Kitagawa, *Nihon Hōgaku No Rekishi To Riron* [History and theory of Japanese jurisprudence] (Tokyo 1968) 67; Y. Hirai, *Songai Baishōhō No Riron* [Theory of damages] (Tokyo 1971) 150. This U.K. case law principle further goes back to *Robert Joseph Pothier's* theory in France: T. Maeda, *Kōjutsu Saiken Sōron* [Dictation of generalities on credits] (3rd ed., Tokyo 1993) 186.

3 K. Fujikura, 'Nihon ni okeru Amerikahō kenkyū' [U.S. law research in Japan] *Jurisuto* no. 600 (1975) 66 indicates that, sometimes legal theories that are inherent to the United States are imported by Germany, and are introduced to Japanese law as new interpretation theories of German law as if they are extremely worthy of reference.

theories of German civil law have often developed based on the results of such studies. Japanese academic circles generelly do not respond to reports on U.S. law, believing that U.S. law is not directly related to Japanese law, but they tend to be convinced by reports on German law for some reason. This must be the difference in the ability to digest and absorb between German civil law study and Japanese civil law study, which is strongly influenced by German civil law study. However, when thinking about this point, consideration should be given to the fact that, at one time, a very large number of representative U.S. scholars in the fields corresponding to the study of civil law became legal scholars in the United States by migrating or defecting to the United States after studying law in German-speaking countries.

Anglo-American law is used as a collective term, but while U.S. law and U.K. law have the same origin historically, at present, it may be appropriate to regard them as different legal systems. As U.K. law will inevitably be incorporated into the EU and become closer to European law, it may be better to consider modern U.K. law as a part of European law.[4] The following sections mainly examine the relationship of Japanese law with U.S. law.

II. Influence of the Study of U.S. Law at Different Levels

1. Methodological level

Let me begin with a discussion at the methodological level. When looking at the influence that U.S. law or the study of U.S. law has had on the study of civil law in Japan, the influence at the interpretation theory level has been extremely limited; meanwhile, the most remarkable influence has been observed at the research methodology

4 There are movements toward introducing European contract law and European private law. See Y. Shiomi, 'Yōroppa tōitsu keiyakuhō no kokoromi to genkai' [Attempts and limits of a unified European contract law] *Hokkaidō Daigaku Hōgaku Ronshū* vol. 51 no. 2 (2000) 1; Y. Kawasumi et al. (eds), *Yōroppa Shihō No Dōkō To Kadai* [Trend and challenges of European private law] (Tokyo 2003).

level. One of the influences from the past is *Izutaro Suehiro's* legal study method, which is referenced by the above-mentioned Professor *Shiomi*. As discussed below, the study of civil law in Japan has been influenced at the methodological level in various forms, and lively discussions have been held whenever some matters were raised. The influences mentioned below can roughly be divided into the following: those from (a) to (c) are legal influences, those from (d) to (f) are economic influences, and those in (g) are social/philosophical influences.

a) The case method of teaching and case study

Professor *Izutaro Suehiro* studied in the United States and Europe in 1918, towards the end of World War I. In the United States, he took a class conducted by the case method of teaching at the University of Chicago Law School, and was extremely impressed. After that, he went to Europe, and was even more impressed upon meeting *Eugen Ehrlich*. One of the tasks he engaged in after returning to Japan from this inspiring trip was to establish the Civil Case Study Group at the University of Tokyo for conducting case studies in a Japanese form of the case method. In addition, further efforts were made in the direction of social law.

Introduction of a postgraduate system of legal education was realized recently in Japan with the establishment of Japanese-style law schools, which are educational institutions specializing in nurturing the legal profession. However, introduction of the case method of teaching has not been very successful. The underlying factors include the difference in the quality of court cases, due to the difference between the case law system and the statute law system, and the fact that most Japanese judical opinions from court judgments do not sufficiently discuss their relationships with precedential cases; and therefore, they would not have much educational merit for students if they were presented as they were prepared.[5] Thus, *Hanrei Hyakusen* (100 se-

[5] Professor *Takayuki Higashi* (a former judge) has proposed having students read written judgments and prepare their own case notes (memos on the case) as a preliminary step of education on ultimate facts at law schools. See T. Higashi, 'Hōka daigakuin ni okeru yōken jijitsu kyōiku ni tsuite (sono 2) (sono 3) (sono 4)' [Education on ultimate facts at law schools (Part 2) (Part 3) (Part 4)] *Kurume Hōgaku* no. 43 (2002) 31; no. 44 (2002) 63; no. 48 (2003) 1; no. 49 (2004) 1. In-

lected court cases) annotated with commentary is used in class, in place of the actual court cases.

At the same time, Professor *Michitaka Kaino*, who is an idelogical successor regarding *Suehiro's* legal study method, has indicated that the lecture method of teaching would create a hotbed for authoritarianism in stating the differences among the U.S.-style of teaching by case method, German-style teaching by the lecture method, and a method in which the university instructor teaches legal dogma from the platform.[6] It is a view that students or apprentices would tend to automatically follow what the teacher said, and would come to compromise their views with the authority position. In this respect, the case method of teaching is irrelevant to the authority of the professor, though there is the authority of court cases, because the students are made to think on their own based on the cases. This point must be the same in Germany as well, but in Japan, this tendency seems to have also connected with the spirit of the traditional *iemoto* system (licensing of the teaching of Japanese traditional art), and has affected the nature of the academic circles and the characteristics of the study.

Although there are many prominent scholars in the United States, they do not seem to have the same degree of authority as German scholars, or, at the least, the nature of authority seems to be different. In the United States, judges have greater authority than scholars. For example, Professor *Richard Posner* at the University of Chicago, who is one of the pioneers in the field of 'law and economics' and who is an authority on antitrust law, currently serves as a judge on the U.S. Court of Appeals. In particular, a judge on the U.S. Supreme Court has extremely great authority. By contrast, Germany is considered to be a legal culture in which scholars have greater authority and stronger influence than judges.

cidentally, T. Isomura, M. Ohashi, K. Kawashima et al., *Hōka Daigakuin Kēsu Bukku: Minpō* [Law school case book: civil law] (Tokyo 2004) also requires students to conduct a similar task before starting the examination of the specific problems of the respective court cases.

6 M. Kaino, 'Saiban no hōshakaigaku-teki kōsatsu to hōritsugaku' [Consideration of court trials from the viewpoint of sociology of law and jurisprudence] *Hōshakaigaku* no. 1 (1951) 26.

b) Legal realism and empirical studies of law

Professor *Takeyoshi Kawashima* has introduced U.S. concepts such as legal realism and empirical studies of law, as a scholar of the generation subsequent to that of Professor *Suehiro*. These concepts have led to the proposal of a practical science of law[7] or 'jurisprudence as empirical science' intended for forecasting the outcome of future court judgments instead of legal interpretation. The study on the 'framework for determination of precedents' which is one of the factors for forecasting future court judgments, has firmly taken root as 'discussions on the scope of the influence of precedent'. However, the personality or social environment of the judge,[8] which are other factors for forecasting future court judgments, have not been accepted outside the sociology of law. Although empirical studies of law have been conducted in some research,[9] they seem to have failed to take root.

c) Balancing of interests

Professor *Ichiro Kato* studied in the United States in the 1960s, and not only raised the matter of the case method of teaching,[10] but also proposed the 'balancing of interests' (*rieki kōryō ron*) analysis. The Japanese pronunciation of the translated term is the same as that for 'weighing of interests' (*rieki kōryō ron*) proposed by Professor *Eiichi Hoshino*, but the meaning is slightly different, just as there is a difference in the Chinese characters. The weighing of interests proposed by Professor *Hoshino* is to make determinations by considering the hierarchy of values when no conclusion can be derived from grammatical interpretation, logical interpretation or inquiring into the

7 T. Kawashima, *Kagaku Toshite No Hōritsugaku* [Jurisprudence as science] (new ed.,Tokyo 1964); included in T. Kawashima, *Takeyoshi Chosakushū, Dai 5 Kan, Hōritsugaku I* [Collection of works by Takeyoshi Kawashima, vol. 5, Jurisprudence I] (Tokyo 1982).

8 See J. Frank, *Law and the Modern Mind* (T. Tanase and K. Tanase trans., Tokyo 1974).

9 For example, T. Ota, *Tōjisha Ni Okeru Shoyūken No Ten'i* [Transfer of ownership between the parties] (Tokyo 1963).

10 I. Kato, 'Keisu mesoddo ron' [Case method] in I. Kato, *Minpō Ni Okeru Ronri To Rieki Kōryō* [Logic and balancing of interests in civil law] (Tokyo 1974) 79 (first published in *Jurisuto* no. 287 and no. 288 (1963)).

drafter's intentions, and the weighing of interests is done at the end.[11] However, in the balancing of interests analysis proposed by Professor *Kato*, the balancing is conducted at the beginning of the lawyer's tasks. The concept accepts the indication by legal realism that the conclusion precedes in a court trial, and considers that a reasonable conclusion can only be derived through analysis of the conflicting through interests, and the balancing of these interests in society, and that the theoretical structure is for formally reasoning the conclusion.[12] In short, it is to first think about the appropriate solution to the actual problem without much regard to the provisions of law and to structure the theory thereafter. It corresponds to the 'substantive theory' that has been conventionally discussed in Japanese academic circles.

The balancing of interests approach never received substantial support as a methodology. Perhaps, no scholars have conducted research solely based on such a methodology. Nonetheless, almost all researchers and judges are aware that the interests of the people concerned must be appropriately taken into account as part of the research, or in the process of deriving at a court judgment. In the sense that only a limited number of researchers and judges would now consider it sufficient to derive a conclusion solely based on logical inter-

11 E. Hoshino, 'Minpō kaishakuron josetsu' [Introduction to interpretation of civil law] in E. Hoshino, *Minpōron-shū Dai Ikkan* [Collection of theories on civil law: vol. 1] (Tokyo 1970) 1 (first published in *Annals of Legal Philosophy 1967*, 'Hō no kaishaku to unyō' [Interpretation and operation of law] (Tokyo 1968)).

12 I. Kato, 'Hō kaishaku-gaku ni okeru ronri to rieki kōryō' [Logic and balancing of interests in legal interpretation] in Kato, n 10 *supra,* 3 (first published in *Iwanami Kōza Gendaihō 15 Kan* [Iwanami lecture: modern law vol. 15] (1966)); I. Kato, 'Minpō no kaishaku to rieki kōryō' [Interpretation and balancing of interests in civil law] *Hōgaku Kyōshitsu* vol. 25 (1982) 16. With regard to the weighing/balancing of interests and the study on U.S. law at the time, see K. Yoshida, 'Riarizumu hōgaku to rieki kōryōron ni kansuru 'kiso riron' teki kōsatsu: minpō kaishaku-gaku hōhōron no shisōteki keifu' [Consideration of interpretation of civil law and weighing of interests from the perspective of 'basic theory": ideological genealogy of the methodologies of civil law interpretation] in K. Yoshida, *Minpō Kaishaku To Yureugoku Shoyūron* [Interpretation of civil law and the wavering property theories] (Tokyo 2000) 3 (first published in N. Segawa (ed), *Shihōgaku No Saik*ōchiku [Restructuring of the study of private law] (Sapporo 1999)).

pretation, while neglecting the balancing of the interests of the parties concerned, the idea seems to have taken root at the conceptual level discussed later in this article.

d) Law and economics

The field of 'law and economics' thrived in the 1970s and many U.S. law schools began to provide classes on this theoretical approach in the 1980s. Also in Japan, economists were early in introducing it,[13] and later, civil law researchers made some attempts to introduce this approach as well.[14] However, the theory has not become as established in Japan as in the United States. The major reason seems to be the fact that an economy and society compliant with neoclassical economic principles, which is the theoretical basis for 'law and economics', did not sufficiently exist in Japan (even today when deregulation is under way).

At present, the concept of 'law and economics' is not used on its own to derive a conclusion, but it is mainly used to justify existing law systems or conclusions of court judgments, or used as a tool along with other reasoning methods in legislation or legal interpretation.

e) Game theory

Game theory, which is also known by the term 'prisoner's dilemma', is one of the elements of 'law and economics'. This method has been used for the analysis of contract law from the perspective of legal philosophy.[15] In addition, civil law scholars have evaluated it favourably, as game theory, which places emphasis on incomplete information and transaction costs, is better applicable to jurisprudence that

13 K. Hamada, *Songai Baishō No Keizai Bunseki* [Economic analysis of compensation for damages] (Tokyo 1977); K. Miyazawa (ed), *Seizōbutsu Sekinin No Keizaigaku* [Economics of product liability] (Tokyo 1982).
14 Apart from the large number of translations, there are H. Kobayashi & H. Kanda, *'Hō To Keizaigaku' Nyūmon'* [Introduction to 'law and economics'] (Tokyo 1986); ; J. Mark Ramseyer, *Hō To Keizaigaku: Nihon Hō No Keizai Bunseki* [Law and economics: economic analysis of Japanese law] (Tokyo 1990); S. Hayashida, *Hō To Keizaigaku: Atarashii Chiteki Teritor* (Dai 2 Han) [Law and economics: New intellectual territory (2nd ed.)] (Tokyo 2002); etc.
15 I. Kobayashi, *Gōriteki Sentaku To Keiyaku* [Rational choices and contracts] (Tokyo 1991).

deals with normative matters, than economic theories based on neo-classical market theories.[16]

f) Law and policy

Professor *Yoshio Hirai's* ideas on law and policy have been developed by integrating normative elements using welfare economics theory, while also being influenced by 'law and economics'.[17] However, while the study of law and policy at the time was greatly influenced by neoclassical economics, recent textbooks consider the limitations of economics and accordingly place emphasis on the perspectives of organization theory and procedural justice.[18] At the same time, 'market-based decision-making', 'authoritative decision-making', and 'procedural decision-making' are presented together as the basic theories for designing legal systems.

g) Critical legal studies

Critical legal studies, which were mainly led by law school students at the time of movements against the Vietnam War in the 1960s, include not so much dissident ideas, but various ideas that are outside of the mainstream in the United States. In Japan, the core of such ideas used to be Marxism. Critical legal studies include Marxism, but

16 K. Yoshida, 'Keizokuteki torihiki to gēmu riron' [Continuous transactions and game theory] *Hokkaidō Daigaku Hōgaku Ronshū* vol. 44 no. 1 (1993) 151; O. Morita, 'Gēmu riron to keiyakuhō: hō to shijō no seido bunseki no tameni (sono 2)' [Game theory and contract law: for analysis of the systems of law and market (Part 2)] *Shakai Kagaku Kenkyū* vol. 49 no. 3 (1999) 29. Also see O. Morita, 'Wiriamuson no keiyaku rikai ni tsuite: hō to shijō no seido bunseki no tameni (sono 1)' [Williamson's understanding of contracts: for analysis of the systems of law and market (Part 1)] *Shakai Kagaku Kenkyū* vol. 48 no. 1 (1996) 182. O. Morita, 'Teiki shakuyaken to kōshō' [Term tenant right and negotiation] *Jurisuto* no. 1124 (1997) 66 criticizes the view to introduce the term tenant right, based on the idea of 'transactions in the shadow of law', which has been influenced by game theory.

17 Y. Hirai, 'Hōseisakugaku josetsu (1)–(9)' [Introduction to law and policy (1) – (9)] *Jurisuto* nos. 613–622 (1976); Y. Hirai, 'Hōseisakugaku josetsu' sairon' ['Introduction to law and policy review'] *Jurisuto* no. 668 (1978) 92; Y. Hirai, *Gendai Huhō Kōi Riron No Ichi-Tenbō* [Prospect for the modern tort theories] (Tokyo 1980).

18 Y. Hirai, 'Dai ni han hashigaki' [Preface for the second edition], in Y. Hirai, *Hōseisakugaku* (Dai Ni Han) [Law and policy (2nd ed.)] (Tokyo 1995).

that is not necessarily the mainstream view. The studies also include feminism and various European post-modern theories. Professor *Kunihiko Yoshida* actively introduces the trend of such critical legal studies in the United States[19] and advocates the critical implementation of law in the study of civil law.[20] Nevertheless, for the study of civil law in Japan, which has been affected by Marxist law since Pre-World War II,[21] the impact of this school of thought would be not significant except in certain respects, including feminist law.[22]

[19] T. Uchida, 'V Keiyakuhō to ideorog ' [V Contract law and ideology], in T. Uchida, *Keiyaku No Saisei* [Recovery of contract] (Tokyo 1990); K. Yoshida, 'Amerika ni okeru hihanhō shisō no tenkai to waga minpōgaku no uukue: minpō kaishakugaku hōhōron no shisōteki keifu' [Development of critical legal thought in the United States and future direction of the study of civil law in Japan: ideological genealogy of the methodologies of civil law interpretation], in K. Yoshida, *Minpō Kaishaku To Yureugoku Shoyūron* (Tokyo 2000) 71 (first published in *Minshōhō Zasshi* vol. 119 no. 2 and no. 3 (1998)).

[20] K. Yoshida, 'Zainichi gaikokujin mondai to jikō hōgaku: sengo hoshō (1)–(6)' [Issue of foreign residents in Japan and prescription: war reparation (1)–(6)] *Jurisuto* no. 1214 (2001) 60, no. 1215 164, no. 1216 119, no. 1217 96, no. 1219 128, no. 1220 92; K. Yoshida, 'Amerika no kyojū jijō to hōkainyū no arikata (tokuni Bosuton no baai) (1)–(3): kyojū kakuri to rento kontorōru, kyojū tekikaku hoshō, komyunit saisei undō' [Residential circumstances in the United States and how laws should intervene (particularly in the case of Boston) (1)–(3): residential isolation and rent control, guarantee of residential qualification, and community revival movement] *Minshōhō Zasshi* vol. 129, no. 1 (2003) 1, no. 2 161, no. 3 297; K. Yoshida, 'Iwayuru 'hoshō' mondai heno apurōchi ni kansuru ichi kōsatsu (jō) (ge): minzokukan kōsō no huhō kōi no kyūsai hōhō (nichibei hikaku wo chūshin to shite)' [Consideration of the approach to the 'compensation' issue (vol. 1) (vol. 2): remedies for acts of tort in racial disputes (focusing on Japan-U.S. comparison)] *Hōritsu Jihō* vol. 76 (2005), no. 1 64, no. 2 107.

[21] Y. Yamanaka, *Shimin Shakai To Minpō* [Civil society and civil law] (Tokyo 1947); T. Kawashima, *Shoyūkenhō No Riron* [Theories of ownership law] (Tokyo 1949) (now contained in *Kawashima Takeyoshi Chosakushū, Dai 7 Kan: Shoyūken* [Collection of works by Takeyoshi Kawashima, vol. 7: Ownership] (Tokyo 1981)); Y. Watanabe, *Hōshakaigaku To Marukusu-shugi Hōgaku* [Sociology of law and Marxist law] (Tokyo 1984).

[22] For example, see Y. Terao, 'Jend hōgaku ga kirihiraku chihei' [Horizons opened up by gender law] *Jurisuto* no. 1237 (2003) 11.

2. Conceptual level

Though it is relatively close to the discussion at the methodological level, there is an influence at the conceptual level, which is not as systematized as methodologies, but is at the base of methodologies and is more ambiguous. It is considered to be quite close to foreign law as a 'conceptual source', which was indicated by Professor *Kogayu*.

a) Pragmatism

Specifically, this approach to issues is extremely pragmatic. For example, the practical research of contracts is conducted actively.

b) Property theory

Property is one of the core principles of common law in the narrow sense, and it is a compulsory subject in the first year of law school. In Japanese law, this field roughly corresponds to the law on real rights, centering on ownership. However, the property theory at the conceptual level, which has its root in Lockean theory, has developed into a broader scope of discussion.[23] When it comes to property rights with respect the human body, it is linked with discussions on privacy or personality rights,[24] while the discussion on property

23 S. Morimura, *Zaisanken No Riron* [Theory of property rights] (Tokyo 1995); S. Morimura, *Rokku Shoyūron No Saisei* [Revival of the Lockean property theory] (Tokyo 1997). The former book is reviewed by K. Yoshida, 'Nihonban Ribatarianizumu shoyūkenron ni kansuru ichi kōsatsu: tokuni Hēgeru no jinkakuteki shoyūron wo tegakari to shite' [Consideration of Japanese Libertarian ownership: using Hegel's private property theory as a clue] in Yoshida, n 19 *supra*, 534 (first published in *Minshōhō Zasshi* vol. 115 no. 1 (1996)).

24 K. Yoshida, 'Amerikahō ni okeru 'shoyūkenhō no riron' to dairi haha: feminizumu hōgaku/hihanteki jinshu riron/puragumatizumu hōgaku ni kansuru kenkyū nōto' ['Theory of ownership law' under U.S. law and surrogate mothers: research note concerning feminist law, critical ethnic studies, and pragmatist jurisprudence] in Yoshida, n 19 *supra*, 337 (first published in H. Eiichi and S. Koki Shukuga: *Nihon Minpōgaku No Keisei To Kadai (Ge)* [Celebration for the 70th birthday of Professor Eiichi Hoshino: Formation and challenges of the theory of civil law in Japan (vol. 2) (Tokyo 1996) and in *Yamahata Masao Sensei/ Igarashi Kiyoshi Sensei/Yabu Shigeo Sensei Koki Kinen: Minpōgaku To Hikakuhōgaku No Shosou I* [Celebration for the 70th birthday of Professor Masao Yamahata, Professor Kiyoshi Igarashi and Professor Shigeo Yabu: Aspects of civil law and comparative jurisprudence I] (Tokyo 1996).

rights and the environment is linked with theories of environmental law.[25] There are cases where a question relating to intellectual property law, such as the reason for the protection of intellectual property, is answered by property law theory.

c) Principle of equity

Equity or equity law is a source of law comparable to common law in Anglo-American law systems, but it is treated as a conceptual issue by Japanese civil law. Professor *Tomohei Taniguchi*, who was engaged in a myriad of activities, studied not only Anglo-American law, but also continental law and Soviet law, which were emerging at the time. When looking at his interpretation of civil law, interpretation based on the principle of equity, in other words, selecting the interpretation that seems to be the best rather than logically explaining an interpretation, is frequently observed.[26] This is probably because a very deep part of his conception of legal studies has been influenced by Anglo-American law.

d) Fiduciary

The idea of trust or fiduciary also has an influence on a variety of aspects. Although hesitant expressions such as 'a theory of trust-like transfers is prevalent in the theoretical structure of mortgage by

25 K. Yoshida, 'Kankyōken to shoyū riron no shintenkai: kankyōhōgaku no kiso riron josetu' [New developments in environment right and property theory: introduction to basic theory of environmental jurisprudence] in Yoshida, n 19 supra 422 (first published in Y. Takao & H. Daihyō, *Shin Gendai Songai Baishōhō Kōza (2): Kenri Shingai To Hi-Shingai Rieki* [New lecture on modern damage compensation law [2]: infringement of right and infringed interests] (Tokyo 1998)).

26 For example, T. Taniguchi, 'Bukken kōi no yūin/muin' [Presence/absence of a cause in transfer of real right], in T. Taniguchi & I. Kato (eds), *Minpō Enshū II* [Civil law seminar II] (Tokyo 1958) 332 presents a theory that refers to the principle of constructive trust with regard to legal acts and their voidance. In addition, T. Taniguchi, 'Senyū kaitei to sokuji shutoku' [Agreement on possession and immediate acquisition], in K. Yunoki, T. Taniguchi & I. Kato (eds), *Hanrei Enshū Bukkenhō* [Case exercise: real right] (Tokyo 1963) 98 propose an impartial theory that, when a double transfer is conducted through agreement on possession of personal property, the acquirer of the right should refund half of the value to the other party.

transfer' were used in the past due to the presence of the continental-law-based tradition, the term 'fiduciary' has come to be used not only in business law, but also in the world of civil law recently.[27] One of the reasons is the remarkable progress in the research of trust law as a by-product of legislation of the adult guardianship system.[28] In addition, work to discover trust (like) legal principles that are unevenly distributed in civil law has also been carried out.[29]

e) Relational theory

Since long ago, relational contracts or relational theory in contracts have also been pointed out as a contrast between the 'will theory under continental law' and the 'relational theory under Anglo-American law' by Professor *Tsuyoshi Kinoshita*, who specializes in Anglo-American law.[30] However, Professor *Takashi Uchida* proposed the 'relational contract theory' from a completely different perspective, reviving contract law from the death of classical contract law which provided a shock.[31] Professor *Uchida's* relational contract theory is originally based on the theory of Professor *Ian Macneil*, but instead of directly introducing Professor *Macneil's* theory, it articulates Professor *Uchida's* own theory by borrowing the term 'relational contract'. Professor *Uchida's* first book took up continuous contracts such as guarantees, subcontracts, and mandates as relational contracts,[32] but in the subsequent and unique development process of the relational contract theory in Japan, an attempt has been made to de-

27 N. Higuchi, *Fidyushar 'Shinnin' No Jidai* [Age of fiduciary 'trust'] (Tokyo 1999).

28 H. Dogauchi, *Shintaku Hōri To Shihō Taikei* [Trust law principles and structure of private law] (Tokyo 1996). At the same time, H. Dogauchi, A. Ohmura, M. Takizawa (ed), *Shintaku Torihiki To Minpō Hōri* [Law of trust transactions and civil law principles] (Tokyo 2003) sheds light on trust from the aspect of civil law principles.

29 M. Arai, *Kōrei Shakai To* Shintaku [Aging society and trust] (Tokyo 1995); M. Arai, *Seinen Kōkenhō To Shintakuhō* [Adult guardianship law and trust law] (Tokyo 2005).

30 T. Kinoshita, *Eibei Keiyakuhō No Riron (Dai 2 Han)* [Theory of Anglo-American contract law (2nd ed.)] (Tokyo 1985); T. Kinoshita, *Amerika Shihō* [U. S. private law] (Tokyo 1988).

31 Uchida, n 19 *supra*.

32 Uchida, n 19 *supra*, 129 et seq.

velop a general theory as a 'post-modern contract law' for all contracts.[33]

f) Civil issues developing into constitutional litigation

Professor *Norio Higuchi,* who is an expert on Anglo-American law, has pointed out that matters which are regarded as issues of civil law in Japan often develop into constitutional litigation in the United States.[34] One of the reasons is found in the system of U.S. legal proceedings which requires that, in order for a party to appeal to the U.S. Supreme Court, the case include a point at issue that is relevant to federal law. So a party will allege a violation of the U.S. Constitution in the petition for *certiorari* in order for the case to be reviewed by the U.S. Supreme Court (a similar situation is also found in Japan in varying degrees). Another reason is that the norms at the civil law level, such as the principle of the freedom of contract and the principle of negligence liability, are established as norms at the constitutional level, such as the Due Process Clause (the 14th Amendment of the U.S. Constitution) and Equal Protection Clause. He introduces a U.S. Supreme Court judgment from the New Deal period, which held a state law that limited labour hours was unconstitutional, and a state supreme court judgment, which ruled that a state law stipulating vicarious liability of parents for a tort conducted by their child was unconstitutional.[35] Civil cases more frequently develop into constitu-

33 T. Uchida, *Keiyaku No Jidai* [Age of contracts] (Tokyo 2000). In particular, Chapter 1 'Gendai nihon no keiyakuhō to ippan jōkō' [Contract law and general clauses of modern Japan] views the modern contract law as a coexistence of 'formalistic contract law' dominated by market logic and 'relational contract law' centred on the intrinsic norms of the life-world. The drawing out and 'convincing' of the intrinsic norms through the good faith principle are discussed as the interpretational constitution of the relational contract model. For the Uchida theory proposed in the paper that served as the source of Chapter 1, see T. Uchida, 'Gendai Keiyakuhō No Aratana Tenkai To Ippan Jōkō (1)–(5)' [New developments of modern contract law and general clauses (1)–(5)] *NBL* nos. 514–518 (1993), see T. Matsumoto, 'Shohyō' (Review) *Hōritsu Jihō* vol. 65 no. 11 (1993) 119.

34 N. Higuchi, 'Minpō to kenpō no kankei: Amerikahō no shiten' [Relationship between civil law and constitution: from the perspective of U.S. law] *Hōgaku Kyōshitsu* no. 171 (1994) 58.

35 While Professor *Higuchi* points out, 'the principles of case law, which constitutes the basic part of law (including what is referred to civil law in Japan),

tional litigation in the field of tort law, regarding issues such as defamation, privacy, and punitive damages[36] and in the field of family law.[37] Relevance to due process under the Constitution has also been pointed out in discussions on informed consent in medical care, which is a domain where tort law and family law overlap.[38]

In addition to such factors related to litigation techniques, the fact that the Constitution penetrates more deeply among people in the United States than in Japan is also accountable for the development of civil cases into constitutional litigation in the United States. In Japan, even in the field of family law, in which constitutional values are relatively easy to reflect, no court has yet held that distinguishing the legally secured positions between a legitimate child and an illegitimate child is unconstitutional.

3. Interpretation level

a) Tort law

The specific influences at the interpretation level could probably be best defined by the influences on tort law. The provisions of Japanese tort law have the nature of general provisions, as if the 709 articles

sometimes play the role of encouraging determination of constitutionality of other laws' (Higuchi, n 34 *supra*, 60), it is doubtful whether Japanese civil law has such strong vitality. Nevertheless, K. Yoshida, 'Kenpō to minpō: mondai no isō to kōzō' [Constitution and civil law: the phase and structure of the problem] *Hōritsu Jihō* vol. 76 no. 2 (2005) 53 suggests 'supplementing of the constitutional norms by civil law' by using the court judgment ruling on the unconstitutionality of the Forest Law (Supreme Court judgment on 2 April 1987, *Saikō Saibansho Minji Hanreishū* vol. 41 no. 3408) as a material.

36 T. Shibuya, 'Amerika Gasshūkoku ni okeru chōbatsuteki baishō ni kansuru saikin no dōkō (1) (2): renpō kenpō dyū purosesu jōyaku ni yoru chōbatsuteki baishōgaku no seigen wo chūshin ni' [Recent trend of punitive damages in the United States [1] [2]: centering on limitation to the amount of punitive damages based on the due process provisions of the U.S. Constitution] *NBL* no. 782 (2004) 23, no. 783 70, no. 784 49.

37 See K. Yonezawa, *Kodomo/Katei/Kenpō* [Children/family/constitution] (Tokyo 1992).

38 I. Niimi, 'Ishi to kanja no kankei (3): setumei to dōi no hōteki sokumen' [Relationship between doctors and patients (3): the legal aspect of informed consent] *Meidai Hōseironshū* no. 66 (1976) 153 et seq.

were a single article. Everything must be dealt with by these provisions. Conversely, there was room for influence, even that by U.S. law, in tort law. In particular, U.S. ideas have had a significant influence on interpretation theories for modern torts, such as pollution, traffic accidents, product liability, defamation,[39] medical malpractice, privacy, and sexual harassment.

However, such influence from U.S. law is restricted to the level of specific tort issues, and not much influence is observed at the level of general tort principles.[40] This is considered to be due to the idea of pragmatism and because there were no generalities regarding U.S. tort law in the first place.

b) Contract law

With regard to contract law, France has a unique contract law theory, and Germany also has an original contract law theory. As a matter of course, Anglo-American law also has its own contract law theory. It may not be too much to say that contract law theories express the characteristics of the legal systems of their respective countries. In that sense, Anglo-American-style contract law is not easily adopted in Japan, or to put it another way, it is difficult to import such law into Japan. It is notable that U.S. contract law, to a great extent, still retains the archaic concepts and terminology of U.K. contract law. In fact, U.K. contract law may now be more modern than U.S. contract law.

Because of such circumstances, Anglo-American contract law is hard to conciliate with Japanese law. Nonetheless, a considerable amount of research has been conducted on new types of contracts (particularly those related to finance) by referring to U.S. practices.

39 The series of Supreme Court judgments on the case of *Kazuyoshi Miura's* alleged murder of his wife in Los Angeles had an effect of considerably furthering Japan's legal principles on defamation. As the grounds for *Jokoku* appeal for one of these judgments, Supreme Court judgment on 9 September 1997, *Saikō Saibansho Minji Hanreishū* vol. 51 no. 8 3804, Mr. *Yoichi Kitamura*, attorney at law, set forth an argument by citing U.S. federal court judgments.

40 Although Japan adopts the statute law system, it is as if the case law system is adopted for torts. Therefore, an attempt has been made to restate the Japanese case law principles, following the Restatement in the United States. F. Kenkyū-kai, *Nihon Fuhōkōihō Risuteitomento* [Restatement of Japanese tort law] (Tokyo 1989) (first published in *Jurisuto* nos. 879–914 (1987–1988)).

c) Damages law

Although it is part of contract law, damages law has been considerably influenced by Anglo-American law. Professor *Yoshio Hirai's* proposal to dismantle the adequate causality theory[41] was developed by using the ideas of U.S. law as motifs. Since *Hirai's* theory seems to have taken root in the field of civil law in Japan, U.S. law is likely to have had a large influence on issues concerning compensation for damages.

Recently, the principle of 'mitigation of damages' has been drawing attention in Japanese academic circles.[42] In the framework of Japanese law, this issue is discussed as an issue of comparative negligence based on the negligence of the creditor. Professor *Takashi Uchida* has surmised that this concept has already been established in Japanese court judgments as a part of relational contract theory and developed a new interpretation from it, which is to calculate the amount of damages based on the time when fungible goods should have been dealt for the mitigation of damages if the fungible goods had a market, and when there were fungible goods that had a market, specific enforcement should only be allowed when mitigation by the dealing of the fungible goods cannot be expected.[43] It is interesting that Professor *Osamu Morita* criticized this view on the basis that it denies the right to performance without mediation of termination of the contract, from the viewpoint of the 'theory of transformation of obligations', which is the idea that the right to performance transforms itself to a right to claim damages under certain conditions.[44]

41 Hirai, n 2 *supra*.

42 In the initial phase, it was introduced in papers including T. Taniguchi, 'Songaibaishō santei ni oekru songai hiyoku gimu' [Mitigation of damages in calculating the amount of damages], in *Wagatsuma Sensei Kanreki Kinen: Songai Baishōhō No Kenkyū (Jō)* [Commemoration of the 60th birthday of Professor Wagatsuma: *Study on damage law (vol. 1)*] (Tokyo 1957) 235.

43 Uchida, n 33 *supra*, 'Dai 4 shō Keiyaku no kōsokuryoku: kyōseirikō to songai baishō' [Chapter 4 Binding force of contracts: performance by enforcement and compensation for damages] (first contained in *Hōsō Jihō* vol. 42, no. 10 (1990)).

44 O. Morita, 'Songai keigen gimu' ni tsuite: rikō seikyūken no igi ni kansuru oboegaki (sono 2)' ['Mitigation of damages: memorandum on the significance of the right to performance (part 2)] *Hōgaku Shirin* vol. 91 no. 1 (1990) 119. He supports the following view in this respect: A. Saito, 'Keiyaku furikō ni okeru

However, Professor *Uchida* counter-argued that although the theoretical framework for the transformation of obligations is applicable to legislation based on German law, 'a more flexible framework that can conduct relative comparison of the German law-based ideas would be more beneficial as a general analysis framework'.[45]

In an argument over whether or not to recognize the seller's obligation concerning rectification of defects with regard to warranty against defects, the concept of warranty under Anglo-American law has had an influence in Japan, either directly or through *Ernst Rabel's* study of comparative law. Apart from this, however, the idea of the seller's right of rectification of defects has emerged recently. This idea is considered to incorporate its conception under Anglo-American law, via the ideas incorporates into the United Nations Convention on Contracts for the International Sales of Goods.

d) Family law

Family law in Japan and that under Anglo-American law are considerably different. Nevertheless, Anglo-American law presumably has had an influence on particular concepts, such as the issues of child custody and visitation rights. More than twenty years ago, I attended a class on family law at a U.S. law school and was very surprised. The very first class was on child custody pertaining to divorce. A Japanese class would have started from the difference between family law and property law or what a family is, and though this is partly due to the order of provisions in the Civil Code, the class would have definitely held discussions on the establishment of marital status first. Starting with discussions on child custody appeared to me as being a very American approach.[46] The class was taught by a team of three: a

songai keigen gimu: songai baishōgaku santei no kijunji tono kanren ni oite' [Mitigation of damages in calculating the amount of damages: in relation with the base time for calculating the amount of damages], in *Ishida Kikuo/Nishihara Michio/Takagi Takio Sensei Kanreki Kinen [chūkan]: Songai Baishōhō No Kadai To Tenbō* [Commemoration of the 60th birthday of Professor Kikuo Ishida, Professor Michio Nishihara, and Professor Takio Takagi (vol. 2): Challenges and prospects of damage law] (Tokyo 1990) 51.

45 Postscript of Uchida, n 33 *supra*, 197.

46 A. Yonekura, *Amerika No Kazoku* [American families] (Tokyo 1982) conveys the situation of U.S. family law at the time.

family law professor, a judge, and a counselor. It was as if family law was practically viewed as a clinic.

4. Legislative level

U.S. law has not been adopted into Japanese civil law. However, it is now possible to include it in civil law, or to introduce it as a special civil law, to set aside the problem of whether consistency can be achieved with the existing civil law system. Indeed, many such proposals at the legislative level have materialized recently. In this respect, the influence of U.S. law on globalization seems to be extremely strong. The following influences can be characterized as follows: (a) to (d) are financial influences; (e) and (f) are IT influences; and (g) is influence on consumer affairs.

a) Corporations

A substantial influence from U.S. law can be observed regarding corporations. In the United States and/or the United Kingdom, various new corporate forms have been introduced, such as the limited partnership, the limited liability partnership (LLP), the limited liability limited partnership (LLLP), and the limited liability company (LLC), which are modified forms of partnerships, in order to avoid the unlimited liability of the members and corporate taxation. Also in Japan, partial legislation has been enacted such as an amendment of the law on the Limited Partnership Act for Investment. In the sweeping revision of company law, the minimum amount of capital required will be one yen, which means the capital maintenance principle will be completely abandoned. The corporation system has developed an aspect of being the ultimate in legal fiction theory by excessively taking on the nature of a tool (pipe), while on the other hand developing an aspect of real entity theory, which is to place emphasis on corporate social responsibility (CSR). Therefore, it is now time that the significance of the corporation system itself needs to be reviewed.

b) Trust

The trust business law, which is related to the corporation system in terms of the separation of non-exempt property, is currently moving towards amendment (enacted in an extraordinary session of the Diet in the autumn of 2004), and the Trust Law, which is the substantive law, is scheduled to be amended next. If the nature of the Trust Law as a dispositive law becomes stronger,[47] the law is expected to become more integrated with civil law.

c) Asset liquidation

Real estate law is not easily influenced by other countries' laws, because each country has a unique land system. However, there has been a considerable influence in Japan with respect to the legislative aspect through the modern phenomenon – securitization of real estate – such as introduction of the real-estate investment trust (Japanese REIT). Legislative arrangements for liquidating assets other than real estate are also under way.[48]

d) Personal property security/pledge of claim as security

Improvements in the law were made to relax the requirements for countering third parties for promoting liquidation of claims as part of an asset liquidation by the enactment of the Law on Regulation of Businesses Concerning Specific Claims (1992), which provides for specific claims, including lease payment claims, and the Law on Exceptions to the Civil Code Concerning Requirements for Countering Third Parties with Regard to Transfer of Claims (1998), which provides for claims transferred by corporations. At the same time, deliberations are also under way towards enabling a transferor of personal property to counter third parties by registration (amended as the Special Law on Transfer of Personal Property and Claims at an extraordinary session of the Diet in the autumn of 2004). Article 9 of the Uniform Commercial Code (UCC) of the United States was referenced to a considerable degree in the legislations of these law.[49]

47 See H. Kansaku, 'Shintakuhō to minpōhō no kōsaku; hōkoku II; soshiki' [Intertwining of trust law and civil law; report II; organization] *NBL* no. 791 (2004) 26.

48 My following paper, though quite dated, discusses this point: 'Fudōsan no shōkenka ni tsuite no minpōgaku karano kentō' [Study of real estate securitization from civil law perspective] *Shintakuhō Kenkyū* no. 15 (1991) 139.

49 K. Kado, 'Amerika Gasshūkoku ni okeru saiken jōto to taikō yōken: UCC fairu seido to honpō heno dōnyū kanōsei' [Transfer of claims and requirement

e) Electronic contracts

Electronic contracts first became the subject of active debate in the United States. The reafter, the Model Law on Electronic Commerce was adopted by the United Nations Commission on International Trade Law (UNCITRAL).[50] Within the United States, the Uniform Electronic Transaction Act (UETA) was adopted by the National Conference of Commissioners on Uniform State Laws (NCCUSL).[51] Furthermore, the Law concerning Electronic Signatures and Certification Services was enacted on one hand, and the Law Concerning Exceptions to the Civil Code Related to Electronic Consumer Contract and Electronic Notice of Acceptance was enacted in 2001 on the other. However, these laws only provide partial legislation concerning electronic contracts, specifically, by changing the time when a contract is deemed to have been established to the time when the notice on consent of the contract reached the other party, and extending stronger protections when there is a mistake in the electronic offer or acceptance.

f) Information license agreements

In the United States, the Uniform Computer Information Transactions Act (UCITA) has been adopted by NCCUSL, along with UETA. At the beginning, the provisions were supposed to be added to the UCC as Article 2B, but because they faced a lot of objections, they were compiled as an independent uniform state act, which does not require the support of the American Law Institute (ALI), as many of its mem-

for countering third parties in the United States: the UCC filing system and the possibility for its introduction in Japan] *Jurisuto* no. 1040 (1994) 31; K. Kado, 'Saiken ryūdōka to saiken jōto no taikō yōken (1)–(4): UCC tōroku seido wo sankō toshite' [Requirements for countering third parties with regard to liquidation of claims and transfer of claims (1)–(4): by referring to the UCC registration system] *NBL* no. 595 (1996) 6, no. 597 24, no. 598 53, no. 599 33; O. Morita, 'Amerikahō ni okeru dōsantanpoken no kōji to senyū (1)–(5): UCC fairingu no datsu shinwaka no tameni' [Publication and possession of security interest under U.S. law (1)–(5): to break away from the myth of the UCC filing] *NBL* no. 781 (2004) 6, no. 782 39, no. 783 56, no. 784 37, no. 785 29.

50 See T. Uchida, 'Denshi shōtorihiki to minpō' [Electronic commerce and civil law] *Bessatsu NBL* no. 51 (1998) 269.

51 With regard to the UETA, see H. Sono, 'Denshi torihiki no hōteki kiban seibi: Amerika ni okeru torikumi' [Development of legal infrastructure for electronic commerce: efforts made in the United States] *Jurisuto* no. 1183 (2000) 144.

bers were skeptical about the provisions.[52] The UCITA structures information transactions, which are not transactions of tangible goods, as one kind of license and provides default rules for them. Discussions were also held in Japan concerning the measures to be taken in response to such a trend, but legislation was not enacted in the end. Instead, the Ministry of Economy, Trade and Industry (METI) published guidelines for interpreting the current law called the 'Interpretative Guidelines on Electronic Commerce' by establishing a section called 'License Agreement' on information license transactions.[53]

g) Consumer contracts

The Consumer Contract Act, which was established in 2000, consists of three rules of substantive law: avoidance in the case of a mistake; avoidance in the case of being distressed; and nullification of unfair clauses. Among these, avoidance in the case of a mistake has the role of filling in the space between a fraud and a mistake, which had not been subject to protection in the past. The concept of misrepresentation under Anglo-American law had an influence in this respect, along with the easing of the requirements for establishment of fraud

52 With regard to the background history up to the adoption of the UCITA, see H. Sono, 'Jōhōtorihiki ni okeru keiyaku hōri no kakuritsu ni mukete (chūkan hōkoku): UCC dai 2B hen (raisensu) kisō sagyō no mezasumono (jō) (ge)' [Toward establishment of contract law principles for information transactions (interim report): what the drafting of UCC Article 2B (License) aims at (vol. 1) (vol. 2)] *NBL* no. 626 (1997) 24, no. 628 32; S. Nakashima, 'Shurinkurappu keiyaku no yūkōsei: uniform Commercial Code 2B dorafuto no tokuchō to sono igi (jō) (ge)' [Effectiveness of shrinkwrap licenses: characteristics and significance of the draft of Uniform Commercial Code 2B (vol. 1) (vol. 2)] *NBL* no. 634 (1998) 22, no. 637 53; H. Sono, 'Jōhō keiyaku ni okeru jiyū to kōjo' [Freedom and public order in information contracts] *Amerikahō* 1992 (2) 181; H. Sono, 'Jōhō keiyaku to chiteki zaisanken' [Information contracts and intellectual property rights] *Jurisuto* no. 1176 (2000) 88; H. Sono, 'Shiryō: NCCUSL nenji sōkai (2000) ni okeru UCC dai 2 hen to UCITA no shingi' [Material: discussions on UCC Article 2B and UCITA at the NCCUSL Annual Meeting (2000)] *Hōsei Kenkyū* vol. 67, no. 3 (2001) 922. With regard to the content of the UCITA, see K. Kokusho, *Beikoku No Denshi Jōhō Torhikihō* [Law on electronic information transactions in the United States] (Tokyo 2001).

53 For full text of the Interpretative Guidelines, see N. Nakayama, 'Kaitei: Denshi Shōtorihiki Ni Kansuru Junsoku to sono kaisetsu' [Revised: Interpretative Guidelines on Electronic Commerce and its commentary] *Bessatsu NBL* no. 93 (2004).

and mistake in France.[54] In fact, the first paper I wrote as a graduate student was on the subject of misrepresentation under Anglo-American law.[55] About 25 years later, a part of it has finally been realized in Japan in the form of the Consumer Contract Act.

III. Close Encounters with U.S. Law in Supporting the Development of Laws

1. Civil law systems

While the influence at the legislative level, discussed above at II. 4 of this report, has been conspicuous recently, the close encounters with U.S. law in supporting the development of laws in developing countries in Asia, discussed in this section, is a very interesting phenomenon currently in progress. The discussions in the previous sections were unilateral topics regarding the research and legislation conducted in Japan by referring to U.S. law and the influences U.S. law has had in Japan. However, this is a topic where Japanese and U.S. law mutually come in contact in a more realistic form.

For the past several years, I have been engaged in supporting the development of laws in developing countries in Asia through the Japan International Cooperation Agency (JICA) as part of ODA (Official Development Assistance). The specific operations were to support the amendment of the Civil Code in Vietnam and the enactment of the Civil Code in Cambodia.[56]

54 With regard to U.S. law, see H. Aizawa, 'Amerika keiyakuhō kara mita shōhisha keiyakuhō' [Consumer contract law from the perspective of U.S. contract law] *Jurisuto* no. 1200 (2000) 294. With regard to U.K. law, see E. Sudo, 'Shōhisha keiyakuhō no hikakuhōteki kenkyū: Igirisuhō no shiten kara (1)–(4)' [Comparative law study of consumer contract law: from a U.K. law perspective (1) – (4)] *Sōka Hōgaku* vol. 31, no. 1–2 (2001) 111, vol. 32, no. 1–2 (2002) 39, no. 3 (2003) 1, vol. 33, no. 1 (2003) 1. Also see the indication in Y. Shiomi, 'Hikakuhō no shiten kara mita 'shōhisha keiyakuhō' ['Consumer contract law' from the viewpoint of comparative law] *Minshōhō Zasshi* vol. 123 no. 1–2 (2001) 643.
55 T. Matsumoto, 'Eibeihō niokeru jōhō teikyōsha no sekinin (1) (2)' [The responsibilities of information providers under Anglo-American law (1) (2)] *Hōgaku Ronsō* vol. 100 no. 3 (1976) 35, vol. 101 (1977) 260.
56 With regard to the support in the civil law field in Cambodia and Vietnam, persons involved in the support activity have written the following: A. Mori-

In Vietnam, the Ministry of Justice is in charge of amending the current Civil Code that was enacted in 1995, but Japan has organized a joint study group with the Vietnamese government for the amendment work and provides advice. The advice mainly consists of providing comments on the current Civil Code in Vietnam and on the draft amendments prepared by the Vietnamese government.

In Cambodia, on the other hand, there is shortage of competent human resources as most of the intellectuals, including lawyers, were killed under the *Pol Pot* administration. Therefore, the Japanese contingent has taken the initiative by presenting draft provisions it has prepared by considering the situation and the needs of Cambodia, and hammering out the details through discussions with the Cambodian side. The first thing that the draft support team had to consider was an appropriate framework for the Civil Code. Although there is no Civil Code in Cambodia at present, in 1964, at the time of the *Sihanouk* administration, a Civil Code had been enacted by adding some original provisions of Cambodia to French Civil Code. Moreover, many of the current high-ranking officials of the Ministry of Justice had escaped to France during the *Pol Pot* administration. So in Cambodian society, including the judicial system, there are slight traces of French law concepts. In addition, the Land Law, which aims at restructuring the land ownership system – the top priority issue –, has already been enacted by incorporating a large portion of the old Civil Code. Therefore, the ideas of the French Civil Code were re-

shima, 'Betonamu ni okeru hō seibi to wagakuni hōritsuka no yakuwari' [Development of laws in Vietnam and the role of Japanese lawyers] *Jiyū To Seigi* vol. 47, no. 7 (1996) 14; A. Morishima, 'Hōseibi shien no rinen to sono kadai' [Philosophy and challenges of support for development of laws] *Hōritsu No Hiroba* vol. 54, no. 10 (2001) 12; I. Niimi, 'Hōseibi shien' ni okeru hōgainen: minpō wo chūshin to shite' [Legal concept in 'support for development of laws': centering on civil law] *Hikakuhō Kenkyū* no. 62 (2001) 88; S. Muto, *Betonamu Shihōshō Taizai Taikenki* [Report on a visit to the Ministry of Justice of Vietnam] (Tokyo 2002); T. Matsumoto, 'Indoshina shokoku ni okeru minpōten no seibi to kaihatsu: minjihō seibi shien heno sanka wo tsūjite kanjita koto' [Establishment and development of the Civil Code in Indochinese countries: impressions after participating in the support for development of the Civil Code] *Hitotsubashi Hōgaku* vol. 2 no. 1 (2002) 390; I. Niimi, 'ODA=Hōseibi shien no ippan (1) (2/mikan): Betonamu to Kanbojia deno keiken' [A part of the ODA support for development of laws (1) (2/incomplete): Experience in Vietnam and Cambodia] *Toki No Hōrei* no. 1729 (2005) 53, no. 1731 45.

spected to a great extent. The old Japanese Civil Code based on *Boissonade's* draft provided some significant hints. Nevertheless, unlike the French Civil Code, the draft Civil Code of Cambodia divides between real rights and obligations. Furthermore, with regard to contract law and sales law, the trend of the United Nations Convention on Contracts for the International Sales of Goods was taken into consideration; and while the structure of the sections did not take on the German Civil Code style (pandect system), it does include legal acts, general statements on contracts and general statements on claims together in the obligation section. The general provisions for the entire Civil Code are not like those of the Japanese Civil Code, but they declare some general principles as can be seen in the new Civil Code of the Netherlands.[57]

[57] The draft of the Civil Code of the Kingdom of Cambodia, which was submitted to the lawyers committee of the Council of Ministers in July 2003, was structured as follows.

Book 1: General Provisions

Book 2: Persons

Chapter 1: Natural Persons; Chapter 2: Juristic Persons

Book 3: Real Rights

Chapter 1: General Provisions; Chapter 2: Ownership; Chapter 3: Possessory Rights; Chapter 4: Emphyteusis; Chapter 5: Usufruct; Chapter 6: Right of Use and Right of Residence; Chapter 7: Servitude; Chapter 8: Ownership and Other Real Rights of the State, Buddhist Temples, Ethnic Minorities, and Other Communities; Chapter 9: Rights Established by Concession of Land

Book 4: Obligations

Chapter 1: General Provisions; Chapter 2: Declaration of Intention and Contract; Chapter 3: Performance of Contract; Chapter 4: Remedies for Breach of Contract; Chapter 5: Risk; Chapter 6: Effectiveness of Claim against Third Parties; Chapter 7: Expiration of Obligation; Chapter 8: Extinctive Prescription; Chapter 9: Transfer of Claim

Book 5: Contract, Unlawful Act, etc.

Chapter 1: Sale; Chapter 2: Exchange; Chapter 3: Gift; Chapter 4: Loan for Consumption; Chapter 5: Lease; Chapter 6: Loan for Use; Chapter 7: Mandate; Chapter 8: Contract for Work; Chapter 9: Service; Chapter 10: Bailment; Chapter 11: Partnership; Chapter 12: Life Annuity; Chapter 13: Compromise; Chapter 14: Management of Affairs Without Mandate; Chapter 15: Unjust Enrichment; Chapter 16: Unlawful Act

Book 6: Security

Chapter 1: General Provisions; Chapter 2: Lien; Chapter 3: Preferential Right; Chapter 4: Pledge; Chapter 5: Mortgage; Chapter 6: Mortgage by Transfer; Chapter 7: Surety; Chapter 8: Joint and Several Obligation

2. Problems of adjustment between multiple donors

One of the serious problems that arise in the process of supporting the development of laws is the adjustment between multiple donors. This problem does not occur when one organization belonging to a single country is supporting the development of laws of a single country. In reality, however, several organizations from multiple countries can be found engaged in the support activity. The partner organizationon on the side of the country receiving support varies. Japan always cooperates with the Ministry of Justice of the country receiving support as its main partner. In Cambodia, donors include not only Japan, but France, Sweden, Australia, the World Bank, and the Asian Development Bank. Each of these donors works with a specific ministry or agency of the Cambodian government as its partner. With regard to matters subject to civil law, the Ministry of Commerce is making an effort to legislate the matters on commerce, the Ministry of Land Management, Urban Planning & Construction is working on matters relating to land and housing issues, and the Ministry of the Interior is working family matter-related issues with the support of the respective donors.

For example, the Ministry of Commerce has the World Bank and the Asian Development Bank (ADB) as its partners. Since both organizations are under the strong influence of the United States, American attorneys are hired as expert consultants as a natural consequence. The Ministry of Commerce has entrusted these American attorneys to create drafts of commerce-related laws one after another. The Commercial Contract Law is one of them, but because it directly tries to introduce U.S. contract law, which is based on the consideration theory, it is incompatible with the basic principles of the contract

Book 7: Relatives
Chapter 1: General Provisions; Chapter 2: Engagement; Chapter 3: Marriage; Chapter 4: Parents and Children; Chapter 5: Parental Power; Chapter 6: Guardianship; Chapter 7: Curatorship; Chapter 8: Support
Book 8: Succession
Chapter 1: General Provisions; Chapter 2: Legal Succession; Chapter 3: Testamentary Succession; Chapter 4: Legally Secured Portions; Chapter 5: Acceptance and Renunciation of Succession; Chapter 6: Management and Division of Inherited Property; Chapter 7: Non-existence of Successors; Chapter 8: Request for Recovery of Succession.

law that is being drafted by the Japan team. This point has not been conciliated between the donors, but rather it is left to the deliberation of the Cambodian government or the parliament. In the worst-case scenario, both laws may pass parliament and enter into force.

The same applies to the Secured Transactions Law. American attorneys acting as consultants have drawn up a draft of the Secured Transactions Law, which seems to have been based on the Model Law on Secured Transactions[58] created by the European Bank for Reconstruction and Development (EBRD). This model law itself has been created based on Article 9 of the UCC of the United States, and it allows all present and future property to be used as security and premises the filing. While the Commercial Contract Law had the limitation of 'commerce', the Secured Transactions Law has no limitation in the scope of application, so the Civil Code provisions on pledge, mortgage by transfer, and transfer of claims may practically become eviscerated. The Japan team has proposed to limit the scope of the Secured Transactions Law to cases where the grantor of security is a trader, but the matter remains unsettled.

The Japan team is drafting rules of the Civil Code as a general private law system. In this process, the team also proposes provisions that are quite different from Japanese civil law by examining the development of civil law in various countries to date, instead of directly importing Japanese civil law. Nevertheless, the Commercial Contract Law and the Secured Transactions Law, which are incompatible with such Civil Caw as a general private law, have abruptly emerged from the Ministry of Commerce side.

3. Problems of adjustment concerning transfers of real rights

The largest legal problem in Cambodia at present is the dispute concerning the ownership of land and housing. Therefore, the Land Law

58 For the Model Law on Secured Transactions, see Y. Sato, T. Akahane & H. Dogauchi, 'Ōshū hukkō kaihatsu ginkō/mohan tanpohō no shōkai to kaisetsu (jō) (ge)' [Introduction of and commentary on the Model Law on Secured Transactions of the European Bank for Reconstruction and Development (vol. 1) (vol. 2)] *NBL* no. 695 (2000) 75, no. 696 79.

was enacted in 1992, far earlier than the Civil Code, and in 2001, the amended Land Law was enacted with the support of the Asian Development Bank. The Land Law is a comprehensive law including public law provisions, private law provisions, as well as criminal law provisions, regarding matters such as private property, public property, and communal property of land, recognition of the ownership during the transition period, concession, acquisition through transactions such as purchase, acquisition through heritage, rights and obligations of the owners, conformity, lease, usufructuary, rights to use and to stay, easement, co-ownership, mortgage, pledge, mortgage by transfer, cadastral register, and penalties for infringement of the ownership. It is obvious that a considerable part of it overlaps with the Civil Code. In drafting the real right section, therefore, the foregoing Land Law is respected, and the rules under the Land Law are incorporated to a large extent.

Nevertheless, with regard to the section concerning transfer of real rights, there is concern about whether transactions can be conducted properly under a system that requires registration for effectiveness of the transactions, in a country where real estate registration and the cadastral map based on which the registration is made are hardly developed.[59] At the same time, there is a view that common principles for the transfer of real rights for both personal property and real estate should be indicated in the Civil Code. Due to these reasons, the draft support team drafted the Civil Code by requiring registration for countering third parties, similar to Japanese law, based on the stance that it would be sufficient to promote registration by requiring registration for countering third parties. The Land Law includes both provisions that can be read as requiring registration for effectiveness of the transactions and those that can be read as requiring registration for countering third parties, so its adjustment with the Civil Code has presented a major problem. The Asian Development Bank side takes

59 Under the Land Law, if any person possesses unrecorded land that belongs to nobody peacefully, publicly, and with good faith for five years, he/she may receive a possession certificate upon application, and when he/she registers based on the certificate, his/her ownership will be recognized for the first time, and a land registration certificate will be issued. However, the land for which the cadastral map and the register have been created is still scarce.

an attitude that the Land Law is based on the Torrens system,[60] and requires registration for effectiveness of the transactions. Its aim seems to be to rapidly promote registration by requiring registration in order for transactions to be effective.[61]

In this manner, there is a sense that problems of adjustment are emerging beyond the mere level of influence or as subjects of debate.

IV. Closing Remarks

This report presented an overview of the influences of Anglo-American law, particularly U.S. law research, on the study of civil law in Japan. I intended to completely rewrite my previous paper, which was written 20 years ago, by reviewing the research results of various professors, but due to time constraints, I was only able to incorporate some papers that raise certain issues, which were published during the past 20 years and are likely to have a large impact.

The vastness of U.S. law both in quantity and quality is truly astonishing. In terms of quantitative vastness, the 50 states all constitute respective jurisdictions, and have their own case law and statute law, but there are also a large number of federal statutory laws, and many

60 The Torrens system is a land registration system that was first introduced in Australia and later introduced in the United Kingdom. Under this system, the government first determines, registers, and issues a certificate to the property owner with responsibility, and any later transfer of the right requires registration to be effective. The registration is given the public-reliance effect so that a person who conducts transaction by trusting the registration may acquire the land ownership.

61 In September 2004, a meeting for adjustment was held between the Japan team and the Asian Development Bank team in Washington. It was agreed that the draft Civil Code would be partially amended so that registration would be required for effectiveness of a transfer of the ownership in the case of registered land, and registration would be required for countering third parties for transactions of unregistered land, and that all private law provisions would be deleted from the Land Law. However, registration were to be required for countering third parties, as in the original draft, concerning transfer of real rights other than land ownership, such as establishment of mortgage, establishment of usufructuary right, and inheritance. It was also agreed that registration would be required for countering third parties with regard to transfer of real rights on personal property, but adjustment with the draft Secured Transactions Law still remains.

court judgments are rendered on a daily basis. Therefore, the first question would be, what should be regarded as U.S. law? In fact, however, there exists an ambiguous consensus on U.S. law.

In terms of qualitative vastness, substantial discussions based on diverse legal ideas are endlessly conducted at the methodological level and the conceptual level, which were referred to in II.1 and II.2 of this report. This is likely to be because U.S. society itself, which nurtures U.S. law, is established as a pluralistic society, rather than a monistic society. Professor *Takashi Uchida* expressed his thoughts on his experience of such a United States as follows:

> 'I stayed at Cornell University in the United States from 1983 to 1985, and during this stay, I was struck by the brisk situation of the study of law in the United States. In particular, I was envious of the spectacular debates on study of contract law. It was as if, a magnificent experiment was being conducted in which various concepts of contract law were boiled down as ideas detached from history or tradition, and were squarely debated.'[62]

In addition, Professor *Kunihiko Yoshida* commented as follows after reading a paper on default rules for contracts:

> 'I was intellectually stimulated by the innovative ideas that could not have been gained from the conventional discussions in Japan and the various views on German and France law studies referenced in those discussions.'[63]

I would like to conclude this report by pointing out that research of U.S. law is important, especially, for civil law scholars who have been mainly studying German law and French law in that it helps to develop a spirit to see things from a slightly different angle without being carried away by authority, and in that it teaches us the need for thinking from multiple viewpoints.

62 Uchida, n 31 *supra*, 2.

63 K. Yoshida, *Keiyaku no kaishaku/hojū to nin'i kitei no igi* [Interpretation/ complement of contracts and the significance of discretionary provisions] in K. Yoshida, *Keiyakuhō/Ijihō No Kankeiteki Tenkai* [Relational development of contract law and medical jurisprudence] (Tokyo 2003) 126 (first published in E. Hoshino & T. Hironaka (eds), *Minpōten No Hyakunen: Zenpanteki Kōsatsu* [100 years of the Civil Code: overall consideration] (Tokyo 1998)).

Part 2: The Identity of Japanese and German Civil Law

Chapter 6: Deutsches Bürgerliches Recht und Europäisches Zivilrecht in Gegenwart und Zukunft

Dieter Leipold

Übersicht

I. Vorbemerkung

Die ehrenvolle Einladung durch Herrn Prof. *Kitagawa*, an diesem Symposium teilzunehmen, habe ich mit großer Freude, aber auch mit einem gewissen Zögern angenommen. Mit Zögern deshalb, weil ich nicht sicher bin, ob ich überhaupt etwas Nützliches und Förderliches zum Thema des Symposiums beitragen kann. Die Zielsetzung meines Vortrags ist es in erster Linie, einen Blick auf den gegenwärtigen Zustand des Europäischen Zivilrechts zu werfen und die besondere Wirkungsweise dieser Rechtsmaterie zu erläutern. Die vielfältigen Bemühungen, über den heutigen Stand hinaus ein umfassendes Europäisches Vertragsrecht oder gar ein Europäisches Zivilgesetzbuch zu schaffen, wird dagegen Herr Kollege *Lorenz* im Einzelnen schildern. Ungeachtet dieser Aufgabenteilung will ich aber im zweiten Teil des Referats auch einige allgemeine Überlegungen zur künftigen Rolle des deutschen Zivilrechts im europäischen Kontext vortragen. Von meiner fachlichen Ausrichtung her bin ich nun freilich kein Vertreter der Rechtstheorie oder der juristischen Methodenlehre, sondern in erster Linie dem Umgang mit dem geltenden Zivilrecht und Zivilprozessrecht und der Lösung konkreter Rechtsfragen verpflichtet. Damit hängt es zusammen, wenn ich auch im Rahmen dieses Referats nicht darauf verzichten will, einige konkrete Problemfelder anzusprechen, um auf exemplarische Weise die Wechselwirkungen zwischen dem Europäischen und dem deutschen Zivilrecht darzustellen.

II. Der gegenwärtige Zustand

1. Einführung

a) Begriff des Europäischen Zivilrechts

Europäisches Zivilrecht ist ein ungenauer, schillernder Begriff, so dass vorweg zu erklären ist, wie der Begriff im Rahmen dieses Vortrags verstanden wird. Gemeint ist das von der Europäischen Gemeinschaft geschaffene Zivilrecht, also das Zivilrecht europäischen Ursprungs. Europa, das sind in diesem Zusammenhang die Mitgliedstaaten der Europäischen Union, mittlerweile 27 an der Zahl, also (noch) nicht das gesamte Europa im geographischen Sinn, aber ein Bereich, der sich von Großbritannien bis Griechenland, von Portugal bis Litauen erstreckt. Europäisches Zivilrecht in diesem Sinn bezeichnet also nicht etwa die Gesamtheit des in Europa geltenden Zivilrechts, was ja auf die Summe der nationalen und europäischen Gesetze sowie des hinzutretenden internationalen Einheitsrechts hinausliefe.

Der Begriff des Zivilrechts umfasst dabei den Kernbestand des Privatrechts, in Deutschland also die im BGB geregelten Materien. Der allgemeinere Begriff ist, jedenfalls bei exaktem Sprachgebrauch, derjenige des Privatrechts als Gegenbegriff zum Öffentlichen Recht. Mein Beitrag bezieht sich somit nicht auf das gesamte Europäische Privatrecht, nicht also auf die Europäischen Rechtsnormen auf dem Gebiet des Handelsrechts, des Gesellschaftsrechts, des Arbeitsrechts usw. Freilich liegt in der Abgrenzung – was gehört zum Zivilrecht als dem ‚für alle' geltenden Teil des Privatrechts, was kann oder soll auch in Zukunft dazu gehören und damit im BGB geregelt bleiben? – bereits ein Teil der Frage nach dem Sinn der zivilrechtlichen Kodifikation gerade im Europäischen Kontext.

b) Der punktuelle, unsystematische Charakter des heutigen Europäischen Zivilrechts

Von einer einheitlichen europäischen Kodifikation des Zivilrechts, auch nur von einem einheitlichen europäischen Vertragsrecht, sind wir derzeit noch meilenweit entfernt. Ganz im Gegenteil stellt sich das Europäische Zivilrecht als eine Anhäufung einzelner Rechtsakte[1] dar, die sich auf recht spezielle Fragen beziehen. So regelt die älteste der zivilrechtlichen Richtlinien auf dem Gebiet des Vertragsrechts, die Haustürgeschäfts-Richtlinie,[2] nichts anderes als das Widerrufsrecht des Verbrauchers bei Verträgen, die ein Verbraucher in seiner Wohnung, an seinem Arbeitsplatz oder bei einem vom Gewerbetreibenden organisierten Ausflug geschlossen hat. Selbst die Richtlinie zum Verbrauchsgüterkauf[3] enthält nicht etwa eine geschlossene

[1] S. die Zusammenstellung der hier in Betracht kommenden Richtlinien im Anhang.
[2] Anhang Nr. 2.
[3] Anhang Nr. 10.

Normierung für Kaufverträge zwischen Verbrauchern und Unternehmern über Verbrauchsgüter, sondern begnügt sich damit, wie es schon in der offiziellen Bezeichnung der Richtlinie heißt, ‚bestimmte Aspekte' des Verbrauchsgüterkaufs und der Garantien für Verbrauchsgüter zu regeln. So sind zwar die Anforderungen an die Vertragsmäßigkeit der gelieferten Güter und die Ansprüche auf Nachbesserung, Ersatzlieferung, Minderung des Kaufpreises oder Auflösung des Vertrages in dieser Richtlinie festgeschrieben, aber die Frage, ob dem Käufer auch Schadensersatzansprüche zustehen, bleibt ungeregelt.

Die einzelnen Richtlinien, die sich dem Europäischen Zivilrecht zurechnen lassen, stehen auch untereinander nicht in einem systematischen Zusammenhang. Sie sind nach und nach entstanden und nicht durch übergreifende, dann etwa für alle oder doch mehrere der Richtlinien geltende Begriffe mit einander verknüpft. Jedenfalls ergibt sich eine solche systematische Verbindung nicht aus dem Inhalt der Richtlinien – ob und in welchem Umfang es möglich ist, durch rechtswissenschaftliche Analyse gleichwohl eine Art von System zu entwickeln, ist eine andere Frage.

Auch die einzelnen Themen, mit denen sich das gegenwärtige Europäische Zivilrecht befasst, wirken sehr disparat. Immerhin lässt sich aber der größere Teil dieser Richtlinien dem Bereich des Verbraucherschutzes zuordnen. Dies ergibt sich bei fünf Richtlinien[4] explizit daraus, dass sie auf Rechtsbeziehungen zwischen Unternehmen und Verbrauchern begrenzt sind, bei zwei weiteren Richtlinien daraus, dass sie Vertragsinhalte betreffen, die typischer Weise in Verträgen mit Verbrauchern vorkommen. Gemeint sind die Richtlinien über Pauschalreisen[5] und über Teilnutzungsrechte an Immobilien.[6] Auch die Produkthaftungsrichtlinie[7] ist in ihrem Inhalt in erster Linie auf den Schutz des Verbrauchers ausgerichtet. Man kann also in einem ersten groben Schritt der Systembildung von einem Europäischen

4 Es geht um die Haustürgeschäfts-Richtlinie (Anhang Nr. 2), die Verbraucherkredit-Richtlinie (Anhang Nr. 3), die Klausel-Richtlinie (Anhang Nr. 5), die Fernabsatz-Richtlinie (Anhang Nr. 8) und die Verbrauchsgüterkauf-Richtlinie (Anhang Nr. 10).

5 Anhang Nr. 4.

6 Anhang Nr. 6.

7 Anhang Nr. 1.

Verbraucherschutzrecht sprechen. Einen eigenen Bereich bilden diejenigen Richtlinien, die einen Schutz gegen Benachteiligungen aus Gründen des Geschlechts, der Rasse usw. gewährleisten sollen.[8] Sie beziehen sich teils auf das Arbeitsrecht (das an sich außerhalb des Vortragsthemas liegt), aber teils auch auf das allgemeine Zivilrecht. Ich komme später auf diese Anti-Diskriminierungs-Richtlinien und ihre Umsetzung in das nationale Recht zurück.

Zweifellos liegt in der Herausbildung des Verbraucherschutzrechts die wichtigste Entwicklung des Privatrechts in den letzen drei Jahrzehnten. Um Missverständnisse zu vermeiden, sei darauf hingewiesen, dass der Verbraucherschutz als zentrale Aufgabe des Zivilrechts zunächst innerhalb der nationalen Rechtsordnungen entwickelt wurde, und gerade das deutsche Recht nahm hierbei, vor allem mit dem Gesetz über Allgemeine Geschäftsbedingungen aus dem Jahre 1974, eine wichtige Schlüsselposition ein (Dieses Gesetz stieß sowohl mit seinen materiell-rechtlichen wie mit seinen prozessrechtlichen Regelungen – Stichwort Verbandsklage – auch in Japan auf großes Interesse; ich erinnere mich gerne daran, dass ich schon bei meinem ersten Besuch in Japan im Jahre 1976 gebeten wurde, über dieses Gesetz zu referieren!). Später wurde der Verbraucherschutz von der Europäischen Gemeinschaft als wichtiges Tätigkeitsgebiet gleichsam ‚entdeckt'. Während die erwähnte Haustürgeschäfts-Richtlinie des Jahres 1985 in etwa parallel zum deutschen Haustürgeschäftewiderrufsgesetz (HtWG) entwickelt wurde, übernahm später mehr und mehr die Europäische Gemeinschaft das Kommando, und die Tätigkeit des nationalen Gesetzgebers setzte erst bei der Umsetzung der Europäischen Richtlinien in das nationale Recht ein.

Nur eine Richtlinie, diejenige über den Zahlungsverzug,[9] bezieht sich gerade umgekehrt allein auf Geschäfte zwischen Unternehmen. Die Richtlinie über grenzüberschreitende Überweisungen[10] hat einen allgemeinen, d.h. Rechtsbeziehungen mit oder ohne Beteiligung von Verbrauchern umfassenden Geltungsbereich. Dasselbe lässt sich über die E-Commerce-Richtlinie[11] sagen, soweit darin überhaupt zivil-

8 Anhang Nr. 13, 14, 16 , 17.
9 Anhang Nr. 12.
10 Anhang Nr. 7.
11 Anhang Nr. 11.

rechtliche Fragen geregelt sind. Dies ist der Fall für den Abschluss von Verträgen auf elektronischem Weg.

c) Der Richtliniencharakter und die Kompetenzgrundlagen

(1) Verordnungen und Richtlinien als Formen des sekundären Europäischen Rechts

Dass das Europäische Zivilrecht sich als bloßes Konglomerat von Einzelakten darstellt, die sich auf recht enge Sachbereiche beziehen und selbst diese nicht umfassend regeln, hängt in einem gewissen Umfang mit dem Charakter der Europäischen Richtlinien und den dafür bestehenden Kompetenzgrundlagen zusammen. Beides ist daher kurz zu erläutern.

Die Rechtsquellen des Europäischen Rechts weisen, verglichen mit dem herkömmlichen nationalen Recht, aber auch mit dem Völkerrecht, große Besonderheiten auf. Als primäres Europäisches Recht pflegt man die Gründungsverträge (also vor allem den Vertrag über die Europäische Union und den Vertrag über die Europäische Gemeinschaft) zu bezeichnen – diese sollen bekanntlich durch eine Europäische Verfassung ersetzt werden, ein Plan, der freilich durch die ablehnenden Volksabstimmungen in Frankreich und den Niederlanden einen schweren Rückschlag erlitten hat. Das im gegebenen Zusammenhang interessierende sog. sekundäre Europäische Recht präsentiert sich vor allem in Gestalt von Verordnungen und Richtlinien. Verordnungen enthalten gemäß Art. 249 Satz 2 EG unmittelbar geltendes Recht, d.h. die in einer Europäischen Verordnung gesetzten Normen sind vom Inkrafttreten der Verordnung an in allen Mitgliedstaaten anzuwenden, ohne dass es irgendwelcher Akte des einzelnen Mitgliedstaates bedarf. Ihrer Wirkung nach könnte man diese Rechtsakte als Europäische Gesetze bezeichnen. Der Ausdruck Verordnung ist jedenfalls innerhalb der deutschen Rechtsterminologie verwirrend, da im innerdeutschen Recht Verordnungen nur Rechtsnormen mit Rang unter den Gesetzen sind. Auf europäischer Ebene wurde der Ausdruck Gesetz wohl deshalb nicht gewählt, weil sie nicht in erster Linie auf Akte eines Parlaments als Gesetzgeber zurückgehen, mag auch im Zuge der Entwicklung die Rolle des Europäischen Parlaments bei der Schaffung sekundären europäischen Rechts deutlich gestärkt worden sein.

Während Verordnungen allgemeine und unmittelbare Geltung in allen Mitgliedstaaten besitzen, wenden sich Richtlinien an den Mitgliedstaat, nicht an die Unionsbürger. Nach Art. 249 Abs. 3 EG ist eine Richtlinie für jeden Mitgliedstaat, an den sie gerichtet ist, hinsichtlich des zu erreichenden Zieles verbindlich, während die Wahl der Form und der Mittel den innerstaatlichen Stellen überlassen bleibt. Eine Richtlinie bedarf daher der Umsetzung durch den nationalen Gesetzgeber, und wenn diese, beispielsweise durch ein in der Bundesrepublik Deutschland erlassenes Gesetz, erfolgt ist, erlangen die darin enthaltenen Normen unmittelbare Geltung zwischen den Normadressaten, insbesondere zwischen den Bürgern. Berücksichtigt man die Formulierung in Art. 249 Abs. 3 EG, so sollte man meinen, dass eine Richtlinie sich auf allgemeine Vorgaben beschränkt und alle Einzelheiten dem nationalen Gesetzgeber überlassen bleiben. Die Wirklichkeit sieht jedoch anders aus. Die zivilrechtlichen Richtlinien enthalten zu einem guten Teil sehr detaillierte Vorschriften, die im Grunde unverändert in das nationale Recht übernommen werden müssen. Man fragt sich dann natürlich, warum vom Instrument der Richtlinie Gebrauch gemacht wird und nicht gleich Verordnungen erlassen werden. Zum Teil hängt dies mit den Kompetenzgrundlagen zusammen, die kurz zu betrachten sind.

(2) Die Kompetenzgrundlagen für das Europäische Zivilrecht

Die Zuständigkeiten der Europäischen Gemeinschaft (ursprünglich hieß sie bekanntlich Europäische Wirtschaftsgemeinschaft – EWG) auf dem hier interessierenden Gebiet wurden im Laufe der Entwicklung sehr stark erweitert. Art. 94 EG sieht nur den Erlass von Richtlinien, nicht von Verordnungen, vor, um eine Angleichung derjenigen Vorschriften der Mitgliedstaaten zu erreichen, die sich unmittelbar auf die Errichtung oder das Funktionieren des Gemeinsamen Marktes auswirken. Richtlinien auf der Grundlage dieser Vorschrift können nur durch einen einstimmigen Beschluss des Rates (d.h. mit Zustimmung aller Mitgliedstaaten) zustande kommen. Diese Bestimmung wurde in der Frühzeit des Europäischen Zivilrechts als Rechtsgrundlage verwendet, so etwa für Haustürgeschäfts-Richtlinie, die Produkthaftungs-Richtlinie und die Verbraucherkredit-Richtlinie. Später trat Art. 95 EG (ursprünglich Art. 100a EGV) hinzu, der ‚Maßnahmen', d.h. sowohl Richtlinien als auch Verordnungen, erlaubt, um eine Angleichung der Vorschriften der Mitgliedstaaten zu erreichen, welche die Errichtung und das Funktionieren des Binnenmarktes zum Gegenstand haben. Dabei darf man den ‚Binnenmarkt' als einen besonders verdichteten Teilbereich des ‚Gemeinsamen Marktes' verstehen. Dass eine exakte Unterscheidung beider Begriffe auf Schwierigkeiten stößt, mag hier auf sich beruhen. Für den Erlass der Maßnahmen gilt das Verfahren nach Art. 251 EG, innerhalb dessen auch eine (freilich qualifizierte) Mehrheitsentscheidung des Rates genügt. Obgleich Art. 95 EG auch den Erlass von Verordnungen erlaubt, wurde auch bei den jüngeren zivilrechtlichen Rechtsakten, die auf diese Rechtsgrundlage gestützt wurden, die Form der Richtlinie gewählt. Dies dürfte damit zusammenhängen, dass sich die Mitgliedstaaten in einem Protokoll über die Anwendung der Grundsätze der Subsidiarität und der Verhältnismäßigkeit darauf einigten, im Regelfall verdiene das Instrument der Richtlinie den Vorrang.[12] Dadurch sollte wohl zu weit reichenden Eingriffen in die Rechte des nationalen Gesetzgebers vorgebeugt werden. Jedenfalls sind, beginnend mit der Pauschalreisen-Richtlinie des Jahres 1993, nahezu alle weiteren zivilrechtlichen Richtlinien auf Art. 95 EG gestützt worden.

Fragt man, ob die begrenzte Reichweite des bisherigen Europäischen Zivilrechts auf die Eigenheiten der Kompetenzgrundlagen zurückzuführen ist, so ist dies zweifellos insofern zu bejahen, als sowohl der ältere Art. 94 als auch der neuere Art. 95 EG nur eine Rechtsangleichung mit Bezug zum Markt gestatten. Macht man sich klar, dass der ‚Markt' den entgeltlichen Umsatz von Gütern und Dienstleistungen zum Gegenstand hat, so wird rasch deutlich, dass die Europäische Gemeinschaft nicht etwa zum Erlass eines vollständigen Europäischen Zivilgesetzbuchs ermächtigt ist; denn den Regeln des Familienrechts und des Erbrechts fehlt in aller Regel ein hinreichender Marktbezug. Auf dem Gebiet des Schuldrechts und zumindest teilweise auch des Sachenrechts wird dagegen der punktuelle Charakter des Europäischen Rechts nicht durch die Kompetenzgrundlagen erzwungen. Dabei ist auch zu beachten, dass Art. 95 Abs. 3 EG die Be-

12 Näher s. S. Leible, in R. Streinz (Hrsg.), *EUV/EGV – Vertrag über die Europäische Union und Vertrag zur Gründung der Europäischen Gemeinschaft* (München 2003) Art. 95 EGV Rn. 33; J. Basedow, ‚Das BGB im künftigen europäischen Privatrecht – der hybride Kodex' *AcP* 200 (2000), 445–492, 479.

reiche Gesundheit, Sicherheit, Umweltschutz und Verbraucherschutz ausdrücklich anspricht und von den Vorschlägen der Kommission erwartet, ein hohes Schutzniveau auf diesen Gebieten anzustreben. Man muss also die bisherige Beschränkung des Europäischen Zivilrechts auf enge Teilbereiche als Ausfluss politischer Entscheidungen verstehen, wonach eben bisher kein hinreichendes Bedürfnis zu einer darüber hinausreichenden Rechtsangleichung artikuliert wurde. Erst recht sind die Kompetenzgrundlagen nicht dafür verantwortlich zu machen, dass es auch dort, wo eine Zusammenfassung und Systematisierung möglich erscheint – vor allem auf dem Gebiet des zivilrechtlichen Verbraucherschutzes – bei dem zersplitterten Rechtszustand verblieben ist. Über die in neuerer Zeit erfreulicher Weise unternommenen Anläufe, diesen misslichen Zustand zu überwinden – das Stichwort lautet: Streben nach einem ‚Gemeinsamen Referenzrahmen' – wird Herr Kollege *Lorenz* ausführlich berichten.

d) Die Systemfeindlichkeit des Europäischen Zivilrechts

Das gegenwärtige Europäische Zivilrecht stellt sich nicht nur als unsystematisch, sondern nach meiner Einschätzung darüber hinaus geradezu als systemfeindlich dar. Es verzichtet selbst auf eine Systembildung. Selbst wenn Begriffe wie die des Verbrauchers und des Unternehmers in einer Reihe von Richtlinien zentrale Bedeutung haben, werden sie nicht in einer allgemeinen Weise definiert, sondern in jeder Richtlinie gesondert, günstigstenfalls inhaltlich übereinstimmend umschrieben, aber auch dies ist nicht ausnahmslos gelungen. Die Systematisierung in Form einer Eingliederung in eine systematisch durchgebildete Rechtsordnung müsste derzeit im Rahmen der Rechtsordnungen der Mitgliedstaaten erfolgen. Hier wirkt sich aber störend aus, dass die Richtlinien vielfach sehr konkrete Bestimmungen enthalten, die für eine Einpassung in den nationalen Kontext keinen genügenden Spielraum belassen. Es kommt hinzu, dass auch bei der Durchsetzung der Geltung des Europäischen Rechts auf systematische oder dogmatische Gesichtspunkte wenig oder keine Rücksicht genommen wird. Das nationale Recht hat sich, so kann man schlagwortartig sagen, dem Europäischen Recht anzupassen, nicht umgekehrt das Europäische Recht dem nationalen. Dieser Zusammenhang schlägt sich vor allem im Grundsatz der richtlinienkonformen Auslegung des nationalen Rechts nieder. Welche Probleme bei der Anwendung des Europäischen Zivilrechts entstehen können und welche Rolle bei ihrer Lösung die nationalen Gerichte und der Europäische Gerichtshof spielen, möchte ich – sozusagen im ‚Besonderen Teil' dieses Vortrags – am Beispiel des Widerrufsrechts bei Immobiliarkrediten veranschaulichen. Anschließend soll betrachtet werden, welche Erfolge der deutsche Gesetzgeber bei seinen Bemühungen erzielt hat, das Europäische Zivilrecht in das BGB zu integrieren. Zuletzt möchte ich auf die Grundlagendiskussion eingehen, die im Zusammenhang mit der Umsetzung der verschiedenen Antidiskriminierungsrichtlinien in Deutschland entfacht wurde, sehen doch viele gerade hier eine fundamentale Gefährdung der zivilrechtlichen Dogmatik.

2. Europäisches und deutsches Zivilrecht in konkreten Zusammenhängen

a) Das Widerrufsrecht bei Immobiliendarlehen – die (fast) unendliche Geschichte von den ‚Schrottimmobilien' als Beispiel für die Rolle der Rechtsprechung

Der Ausdruck ‚Schrottimmobilien' hat in der gegenwärtigen Diskussion unter deutschen Juristen eine ganz spezifische Bedeutung. Es geht um den Erwerb von Eigentumswohnungen oder von Bürogebäuden, der von Privatleuten in der Erwartung vorgenommen wurde, durch steuerliche Vorteile und durch Mieteinnahmen erhebliche Erträge zu erzielen. Vielfach wurde der Erwerb solcher Immobilien weitestgehend kreditfinanziert, also unter gleichzeitiger Aufnahme eines Immobiliarkredits. Die kreditgebenden Banken und die Verkäufer der Immobilien wirkten dem Käufer gegenüber oft zusammen und verstanden es, die zu erwartenden Gewinne höchst attraktiv erscheinen zu lassen. Die Wirklichkeit verlief dann oft ganz anders – viele dieser Immobilien konnten nur zu einem niedrigen Mietpreis oder überhaupt nicht vermietet werden; gleichwohl waren die Erwerber mit hohen Kreditverpflichtungen belastet. So nimmt es nicht wunder, dass von den Käufern und ihren juristischen Beratern in vielen Fällen nach Wegen gesucht wurde, den Kauf und die Darlehensaufnahme rückgängig zu machen. Das ist freilich nicht ganz einfach, denn auch in solchen Fällen gilt der alte Satz *pacta sunt servanda* und eine wirtschaftliche Fehleinschätzung allein erlaubt im allgemeinen keine Durchbrechung der Bindung an einmal geschlossene Verträge. Mag auch die Anpreisung solcher Geschäfte nicht selten unseriös gewesen sein, geradezu eine arglistige Täuschung nachzuweisen, die eine Vertragsanfechtung nach dem BGB erlauben würde, gelingt im Allgemeinen nicht. Die ‚klassische', sogleich mit dem Vertragsschluss einsetzende Bindung wird aber durch das moderne Verbraucherschutzrecht erheblich modifiziert, das unter bestimmten Voraussetzungen dem Verbraucher gestattet, sich durch Widerruf wieder von dem Vertrag zu lösen. Aber geht das auch noch viele Jahre nach Vertragsschluss? Im berühmt gewordenen Fall *Heininger* hatten die später als Kläger auftretenden Eheleute im Jahre 1993 eine Eigentumswohnung erworben und zur Finanzierung ein Bankdarlehen aufgenommen, das durch ein Grundpfandrecht abgesichert wurde. Im Jahre 1997 – bis dahin waren Zins- und Tilgungsleistungen ordnungsgemäß gezahlt worden – kamen die Kläger, besser ihre findigen juristischen Berater, auf die Idee, den Darlehensvertrag nach dem Haustürwiderrufsgesetz zu widerrufen. Zwar war das Widerrufsrecht nach damaliger Rechtslage auf eine Woche befristet, aber das Gesetz sagte auch, dass diese Frist erst mit ordnungsmäßiger Belehrung über das Bestehen eines Widerrufsrechts beginne. Die Kläger beriefen sich darauf, sie seien durch einen Immobilienmakler in ihrer Wohnung aufgesucht und sowohl zum Kauf der Immobilie als auch zur Aufnahme des Darlehens überredet worden; eine Belehrung über ein Widerrufsrecht sei ihnen dabei nicht erteilt worden. Als zweifelhaft erwies sich, ob hier die Regeln des Haustürwiderrufsgesetzs überhaupt anwendbar waren. Denn zugleich handelte es sich um ein Verbraucherkreditgeschäft, und das Verbraucherkreditgesetz enthielt ebenfalls Bestimmungen über das Widerrufsrecht des Verbrauchers. Dem Verhältnis beider Regelungen war eine Bestimmung des Haustürwiderrufsgesetzes gewidmet, wonach dieses Gesetz auf solche Geschäfte keine Anwendung findet, die zugleich die Voraussetzungen des Verbraucherkreditgesetzes erfüllten. Einen Realkreditvertrag, wie er hier vorlag, nahm das Verbraucherkreditgesetz ausdrücklich von seinen Bestimmungen über das Widerrufsrecht aus. Im übrigen sah das Verbrauchskreditgesetz vor, dass das Widerrufsrecht spätestens ein Jahr nach Abschluss des Kreditvertrags entfällt. Das Widerrufsrecht nach dem Haustürgeschäftewiderrufsgesetz sah dagegen für den Fall der fehlenden Belehrung keine Befristung des Widerrufsrechts vor. Den deutschen Gerichten der unteren Instanzen erschien die Sachlage klar: Aufgrund des gesetzlich angeordneten Vorrangs kamen nur die Regeln des Verbraucherkreditgesetzes über das Widerrufsrecht zur Anwendung. Danach bestand aber kein Widerrufsrecht, da es sich um einen Realkreditvertrag handelte. Der BGH[13] bejahte ebenfalls den Vorrang des Verbraucherkreditgesetzes vor dem Haustürgeschäftewiderrufsgesetz, wobei er die Regelung des positiven Rechts mit Hinweisen auf die teleologischen Erwägungen des deutschen Gesetzgebers untermauerte. Dieser hatte den Ausschluss des Widerrufsrechts bei Realkreditverträgen damit begründet, dass durch ein Widerrufsrecht die taggenaue Refinanzierung und damit die günstige Verzinsung von Realkrediten gefährdet werde und außerdem durch die grundpfandrechtliche Absicherung (die auch den Gang zum Notar unumgänglich macht) auch eine hinreichende Warnung vor übereiltem Abschluss gesichert sei. Das gilt nach Ansicht des BGH auch beim Abschluss eines Realkreditvertrages in einer Haustürsituation.

Obgleich also der BGH der Beurteilung durch die Vorinstanzen zustimmte, hinderte ihn der europäische Hintergrund der erwähnten deutschen Gesetze daran, die Sache sogleich selbst zu entscheiden. Es geht um die Haustürgeschäfts-Richtlinie und um die Verbraucherkreditrichtlinie. Die Verbraucherkredit-Richtlinie sieht kein Widerrufsrecht des Verbrauchers vor. Der BGH interpretierte das Verhältnis beider Richtlinien unter Rückgriff auf die Entstehungsgeschichte so, dass die Verbraucherkredit-Richtlinie eine eigenständige Regelung der Verbraucherkreditgeschäfte enthalte, die der Haustürgeschäfts-Richtlinie vorgehe. Danach war der nationale Gesetzgeber berechtigt, für Realkreditverträge auch dann kein Widerrufsrecht vorzusehen, wenn der Vertrag in einer Haustürsituation zustande gekommen war. Da für den BGH die Entscheidung davon abhing, wie das Verhältnis der beiden europäischen Richtlinien zueinander zu verstehen sei, sah er sich genötigt, die entsprechende Frage dem Europäischen Gerichtshof in Luxemburg vorzulegen. Der EuGH hat nach Art. 234 EG im Wege der Vorabentscheidung über die Auslegung des EG-Vertrages, aber auch über die Gültigkeit und die Auslegung der Handlungen der Organe der EG zu befinden. Es ist daher auch Aufgabe des EuGH, über die Auslegung von Europäischen Verordnungen und

13 BGH, *NJW* 2000, 521.

Richtlinien zu entscheiden. Nationale Gerichte der letzten Instanz sind verpflichtet, den EuGH anzurufen, wenn sich in einem vor ihnen schwebenden Verfahren eine solche Auslegungsfrage stellt. Nun könnte man meinen, im Fall der Richtlinien habe das nationale Gericht, hier der BGH, nicht die Richtlinie, sondern das nationale Gesetz anzuwenden und auszulegen; dies aber sei nicht die Aufgabe des EuGH. Mittelbar hängt aber die Auslegung des nationalen Rechts, insbesondere des zur Umsetzung einer Richtlinie ergangenen Gesetzes, oft ihrerseits von der Auslegung der Richtlinie ab. Dies kommt in dem allgemein anerkannten Grundsatz der richtlinienkonformen Auslegung zum Ausdruck. Diese Doktrin geht davon aus, dass der nationale Gesetzgeber bestrebt sein müsse, die Richtlinien korrekt und vollständig umzusetzen. Das nationale Recht sei also im Zweifel so auszulegen, dass es mit den Europäischen Richtlinien übereinstimme. Um dies beantworten zu können, muss man aber wissen, wie die Richtlinie zu verstehen ist – und dies in zweifelhaften Fällen zu klären, ist Aufgabe des EuGH im Rahmen des Vorabentscheidungsverfahrens.

Der BGH legte dem EuGH nicht nur die Frage vor, ob die Haustürgeschäfts-Richtlinie auch bei Realkreditverträgen anzuwenden sei und hinsichtlich des Widerrufsrechts den Vorrang vor der Verbraucherkredit-Richtlinie habe, sondern fragte weiter, ob, falls die Haustürgeschäfts-Richtlinie anwendbar sei, der nationale Gesetzgeber befugt sei, das Widerrufsrecht bei einem Realkreditvertrag auf ein Jahr nach Abgabe der vertraglichen Willenserklärung des Verbrauchers zu begrenzen.

Der EuGH[14] sah die Dinge völlig anders als die deutschen Gerichte. Er bejahte die uneingeschränkte Geltung der Haustürgeschäfte-Richtlinie und verneinte darüberhinaus jegliche Befugnis des nationalen Gesetzgebers, das Widerrufsrecht bei nicht erteilter Belehrung zu befristen. Bemerkenswert ist aber nicht nur das vom EuGH gefundene Ergebnis, über das man geteilter Meinung sein kann, sondern vor allem die Begründung und die darin erkennbare Methode der Rechtsanwendung. Der Stil der Entscheidungen des EuGH ist durchweg und auch in diesem Fall knapp und lapidar – es wird eher dekretiert

[14] Rs. C-481/99 *Georg und Helga Heininger* v. *Bayerische Hypo- und Vereinsbank AG* [2001], Slg. I-9945 = *NJW* 2002, 281 (EuGH).

als diskutiert. Der EuGH prüft, ob die Haustürgeschäfte-Richtlinie eine Ausnahme für Realkreditverträge enthält und verneint dies. Die in der Richtlinie enthaltene Ausnahme für Verträge über den Bau oder den Verkauf einer Immobilie oder über andere Rechte an einer Immobilie greife trotz der Absicherung des Darlehens durch ein Grundpfandrecht für den hier vorliegenden Kreditvertrag nicht ein. Dabei bekräftigt der EuGH seine schon früher formulierte These, Ausnahmen von den Verbraucherschutzvorschriften seien eng auszulegen. Einen Vorrang der Verbraucherkredit-Richtlinie lehnt der EuGH ab, weil sich weder in der Präambel noch im normativen Teil dieser Richtlinie Anhaltspunkte dafür fänden, dass der Gesetzgeber den Anwendungsbereich der Haustürgeschäfte-Richtlinie habe einschränken wollen. Auch die zweite Frage, ob der nationale Gesetzgeber das Widerrufsrecht bei nicht erfolgter Belehrung befristen könne, verneint der EuGH. Dies ist vor allem deswegen bemerkenswert, weil in der Haustürgeschäfte-Richtlinie zwar die Belehrung vorgeschrieben ist, dann aber hinzugefügt wird, es sei Sache der Mitgliedstaaten, dafür zu sorgen, dass ihre innerstaatlichen Vorschriften geeignete Maßnahmen zum Schutz des Verbrauchers vorsehen, wenn die Belehrung nicht erfolgt. Der EuGH verweist darauf, die Richtlinie sehe nur den Wegfall des Widerrufsrechts durch Ablauf einer Mindestfrist von sieben Tagen ab Belehrung vor und erlaube damit dem nationalen Gesetzgeber keine von einer Belehrung unabhängige Befristung. Man sieht an diesem konkreten Beispiel, wie wenig die zivilrechtlichen Richtlinien heute noch als bloße Zielvorgaben für den Gesetzgeber zu verstehen sind. Zur Begründung verweist der EuGH darauf, der Verbraucher könne das Widerrufsrecht schließlich nicht ausüben, wenn es ihm nicht bekannt sei. Auf den Gedanken, dass eine Kenntnis vom Widerrufsrecht auch ohne Belehrung durch den Unternehmer erlangt werden könne, kommt der EuGH nicht – nicht mehr der freie und selbstverantwortliche Bürger, wie ihn das BGB vor Augen hatte, sondern der unmündige, unerfahrene, wirtschaftlich schwache Verbraucher ist heute das Leitbild.

Die Entscheidung des EuGH ist ein gutes Beispiel für die von ihm auch sonst bei der Auslegung des Europäischen Zivilrechts verwendete Methode. Im Vordergrund steht das Ziel, die uneingeschränkte Geltung des Europäischen Rechts zu sichern. Daher werden geschriebene Ausnahmen grundsätzlich eng verstanden und ungeschriebene, aus dem Zweck der Vorschriften hergeleitete Einschränkungen von vornherein nicht in Erwägung gezogen. Man pflegt diese Denkweise des EuGH als die Lehre vom *effet utile* zu kennzeichnen und auf diese Weise mit einem positiv wertenden Etikett zu versehen. Das kann man freilich auch anders sehen. Das Vorgehen des EuGH ist wortlautorientiert, oberflächlich und – soweit teleologisch argumentiert wird – eindimensional.[15] Zu einer systematischen und rechtsdogmatischen Entwicklung des zersplitterten heutigen Europäischen Zivilrechts sind auf diese Weise keine Beiträge des EuGH zu erwarten.

Kehren wir zum Fall *Heininger* zurück, mit dem sich der BGH[16] erneut (mit gehörigem zeitlichem Abstand, denn zwischen seinem Vorlagebeschluss und dem Urteil des EuGH waren zwei Jahre vergangen) zu befassen hatte. Was sollte er nun tun, nachdem das nationale Recht, so wie es der BGH verstanden hatte, nicht den vom EuGH dekretierten Anforderungen der Haustürgeschäfte-Richtlinie entsprach? Die Antwort liegt in der schon erwähnten richtlinienkonformen Auslegung. Der BGH drehte nun die Auslegung der Vorschrift über den Vorrang des Verbraucherkreditgesetzes um 180 Grad. Er stellte fest, unter Beachtung der für die nationalen Gerichte bindenden Auslegung des EuGH sei diese Bestimmung des nationalen Gesetzes richtlinienkonform einschränkend auszulegen. Sie sei so zu verstehen, dass das Verbraucherkreditgesetz nur dann vorgehe, wenn es ein ebenso weit reichendes Widerrufsrecht wie das Haustürgeschäftewiderrufsgesetz einräume. Der Wortlaut sei nicht eindeutig und der (eindeutig entgegengesetzte) Wille des Gesetzgebers spiele keine Rolle, denn der Gesetzgeber sei eben damals davon ausgegangen, dass die von ihm angestrebte Regelung – die Privilegierung von Realkreditverträgen in einer Haustürsituation – richtlinienkonform sei. Man könne dem Gesetzgeber nicht unterstellen, dass er sehenden Auges einen Richtlinienverstoß habe in Kauf nehmen wollen. Also habe dem Willen des Gesetzgebers die Übereinstimmung von nationalem Recht und Richtlinieninhalt entsprochen – und damit steht der Auslegung im Sinne der Rechtsprechung des EuGH nichts entgegen.

[15] Damit wird den überzeugenden Ausführungen von M. Franzen, ‚Heininger und die Folgen – ein Lehrstück Gemeinschaftsprivatrecht' *JZ* 2003, 321–332, 326 gefolgt.

[16] BGH, Urteil vom 9.4.2002, XI ZR 91/99, *NJW* 2002, 1881.

Man sieht, mit welcher Rigorosität das Europäische Recht sich gegenüber dem nationalen Recht durchsetzt, und zwar, um dies nochmals hervorzuheben, nicht nur die Europäischen Verordnungen, sondern auch die Europäischen Richtlinien. Der Wille des deutschen Gesetzgebers wird notfalls beiseite geschoben, um die Konformität mit dem Europäischen Recht zu erreichen.

Was lange währt, wird endlich gut – so lautet ein deutsches Sprichwort, dessen Wahrheitsgehalt man freilich stark bezweifeln kann. Kam denn nun wenigstens der Verbraucher, hier das Ehepaar *Heininger*, zu seinem Recht (wie es der EuGH verstanden hatte), gelang es ihm also, sich durch Widerruf vom Kreditvertrag zu lösen? Ich will Ihnen die nahezu groteske Schlusspointe des Falles nicht vorenthalten.[17] Da die Regeln des Haustürwiderrufsgesetzes anzuwenden waren, hob der BGH die Entscheidungen der Vorinstanzen auf und verwies die Sache an das OLG zurück. Nun war aber im bisherigen Verlauf des Rechtsstreits ungeklärt geblieben, ob der Vertrag überhaupt in einer Haustürsituation abgeschlossen worden war. Die Kläger hatten dies behauptet, die Beklagte hatte es bestritten. Da bei Unanwendbarkeit des Haustürwiderrufsgesetzes die Frage nicht relevant war, hatten die Gerichte hierüber auch keinen Beweis erhoben. Es war aber auch nicht Sache des BGH, diese tatsächliche Frage etwa vor der Vorlage an den EuGH zu klären, erst recht nicht Aufgabe des EuGH, der auch – mit Recht – ausdrücklich klarstellte, dass seine Ausführungen, bezogen auf den konkreten Fall, unter der Prämisse stünden, dass überhaupt ein Haustürgeschäft vorgelegen habe. Das OLG entschied schließlich, es habe keine Haustürsituation nach dem Haustürgeschäftewiderrufsgesetz bestanden und lehnte daher ein Widerrufsrecht der Kläger ab! Wie sich ein solcher Leerlauf vermeiden lässt, ist ein Problem für sich – vielleicht muss man von dem Grundsatz, wonach im Zivilprozess nur über solche Tatsachen Beweis zu erheben ist, die nach Ansicht des Gerichts rechtserheblich sind, dann eine Ausnahme machen, wenn die Rechtsfrage nur durch eine Vorlage an den EuGH geklärt werden kann.[18]

Die ‚Schrottimmobilien' haben die deutschen Gerichte und den EuGH noch etliche Male beschäftigt, und wahrscheinlich ist dabei

[17] Näher s. Franzen, Fn. 15 *supra*, 325.
[18] Vgl. Franzen, Fn. 15 *supra*, 330.

noch immer nicht das Ende erreicht. Selbst wenn der Kreditvertrag mangels Belehrung noch viele Jahre später widerrufen werden kann, ist erst die nächste Frage, ob sich der Käufer damit auch vom Kaufvertrag über die Immobilie lösen kann – worin ja sein eigentliches Ziel liegt. Der BGH lehnte es im Regelfall ab, den Widerruf des Kreditvertrages auch auf den Kaufvertrag übergreifen zu lassen.[19] Der EuGH[20] stellte insoweit fest, die Haustürgeschäfte-Richtlinie beziehe sich nicht auf den Immobilienkaufvertrag, auch wenn er Bestandteil eines kreditfinanzierten Anlagemodells gewesen sei und die Vertragsverhandlungen sowohl hinsichtlich des Immobilienkaufvertrags als auch des ausschließlich der Finanzierung dienenden Darlehensvertrags in einer Haustürsituation erfolgten. Im Grunde blieb der EuGH auch in dieser Entscheidung beim Wortlaut der Richtlinie stehen – diese schließe Kaufverträge über Immobilien ausdrücklich von ihrem Anwendungsbereich aus und enthalte keine Vorschrift über verbundene Verträge. Die Folgen des Widerrufs des Kreditvertrags für den Immobilienkaufvertrag richteten sich daher allein nach nationalem Recht. Die Haustürgeschäfte-Richtlinie verbiete es auch nicht, so der EuGH, dass der Darlehensnehmer, der von seinem Widerruf Gebrauch gemacht habe, aufgrund des nationalen Rechts die Darlehensvaluta sofort an den Kreditgeber zurückzahlen müsse und auch die marktüblichen Zinsen zu leisten habe. Es folgt dann allerdings eine Feststellung des EuGH zu den Folgen bei unterbliebener Widerrufsbelehrung, die einige Rätsel aufgibt. Der EuGH dekretiert, wenn der vom Kreditinstitut ordnungsgemäß über sein Widerrufsrecht belehrte Verbraucher es hätte vermeiden können, sich den Risiken der Kapitalanlage auszusetzen, so müssten die Mitgliedstaaten in ihren Rechtsvorschriften dafür sorgen, dass die Folgen dieses Risikos nicht den Verbraucher treffen. Ist dies ein Ansatz für eine besondere Haftung des nicht belehrenden Kreditinstituts, die man wohl in den

[19] Die Auswirkungen eines Widerrufs auf verbundene Verträge sind nunmehr in der langatmigen Vorschrift des § 358 BGB geregelt. Seit 2002 ist in § 358 Abs. 3 S. 3 BGB im Einzelnen bestimmt, unter welchen Voraussetzungen bei einem finanzierten Erwerb eines Grundstücks der Verbraucherdarlehensvertrag und der Grundstückskauf als wirtschaftliche Einheit und damit als verbundene Verträge anzusehen sind, so dass der Widerruf des Darlehensvertrages auch die Verpflichtungen aus dem Grundstückskauf entfallen lässt.

[20] Rs. C-350/03 *Elisabeth und Wolfgang Schulte* v. *Deutsche Bausparkasse Badenia AG* [2005], Slg. I-9215 = *NJW* 2005, 3551 (EuGH).

Zusammenhang der *culpa in contrahendo*[21] einfügen müsste? Und ist dabei etwa zu unterstellen, dass der Verbraucher, wenn er über das Widerrufsrecht belehrt worden wäre, davon sogleich nach Abschluss der Verträge Gebrauch gemacht hätte?[22]

In einer weiteren Entscheidung[23] ging es um die Frage, ob das Widerrufsrecht bei Immobilien-Kreditverträgen auch dann bestehe, wenn der Abschluss in einer Haustürsituation nicht von der kreditgebenden Bank veranlasst war, sondern von einer Vertriebsfirma und von dieser wiederum selbständige Anlagevermittler eingeschaltet worden waren. Der BGH hatte gemeint, dieses Problem in analoger Anwendung der Regeln lösen zu können, die bei einer Anfechtung wegen arglistiger Täuschung eingreifen. Die Täuschung durch einen Dritten (der nicht etwa Vertreter oder vom Verhandlungsgehilfe des Anfechtungsgegners ist) wird nach § 123 Abs. 2 BGB dem Anfechtungsgegner nur zugerechnet, wenn er sie kannte oder kennen musste. Der BGH wies darauf hin, dass der Widerruf mit der Anfechtung wegen arglistiger Täuschung durchaus verwandt sei, und erklärte daher § 123 Abs. 2 BGB für analog anwendbar. Auf Vorlage des OLG Bremen entschied der EuGH entgegengesetzt,[24] auch hier ganz am Wortlaut der Richtlinie orientiert, die allein auf das Vorliegen einer Haustürsituation abstelle und nicht danach frage, ob der Gewerbetreibende dies wusste oder hätte wissen müssen. Das Beispiel zeigt, wie sich das Europäische Recht in der strikt auf Wirksamkeit und

21 Dafür M. Habersack, ‚Zum Widerruf von an der Haustür abgeschlossenen Realkreditverträgen‘ *JZ* 2006, 91–94, 93, der hierbei (unter Berufung auf den *effet utile*!) auf das sonst geltende Verschuldenserfordernis (§ 280 Abs. 1 S. 2 BGB) verzichten will.

22 *Habersack* will (auch hier unter Berufung auf den *effet utile*) zugunsten des Verbrauchers die Vermutung aufklärungsgerechten Verhaltens anwenden. Aber bedeutet denn die Belehrung über ein Widerrufsrecht eine Aufklärung dahingehend, dass es sinnvoll sei, vom Widerrufsrecht Gebrauch zu machen? A. Staudinger, ‚Die Zukunft der Schrottimmobilien nach den EuGH-Entscheidungen vom 25.10.2005‘ *NJW* 2005, 3521–3525, 3523 will aus dem EuGH-Urteil eine widerlegliche Vermutung entnehmen. Danach soll es der Bank obliegen, zu beweisen, dass der Verbraucher auch bei ordnungsgemäßer Belehrung an den beiden Verträgen festgehalten hätte.

23 Rs. C-229/04 *Crailsheimer Volksbank eG* v. *Klaus Conrads, Frank Schulzke und Petra Schulzke-Lösche, Joachim Nitschke* [2005], Slg. I-9273 = *NJW* 2005, 3555 = *JZ* 2006, 90 (mit Anm. *Habersack*) (EuGH).

24 Zustimmend Habersack, Fn. 21 *supra*, 94; Staudinger, Fn. 22 *supra*, 3522.

uneingeschränkte Geltung bedachten Auslegung durch den EuGH gegen eine Einpassung in den Kontext des BGB gleichsam zur Wehr setzt.

Insgesamt ist festzustellen, dass sich das heutige Europäische Zivilrecht nicht nur aufgrund des Zuschnitts der Richtlinien als unsystematisches Konglomerat darstellt, sondern dass auch der vielfach sehr konkrete Inhalt der Richtlinien in Verbindung mit der Rechtsprechung des EuGH, die strikt die Wirksamkeit des Europäischen Rechts garantieren will, einer Integration in die Systematik und Dogmatik des nationalen Rechts durch die Rechtsprechung entgegensteht.

b) Die Eingliederung des Verbraucherschutzrechts in das BGB

(1) Vom Sonderprivatrecht zurück ins BGB

Gewiss wäre es wünschenswert, dass der nationale Gesetzgeber die zur Umsetzung der punktuellen Richtlinien des Europäischen Zivilrechts erlassenen Normen in die nationale Kodifikation des Zivilrechts einpasst und sie mit dessen Systematik und der zivilrechtlichen Dogmatik in Übereinstimmung bringt. Im deutschen Recht erfolgte die Entwicklung des Verbraucherschutzrechts zunächst im wesentlichen durch besondere Gesetze, die neben dem BGB standen. Dies gilt sowohl für den ursprünglich aus nationaler Quelle stammenden Bereich des AGB-Gesetzes als auch für die späteren Gesetze, die zu einem guten Teil der Umsetzung von Europäischen Richtlinien dienten wie etwa das Verbraucherkreditgesetz. Diese Herausbildung eines Sonderprivatrechts bringt nicht nur praktische Schwierigkeiten bei der Rechtsanwendung mit sich, sondern sie gefährdet schließlich geradezu die Existenzgrundlage einer Kodifikation, die eine grundsätzlich umfassende Regelung der privatrechtlichen Rechtsverhältnisse anstrebt. Es verdient daher höchste Anerkennung, dass der deutsche Gesetzgeber in neuerer Zeit, vor allem anlässlich der Schuldrechtsreform, den Mut und die politische Kraft aufgebracht hat, das Verbraucherschutzrecht unter weitestgehender Aufhebung der Sondergesetze in das BGB zu verlagern.

Ob allerdings mit dieser Rückführung in das BGB über die äußerliche Einbindung in das Gesetzbuch hinaus auch eine echte Einpassung in die Systematik und Dogmatik des BGB gelungen ist, stellt eine andere Frage dar. Nach meinem Eindruck sind insoweit einige Defizite zu verzeichnen.

(2) Die Einfügung der Begriffe Verbraucher und Unternehmer in den Allgemeinen Teil des BGB

Schon durch das Fernabsatzgesetz des Jahres 2000 wurden in den Allgemeinen Teil des BGB zwei Bestimmungen eingefügt, die den Begriff des Verbrauchers (§ 13 BGB) und des Unternehmers (§ 14 BGB) in einer Weise definieren, die innerhalb des deutschen Privatrechts allgemeine Geltung beansprucht. Um dies zu unterstreichen, gab man der Aufnahme in den Allgemeinen Teil den Vorrang vor der zunächst geplanten Zuordnung zum Schuldrecht (in dessen Rahmen die genannten Begriffe freilich die bei weitem größte Bedeutung haben). Ob man diesen Vorgang geradezu als eine Art von Revolution bezeichnen darf,[25] mag dahin gestellt bleiben. Richtig ist zweifellos, dass schon mit der Aufnahme dieser beiden Begriffe die grundsätzliche Ausrichtung des BGB einen Wandel erfahren hat. Das Verbraucherschutzrecht stellt sich nicht mehr als eine systemsprengende Ausnahme von einem ‚eigentlich' geltenden Privatrecht als einem Recht gleichartiger Rechtssubjekte dar, sondern die damit verbundene unterschiedliche Bewertung der Interessenlage auf der Seite des Verbrauchers und des Unternehmers ist ein zentraler Bestandteil des Bürgerlichen Rechts geworden. Der Verbraucherschutz tritt dem Prinzip der vertraglichen Gestaltungsfreiheit nicht bloß auf gleicher Augenhöhe, sondern mit dem Anspruch auf vorrangige Beachtung gegenüber. Dieser grundlegende Wandel wird nicht mehr dadurch verdeckt, dass das BGB neben den Sondergesetzen scheinbar unverändert bei Bestand bliebe.

Es ist hier nicht der Ort, zu den Definitionen des Verbrauchers und des Unternehmers im einzelnen Stellung zu nehmen. Sicher kann man kritisch vermerken, dass es im Grunde nicht um eine personenbezogene Definition, sondern um Merkmale gehe, die beim Abschluss bestimmter Rechtsgeschäfte gegeben sein müssen, um verbraucherschützende Vorschriften anwenden zu können. Niemand ist

25 So H.-W. Micklitz, in J. Säcker & R. Rixecker (Hrsg.), *Münchener Kommentar zum BGB* (5. Aufl., München 2006) vor §§ 13, 14 Rn. 1.

schlechthin Verbraucher oder Unternehmer, sondern entscheidend ist, zu welchem Zweck die jeweiligen Rechtsgeschäfte abgeschlossen werden. Man hat mit vollem Recht von einem situativen Verbraucherbegriff gesprochen, zumal die Geltung der verbraucherschützenden Normen oft genug auch von einer bestimmten Abschlusssituation abhängt. Aber die Herausarbeitung des Verbraucher- und des Unternehmerbegriffs besitzt die Vorteile einer allgemeinen und abstrakten Begriffsbildung, ohne dass damit die Gefahr von Missverständnissen verbunden ist.

(3) Die systematische Einbindung der Widerrufsrechte

Bereits durch das Fernabsatzschutzgesetz wurden die Bestimmungen über das Widerrufsrecht des Verbrauchers aus den bis dahin geltenden Sondergesetzen weitgehend in das BGB verlagert. Im Rahmen der Schuldrechtsreform 2001 wurden diese Vorschriften in verschiedenen Punkten verändert. Auf die Einzelheiten der Entwicklung braucht hier nicht eingegangen zu werden; ich lege den heutigen Gesetzesstand des BGB zugrunde. Das Verbraucherwiderrufsrecht ist in den allgemeinen Teil des Schuldrechts aufgenommen worden und dort an zwei verschiedenen Stellen geregelt. Die Voraussetzungen, unter denen dem Verbraucher ein Widerrufsrecht zusteht, findet man im Abschnitt 3, der den Schuldverhältnissen aus Verträgen gewidmet ist, und dort im Titel 1, der von Begründung, Inhalt und Beendigung der vertraglichen Schuldverhältnisse handelt. Der Untertitel 2, in dem sich die Voraussetzungen der Widerrufsrechte finden, trägt die Überschrift ‚Besondere Vertriebsformen' und enthält die Bestimmungen über die Voraussetzungen der Widerrufsrechte bei Haustürgeschäften, bei Fernabsatzverträgen sowie eine Bestimmung über die Pflichten des Unternehmers im elektronischen Geschäftsverkehr. Die Zusammenfassung unter dem übergreifenden Gesichtspunkt der besonderen Vertriebsformen ist ein bemerkenswerter Versuch der Systematisierung, auch wenn man kritisch einwenden kann, dass die Beschränkung auf Verträge zwischen Unternehmer und Verbraucher und die weiteren Voraussetzungen, die sich auf den Inhalt des Vertrags beziehen, darin nicht zum Ausdruck kommen. Nicht in diesem Abschnitt, sondern im besonderen Schuldrecht findet man das Widerrufsrecht beim Verbraucherdarlehensvertrag, und in einem Sondergesetz, dem Fernunterrichtsschutzgesetz, verblieben sind die

Voraussetzungen des Widerrufsrechts beim Fernunterrichtsvertrag. Im Einzelnen sind die in dem Abschnitt ‚Besondere Vertriebsformen' enthaltenen Vorschriften über die Voraussetzungen des Widerrufsrechts sehr umfangreich und detailliert. Es sind nicht etwa die Voraussetzungen der einzelnen Varianten des Widerrufsrechts zusammengefasst und verallgemeinert worden. Dafür sind zu einem guten Teil die Vorgaben des Europäischen Zivilrechts verantwortlich, die der deutsche Gesetzgeber ebenso wie zunächst in die Sondergesetze, so nunmehr in das BGB übernommen hat. Soweit es um die Informationspflichten des Unternehmers bei Vertragsschluss bei Fernabsatzverträgen, Teilzeit-Wohnrechte-Verträgen, elektronischem Rechtsverkehr und Reiseverträgen geht, wird das BGB auch noch durch eine ‚Verordnung über Informations- und Nachweispflichten nach bürgerlichem Recht' ergänzt, die weitere sehr ins Einzelne gehende Vorschriften sowie Muster (z.B. über die Widerrufsbelehrung) enthält.

Ob es jemals gelingen wird, diese Paragraphenflut – auf einem an sich so schmalen Sektor, wie ihn nun einmal das Widerrufsrecht bei Verbraucherverträgen darstellt – durch einen höheren Abstraktionsgrad zu ersetzen, also durch Vorschriften, die das Prädikat ‚Rechtsdogmatik' verdienen würden, erscheint mir zweifelhaft. Man könnte bei dem erreichten Entwicklungsstand, insbesondere bei der weiten Ausdehnung des Widerrufsrecht durch die Regeln über das Fernabsatzgeschäft, durchaus an eine Verallgemeinerung dahin denken, dass bei Verträgen zwischen Unternehmen und Verbrauchern grundsätzlich ein Widerrufsrecht besteht, und wenn das so allgemein gelten würde, könnte man sich auch die heute vorgeschriebenen umfangreichen Belehrungen des Verbrauchers über das jeweilige Widerrufsrecht sparen und auf das Rechtsbewußtsein der Bevölkerung vertrauen (nebenbei bemerkt: schon heute trifft man bei juristischen Laien zuweilen auf die – natürlich unzutreffende – Ansicht, es gebe ein generelles Widerrufsrecht des Verbrauchers!).

Neben den Voraussetzungen der Widerrufsrechte findet man nunmehr auch die Ausübung des Widerrufsrechts und die Rechtsfolgen des Widerrufsrechts im BGB geregelt. Das Gesetz enthält im Abschnitt 3 ‚Schuldverhältnisse aus Verträgen' einen Titel 5, der im Untertitel 1 den Rücktritt im Allgemeinen, und im Untertitel 2 das Widerrufs- und Rückgaberecht bei Verbraucherverträgen zum Gegenstand hat. Der Zusammenhang mit denjenigen Vorschriften, die das Widerrufsrecht einräumen, wird dadurch hergestellt, dass das Widerrufsrecht (innerhalb oder auch außerhalb des BGB) als ‚Widerrufsrecht gemäß § 355' bezeichnet wird. In dem genannten Bereich der §§ 355 bis 359 BGB ist es dem Gesetzgeber gelungen, Ausübung und Rechtsfolgen der Verbraucher-Widerrufsrechte zusammenfassend zu regeln. Darin liegt ein beachtlicher systematischer Fortschritt. Ohne auf den Inhalt im Einzelnen eingehen zu können, sei doch hervorgehoben, dass sich der Gesetzgeber mit dieser Regelung dazu entschlossen hat, das Widerrufsrecht – jedenfalls im wesentlichen – wie ein gesetzliches Rücktrittsrecht auszugestalten. Damit unterscheidet sich zwar diese Variante des Widerrufs grundlegend von dem Widerruf einer Willenserklärung, wie ihn der Allgemeine Teil in § 130 Abs. 1 S. 2 BGB kennt, aber dies ist doch eher ein Schönheitsfehler, auch wenn man ihn durchaus dadurch vermeiden könnte, dass das Widerrufsrecht des Verbrauchers eben als Rücktrittsrecht bezeichnet wird! Mit der grundsätzlichen Beurteilung der Rechtsfolgen nach Rücktrittsrecht erteilte der Gesetzgeber der zuvor vielfach, insbesondere vom BGH,[26] vertretenen Auffassung eine Absage, wonach der Vertrag schwebend unwirksam bleibe, solange dem Verbraucher das Widerrufsrecht zusteht. Die Beurteilung der Rechtsfolgen nach Rücktrittsrecht bedeutet vielmehr, dass der vom Verbraucher geschlossene Vertrag zunächst wirksam und damit für beide Teile verbindlich ist, und dass erst mit dem Widerruf die Hauptverbindlichkeiten entfallen. Das bedeutet, in Übereinstimmung mit der seit langem anerkannten Dogmatik der Rücktrittsfolgen, nicht etwa, dass der Vertrag rückwirkend vernichtet wird, sondern dass er in ein Rückabwicklungsschuldverhältnis umgewandelt wird. Die Rückabwicklung bei bereits erbrachten Leistungen erfolgt demgemäß nicht nach dem Recht der ungerechtfertigten Bereicherung (wie bei einem von Anfang an nichtigen oder durch Anfechtung vernichteten Vertrag), sondern eben nach den Regeln des Rücktrittsrechts. Damit ist insbesondere eine Berufung auf den Wegfall der Bereicherung ausgeschlossen. Im Einzelnen hat sich der Gesetzgeber bemüht, den Inhalt der Pflichten nach dem Widerruf interessengerecht auszugestalten. Das Europäische Recht hält sich insoweit, glücklicherweise, zurück, und wie bereits oben ausgeführt, hat auch der EuGH (beim Verbraucherdarle-

[26] BGHZ 113, 222, 225; BGHZ 119, 283, 298.

hensvertrag als Haustürgeschäft) insoweit die Zuständigkeit des nationalen Gesetzgebers nicht in Frage gestellt. Insgesamt liegt in dieser Zuordnung der Widerrufsfolgen zum Rücktrittsrecht m.E. ein beträchtlicher Fortschritt und zugleich ein sehr erfreulicher Beweis dafür, dass die Kraft zum systematischen und dogmatischen Rechtsdenken dem deutschen Gesetzgeber noch keineswegs abhanden gekommen ist.

(4) Die Einfügung der materiell-rechtlichen Bestimmungen des AGBG in das BGB

Eine bemerkenswerte Tat des deutschen Gesetzgebers war es auch, das seit 1974 geltende Gesetz über die Allgemeinen Geschäftsbedingungen aufzuheben und dessen materiell-rechtliche Bestimmungen[27] in das BGB zu verlagern. Sie finden sich jetzt im Allgemeinen Schuldrecht in dem Abschnitt 2 ‚Gestaltung rechtsgeschäftlicher Schuldverhältnisse durch Allgemeine Geschäftsbedingungen', seltsamer Weise vor und außerhalb des Abschnitts über Schuldverhältnisse aus Verträgen, obwohl die Allgemeinen Geschäftsbedingungen nur die vertraglichen Schuldverhältnisse betreffen. Inhaltlich stimmen die jetzigen §§ 305 bis 310 BGB mit den Vorschriften des früheren AGBG weitestgehend überein.[28] In der Eingliederung dieser Materie in das BGB kann man durchaus einen Systemwechsel insofern sehen, als das Recht der AGB seinen Ausnahmecharakter gegenüber dem BGB verloren hat und sich nunmehr auch vom Standort her als Normalfall darstellt. Faktisch ist dies natürlich schon lange so, und es hatte immer etwas reichlich Künstliches an sich, den Grundsatz der Vertragsfreiheit als inhaltliche Gestaltungsfreiheit beider Teile herauszustellen, wohl wissend, dass diese Freiheit durch die verbreitete Verwendung von AGB seit langem denaturiert wurde und die Rechtsordnung (zunächst die Rechtsprechung und dann der Gesetzgeber) darauf mit der weitreichenden Inhaltskontrolle der AGB rea-

[27] Die prozessualen Bestimmungen des AGBG, die sich auf die Verbandsklage beziehen, fügte man dagegen nicht in die ZPO ein, sondern hielt es für richtig, ein eigenes Unterlassungsklagengesetz zu schaffen. Auch dieser Bereich steht heute weitgehend unter dem Einfluss des Europäischen Rechts.

[28] Zu den Änderungen zusammenfassend J. Basedow, in J. Säcker, K. Rebmann & R. Rixecker (Hrsg.), *Münchener Kommentar zum BGB* (4. Aufl., München 2001) vor § 305 Rn. 17.

giert hat. Trotz der Einfügung in das BGB steht allerdings das AGB-Recht weiterhin unverknüpft neben der ansonsten grundsätzlich dispositiven Gestaltung des Schuldrechts. Man sollte aber nicht übersehen, dass die Rechtfertigung der Inhaltskontrolle von AGB und Formularverträgen bei gleichzeitiger Aufrechterhaltung der Gestaltungsfreiheit bei sog. Individualverträgen mehr und mehr problematisch erscheint. Dafür ist zum Teil das Europäische Zivilrecht verantwortlich. Der deutsche Standpunkt, der überhaupt die Inhaltskontrolle rechtfertigen sollte, war immer gewesen, dass es die vom AGB-Verwender usurpierte Quasi-Normsetzung sei, die die Inhaltskontrolle rechtfertige. Daher stammt das begriffliche Erfordernis, dass die AGB stets für eine Vielzahl von Verträgen vorformuliert sein müssen, wie es noch heute in § 305 Abs. 1 S. 1 BGB zu lesen steht. Der Europäische Gesetzgeber[29] hat aber schon vor geraumer Zeit eine Inhaltskontrolle auch für solche von einem Unternehmer bei einem Verbrauchvertrag vorformulierten Vertragsbedingungen vorgeschrieben, die nur für eine einmalige Verwendung bestimmt sind, sofern der andere Teil darauf aufgrund der Vorformulierung keinen Einfluss nehmen konnte. Damit sollte ein Kompromiss zwischen der AGB-fixierten Konzeption des deutschen und der umfassenderen Missbrauchskontrolle des französischen Rechts gefunden werden.[30] Das letztgenannte Erfordernis steht praktisch auf dem Papier, denn angesichts der Vorformulierung wird es bei einem Verbrauchervertrag kaum jemals zu einer echten Aushandlung der Vertragsbedingungen kommen.[31] Diese gegenüber der ursprünglichen Dogmatik des deutschen AGB-Rechts im Grunde systemsprengende Vorschrift steht heute in § 310 Abs. 3 BGB. Danach sind die Vorschriften über die inhaltliche Kontrolle von AGB auch auf vorformulierte Indivi-

[29] Art. 3 Abs. 1 der Klausel-Richtlinie unterstellt alle nicht im Einzelnen ausgehandelten Vertragsklauseln der Missbrauchskontrolle, und Art. 3 Abs. 2 erläutert dies dahin, dass eine Vertragsklausel immer dann als nicht im Einzelnen ausgehandelt anzusehen ist, wenn sie im Voraus abgefasst wurde und der Verbraucher deshalb keinen Einfluss auf ihren Inhalt nehmen konnte. Es muss sich dabei nicht notwendigerweise um einen vorformulierten Standardvertrag handeln, auch wenn dieser in der genannten Bestimmung besonders erwähnt wird.

[30] J. Basedow, in J. Säcker, K. Rebmann & R. Rixecker (Hrsg.), *Münchener Kommentar zum BGB* (4. Aufl., München 2001) § 310 Rn. 61 mit Nachweisen.

[31] A.M. ibid, Rn. 62.

dualverträge anzuwenden, und zwar nicht nur die allgemeine Inhaltskontrolle gemäß § 307 BGB, sondern auch die zahlreichen einzelnen Klauselverbote der §§ 308 und 309 BGB. Zwischen der angeblichen Dispositivität des Schuldrechts, oder anders ausgedrückt der inhaltlichen Gestaltungsfreiheit, und der weitreichenden Inhaltskontrolle nicht nur bei AGB, sondern auch bei vorformulierten Individualverträgen besteht eine Spannungsverhältnis, das durch die bloße Einfügung der früheren AGBG-Bestimmungen in das BGB in keiner Weise gelöst worden ist. Man wird überlegen müssen, ob es nicht an der Zeit ist, jedenfalls für Verträge zwischen Unternehmern und Verbrauchern die Dogmatik in dem Sinne zu ändern, dass generell nur eine vertragliche Abweichung zugunsten des Verbrauchers zugelassen wird, dass also das einseitig zwingende Recht zur Regel würde. Insgesamt scheint mir mit der Eingliederung der AGB-Bestimmungen in das BGB die notwendige Weiterentwicklung der Dogmatik noch nicht gelungen zu sein.

3. Privatautonomie und Antidiskriminierung

a) Die Antidiskriminierungs-Richtlinien

Das Verhältnis zwischen den Prinzipien des deutschen Zivilrechts und den Einflüssen des Europäischen Zivilrechts ist in Deutschland in keinem Zusammenhang so intensiv, engagiert, ja leidenschaftlich erörtert worden wie im Hinblick auf das geplante deutsche Antidiskriminierungsgesetz.[32] Trotz zweier Anläufe in der vorletzten und in der letzten Legislaturperiode ist dieses Gesetz bislang nicht zustande gekommen. Die Überschrift zu dem zuletzt vorgelegten Entwurf der damaligen Bundesregierung[33] lautet: Entwurf eines Gesetzes zur Umsetzung europäischer Antidiskriminierungsvorschriften. Als Art. 1 des gesamten Gesetzes findet man dann das ‚Gesetz zum Schutz vor Dis-

[32] Zur Diskussion s. etwa J. Neuner, ‚Diskriminierungsschutz durch Privatrecht‘ *JZ* 2003, 57–66, 57; E. Picker, ‚Antidiskriminierung als Zivilrechtsprogramm?‘ *JZ* 2003, 540–545, 540; G. Thüsing, ‚Religion und Kirche in einem Anti-Diskriminierungsrecht‘ *JZ* 2004, 172–179, 172; K. Riesenhuber & J.U. Frank, ‚Verbot der Geschlechtsdiskriminierung im Europäischen Vertragsrecht‘ *JZ* 2004, 529–538, 529.

[33] BT-Drs. 15/4538 vom 16.12.2004, auszugsweise abgedruckt in *NJW* Heft 1–2/2005, S. XXXV ff.

kriminierungen' (Antidiskriminierungsgesetz), das uns im gegebenen Zusammenhang interessiert, während Art. 2 ein Gesetz zum Schutz von Soldatinnen und Soldaten vor Diskriminierungen enthält. Die Bundesregierung hat sich erst durch die Europäischen Antidiskriminierungsrichtlinien dazu veranlasst gesehen, ein Antidiskriminierungsgesetz auf den Weg zu bringen. Das bedeutet freilich nicht, dass es bisher im deutschen Zivilrecht keinen Schutz vor Diskriminierung gegeben hätte. Eine geschlechtsbezogene Benachteiligung im Arbeitsrecht ist durch eine Reihe von ausdrücklichen Bestimmungen des BGB (insbesondere § 611a, § 611b, § 612 Abs. 3, § 612a) verboten und mit Sanktionen versehen – diese Vorschrift wurden zur Umsetzung der einschlägigen Europäischen Gleichbehandlungs-Richtlinien in ihren früheren Fassungen geschaffen. Soweit im Übrigen Diskriminierungsprobleme auftraten, waren (und sind) sie in erster Linie unter Anwendung der zivilrechtlichen Generalklauseln zu lösen. Diskriminierendes Verhalten kann dazu führen, dass ein Rechtsgeschäft als sittenwidrig und daher gemäß § 138 Abs. 1 BGB als nichtig anzusehen ist. Die Ablehnung eines Vertragsschlusses aus diskriminierenden Gründen kann ebenfalls gegen die guten Sitten verstoßen, woraus sich in entsprechender Anwendung des § 826 BGB (Schadensersatz bei vorsätzlicher sittenwidriger Schädigung) auch ein Anspruch auf Vertragsschluss, also ein Kontrahierungszwang ergeben kann. Im deutschen Recht ist es seit langem anerkannt, dass im Rahmen der Generalklauseln die Grundrechte eine wesentliche Rolle spielen. Dies ist vor allem der Rechtsprechung des BVerfG zu verdanken, die in den Grundrechten nicht nur Abwehrrechte des Bürgers gegen den Staat sieht, sondern sie als Ausdruck einer objektiven Werteordnung versteht, die innerhalb der gesamten Rechtsordnung Beachtung verlangt. Die zivilrechtlichen Generalklauseln sind flexibel genug, um geänderten Wertungen Rechnung zu tragen. So gesehen fehlt es an sich nicht an einem Schutz gegen Diskriminierungen innerhalb des deutschen Zivilrechts. Wann freilich eine unzulässige Diskriminierung vorliegt und wann deshalb die zivilrechtliche Vertragsfreiheit hinter dem Diskriminierungsverbot zurücktreten muss, bleibt der Beurteilung des Einzelfalles überlassen. Da die Vertragsfreiheit im deutschen Recht einen hohen Rang genießt und sich im Übrigen auch ihrerseits einer verfassungsrechtlichen Absicherung im Recht auf freie Entfaltung der Persönlichkeit erfreut, ist man im allgemeinen in der Bejahung der Sittenwidrigkeit aufgrund unzulässiger Diskriminierung zurückhaltend. Der Europäische Gesetzgeber dagegen hat auf diesem Gebiet gerade in den letzten Jahren bemerkenswerte Aktivität entfaltet. Dabei ist er der bereits oben hervorgehobenen Regelungstechnik treu geblieben, nur konkrete Teilgebiete zu normieren. Die vier hier zu erwähnenden Anti-Diskriminierungsrichtlinien sind ein anschauliches Beispiel für diesen Verzicht des heutigen Europäischen Rechts auf eine zusammenfassende, systematische Regelung. Da sich die Richtlinien teils auf bestimmte Diskriminierungsformen, teils auf bestimmte Ausschnitte der Rechtsordnung beschränken, ergibt sich insgesamt ein verwirrendes Bild. Eine alte, aber später geänderte Richtlinie[34] schreibt die Gleichbehandlung von Männern und Frauen im beruflichen Sektor, insbesondere im Arbeitsrecht vor. Eine weitere Richtlinie[35] verlangt aber auch die Gleichbehandlung von Männern und Frauen beim Zugang zu Gütern und Dienstleistungen. Für den Bereich der Beschäftigung und des Berufs, also wiederum vor allem im Arbeitsrecht, verbietet eine dritte Richtlinie[36] eine Diskriminierung aus Gründen der Religion, der Weltanschauung, einer Behinderung, des Alters oder der sexuellen Orientierung. Die ‚Anti-Rassismus'-Richtlinie[37] bekämpft nur Diskriminierungen aus Gründen der Rasse oder der ethnischen Herkunft, dafür aber auf einem sehr breiten Anwendungsgebiet, zu dem neben der beruflichen Tätigkeit (einschließlich des Arbeitsrechts) auch der ‚Zugang zu und die Versorgung mit Gütern und Dienstleistungen gehören, die der Öffentlichkeit zur Verfügung stehen, einschließlich Wohnraum', also im Grund der gesamte Waren- und Dienstleistungsmarkt.

b) Die bislang gescheiterte Schaffung eines deutschen Antidiskriminierungsgesetzes

Der deutsche Gesetzgeber ist verpflichtet, diese Richtlinien in das deutsche Recht umzusetzen – zum Teil sind die dafür geltenden Fristen schon seit gut zwei Jahren abgelaufen. Rechtspolitisch kann man diese Richtlinien kaum kritisieren, denn natürlich kann niemand Diskriminierungen aus den genannten Gründen gut heißen. Immerhin ließe sich fragen, ob es denn eine besondere Notwendigkeit gab,

34 Anhang Nr. 16.
35 Anhang Nr. 17.
36 Anhang Nr. 14.
37 Anhang Nr. 13.

Diskriminierungen gerade auf dem Gebiet des Zivilrechts mit diesem großen gesetzgeberischen Aufwand zu bekämpfen. Auf das deutsche Recht bezogen, könnte man behaupten, dass in Gestalt der Generalklauseln und der erwähnten grundrechtsorientierten Anwendung ohnehin bereits eine hinreichende gesetzliche Regelung bestehe. Es ist aber ziemlich klar, dass dies nicht als eine hinreichende Umsetzung der Richtlinien angesehen würde – die vom Europäischen Gesetzgeber formulierten Diskriminierungstatbestände müssen sich als solche im nationalen Recht wieder finden. Das Europäische Anti-Diskriminierungsrecht erweist sich, könnte man leicht überspitzt formulieren, als Feind der zivilrechtlichen Generalklausel und greift somit auch an dieser Stelle tief in die zivilrechtliche Dogmatik ein.

Dass es dem deutschen Gesetzgeber bislang nicht gelungen ist, die Umsetzung der Antidiskriminierungs-Richtlinien zu bewältigen, hängt nicht damit zusammen, dass es am guten Willen gefehlt hätte. Das Gegenteil ist der Fall. Es war gewissermaßen zu viel des guten Willens vorhanden. Man beschloss über die eher punktuellen Anwendungsbereiche der Europäischen Richtlinien hinauszugehen und eine Diskriminierung aus allen in den Richtlinien vorkommenden Gründen möglichst umfassend zu untersagen. Das bedeutet vor allem, dass nicht nur Diskriminierungen aus Gründen der Rasse, sondern auch aus Gründen der Religion, der Weltanschauung, einer Behinderung, des Alters oder der sexuellen Diskriminierung bei der Versorgung mit Gütern und Dienstleistungen, einschließlich Wohnraums, verboten werden sollen, obgleich dies von den Europäischen Richtlinien nicht gefordert wurde. An dieser überschießenden Umsetzungsabsicht entzündete sich der Protest, der nicht nur von Wirtschaftskreisen, sondern auch von angesehenen Vertretern der Zivilrechtswissenschaft erhoben wurde. Was bleibt, so lautet der nahe liegende Vorwurf, von der Vertragsfreiheit noch übrig, wenn denkbare Entscheidungskriterien in einem so weit gehenden Maße ausgeschlossen werden sollen? Es kam hinzu, dass das geplante Umsetzungsgesetz dann auch in der Gewährung von Schadensersatzansprüchen wegen Diskriminierung äußerst großzügig verfuhr und demjenigen, der solche Ansprüche aufgrund der Verweigerung eines Vertragsschlusses geltend machen wollte, auch mit einer beweiserleichternden Vorschrift zu Hilfe kommen wollte – bei Glaubhaftmachung von Umständen, die eine unzulässige Benachteiligung vermuten lassen, sollte sich die Beweislast zu Lasten der anderen Partei umdrehen. Natürlich bemühten sich die Gesetzesverfasser, die Reichweite des Diskriminierungsverbots auch wieder einzuschränken und unter besonderen Voraussetzungen eine unterschiedliche Behandlung zuzulassen, aber dies im Einzelnen zu regeln, ist schwierig, und, soweit es überhaupt gelingt, läuft es dann eben auf ein Gängelung der Parteien in vielen Einzelheiten hinaus. Die jetzige Bundesregierung hat noch keinen neuen Gesetzesvorschlag vorgelegt. Es bleibt zu hoffen,[38] dass man sich, ganz im Gegensatz zu den bisherigen Entwürfen, auf diejenigen Regelungen beschränkt, die zur Umsetzung der Richtlinie unumgänglich sind, und auf alle Ausweitungen verzichtet – nicht nur, um das Prinzip der Vertragsfreiheit zu wahren, sondern um auch die Anschüttung weiterer Berge von Paragraphen zu vermeiden!

III. Von der Zukunft systematischen und dogmatischen Rechtsdenkens in Europa oder: Was wird aus dem BGB?

1. Systematik und Rechtsdogmatik als erstrebenswerte Ziele

Auch wenn der Systemgedanke in der Welt des Privatrechts allgegenwärtig ist und die Begriffe Rechtssystem oder systematische Auslegung ständig verwendet werden, ist es doch nicht leicht, diesen Begriffen einen exakten Inhalt zuzuweisen. Erst recht gilt dies für die Begriffe der Rechtsdogmatik und des dogmatischen Denkens im Recht. Auf die weit reichende theoretische Diskussion hierüber kann ich hier nicht eingehen. Ich versuche offen zu legen, von welchem, vielleicht etwas simplen Verständnis ich selbst ausgehe. Das kann man natürlich kritisieren, und dann sehen möglicherweise auch die

[38] So auch der Vorschlag von H. Reichold, ‚Umsetzung der Antidiskriminierungsrichtlinien – Zurück zum BGB‘ *NJW* Heft 4/2006, III (Editorial). – Nach Abschluss des Manuskripts wurden das Gesetz zur Umsetzung europäischer Richtlinien zur Verwirklichung des Grundsatzes der Gleichbehandlung vom 14. August 2006, BGBl. I 2006, 1897, und als dessen Artikel 1 das Allgemeine Gleichbehandlungsgesetz (AGG) erlassen. Die oben ausgedrückte Hoffnung ist dabei leider nicht in Erfüllung gegangen.

Schlussfolgerungen für das heutige und künftige Europäische Zivilrecht unterschiedlich aus.

Ein System entsteht durch Zusammenstellung unterschiedlicher Gegenstände unter ordnenden und damit zugleich verbindenden Gesichtspunkten. Die Bildung eines juristischen Systems setzt weiter voraus, dass die große Masse der rechtlichen Aussagen in ein Verhältnis von Regeln und Ausnahmen gebracht wird. Um ein juristisches System errichten zu können, bedarf es der Bildung von rechtlichen Begriffen. Daher ist die Herausbildung eines rechtlichen Systems eng verknüpft mit der Rechtsdogmatik. Dogmatik ist die Formung juristischer Begriffe mit einem festen, unverrückbaren Inhalt. Juristische Begriffe sind von den Begriffen der Alltagssprache zu unterscheiden. Sie müssen sich durch einen präzisen Inhalt auszeichnen und verlangen daher nach Abstraktion gegenüber den konkreten Sachverhalten. Systematisches und rechtsdogmatisches Denken bilden damit eine Einheit. Die von der Rechtsdogmatik geschaffenen juristischen Begriffe sind die ordnenden Gesichtspunkte, die ein juristisches System ermöglichen.

Das heutige Europäische Zivilrecht ist unsystematisch. Die einzelnen Regelungen, verkörpert in den Europäischen Richtlinien, stehen unverknüpft nebeneinander. Sie betreffen konkrete Problemfelder unterschiedlicher Art, zwischen denen durch die Richtlinien selbst kein Zusammenhang hergestellt wird.

Ob gleichwohl durch rechtswissenschaftliche Analyse eine Systembildung möglich ist, erscheint mir sehr zweifelhaft. Das System kann nicht aus dem jeweiligen nationalen Recht entnommen werden, weil die europäischen Normen nicht auf ein solches System hin ausgerichtet sind. Denkbar wäre, die europäischen Normen in das jeweilige nationale System einzufügen und sie in der Begriffsbildung und der Systematisierung entsprechend anzupassen. Dem steht aber entgegen, dass gerade die zivilrechtlichen Richtlinien in weiten Teilen die geregelten Teilaspekte sehr detailliert umschreiben und dass diese Richtlinieninhalte letztlich völlig unverändert in das nationale Recht übernommen werden müssen.

Eher könnte man daran denken, auf europäischer Ebene ein System zu erarbeiten. Auch insoweit ist es aber hinderlich, dass die Regelungen sich nur auf Einzelprobleme beziehen und die verwendeten

Begriffe im Allgemeinen nur einen niedrigen Abstraktionsgrad aufweisen. Die Rechtsprechung des Europäischen Gerichtshofs hat bislang nicht zur Systembildung beigetragen, da sie die Richtlinien isoliert betrachtet, übergreifende juristische Gesichtspunkte kaum in Erwägung zieht und bei der Auslegung der Richtlinien auf einem methodisch unzureichenden Niveau verharrt. Statt teleologischer Interpretation samt Interessenabwägung (und darauf aufbauender dogmatischer Fixierung) dominiert der Blick auf den Wortlaut und das generelle Streben nach möglichst strikter und weitgehender Anwendung des Europäischen Rechts.

Ein weiterer Aspekt des heutigen Europäischen Zivilrechts, der einer systematischen und rechtsdogmatischen Verarbeitung im Wege steht, ist das weithin anzutreffende ‚Günstigkeitsprinzip' der Europäischen Normsetzung. Das gilt vor allem für das Europäische Verbraucherschutzrecht. Durchweg enthalten die Richtlinien ausdrückliche Bestimmungen, wonach die Mitgliedstaaten nicht gehindert seien, einen weiterreichenden Verbraucherschutz vorzusehen. So lautet z.B. Art. 8 der Haustürgeschäfte-Richtlinie: ‚Die vorliegende Richtlinie hindert die Mitgliedstaaten nicht daran, noch günstigere Verbraucherschutzbestimmungen auf dem Gebiet dieser Richtlinie zu erlassen oder beizubehalten.' Auch bei den zivilrechtlichen Richtlinien, die nicht dem Verbraucherschutz zuzuordnen sind, findet man dieses Günstigkeitsprinzip. Es scheint dem Europäischen Gesetzgeber gewissermaßen in Fleisch und Blut übergegangen zu sein, dass seine Aufgabe nur darin bestehe, ein Mindestschutzniveau zu gewähren. So heißt es auch in Art. 6 Abs. 2 der Zahlungsverzugs-Richtlinie: ‚Die Mitgliedstaaten können Vorschriften beibehalten oder erlassen, die für den Gläubiger günstiger sind als die zur Erfüllung dieser Richtlinie erforderlichen Maßnahmen.'. Ich muss bekennen, dass mir diese Regelungsmethode immer problematisch erschien, die freilich, wenn ich recht sehe, im allgemeinen widerspruchslos hingenommen wird. Sie erscheint mir schon deshalb sehr fragwürdig, weil das angebliche Ziel der Richtlinien, die Rechtsordnungen der Mitgliedstaaten im Interesse des Binnenmarktes zu harmonisieren, auf diese Weise zu einem guten Teil wieder aufgegeben wird. In meinen Augen soll der Vorteil einer Rechtsangleichung nicht zuletzt darin bestehen, dass die am Markt handelnden Personen von der europaweiten Geltung einheitlichen Rechts ausgehen können und sich daher, auf den vom Europäischen

Recht erfassten Gebieten, um das jeweilige nationale Recht und dessen Eigenheiten nicht mehr zu kümmern brauchen. Aber wenn das Europäische Recht nur jeweils den Mindestschutz (des Verbrauchers, des Gläubigers) festlegt, dann muss man eben doch im einzelnen prüfen, wie das Recht des Mitgliedstaates beschaffen ist, das im konkreten Fall anzuwenden ist. Wenn etwa ein Gläubiger wissen will, in welcher Höhe er von einem in Deutschland residierenden Kunden-Unternehmen im Verzugsfall Zinsen verlangen kann, dann teilt ihm die Verzugsrichtlinie mit, dass dies mindestens der sog. Bezugszinssatz plus 7 Prozentpunkte sind, aber erst der Blick in das deutsche BGB klärt ihn dann darüber auf, dass er nach § 288 Abs. 2 BGB – über das Europäische Schutzniveau hinausgehend – den Basiszinssatz plus acht Prozentpunkte beanspruchen darf.

Meine Bedenken gegen das europarechtliche Günstigkeitsprinzip gehen aber über diesen eher pragmatischen, auf die Komplizierung der Rechtsanwendung bezogenen Einwand hinaus. Zumindest will ich dies hier einmal zur Diskussion stellen. Wenngleich über die Grundsätze, die für die Auslegung von Rechtsnormen zu gelten haben, weiterhin diskutiert wird, ist doch weitgehend anerkannt, dass der teleologischen Auslegung eine herausragende, wohl sogar dominierende Bedeutung zuzumessen ist. Die Frage ist aber, ob eine teleologische Auslegung einer Norm überhaupt möglich ist, wenn diese nur ein Mindestschutzniveau vorschreibt. Teleologische Auslegung kann in aller Regel nicht bedeuten, nur den auf den Schutz eines bestimmten Interesses bezogenen Zweck einer Norm zu beachten, sondern sie muss selbstverständlich auch die gegenläufigen Interessen berücksichtigen, die der Verwirklichung des anderen Zweckes Grenzen setzen. Verbraucherschutz kann schließlich nicht *ad infinitum* gewährt werden, sondern muss so begrenzt werden, dass auch die Interessen des Unternehmers gewahrt werden. Wenn aber eine Richtlinie nur ein Mindestschutzniveau gewährt, dann verzichtet sie im Grunde völlig auf eine Abwägung mit gegenläufigen Interessen. Vielleicht ist das der tiefere Grund dafür, warum der EuGH aus der Richtlinie dann auch keinerlei Schranken entnimmt, die nicht ausdrücklich im Wortlaut enthalten sind, Würde man den Inhalt einer Richtlinie in der abschließenden Bewertung der gegenläufigen Interessen sehen, dann wäre es auch möglich, aus der Richtlinie heraus ungeschriebene Schranken des Widerrufsrechts zu entwickeln. Bei einem solchen

Ansatz hätte der EuGH beispielsweise sagen können, dass zwar die Richtlinie nichts darüber aussagt, wie lange das Widerrufsrecht ohne erteilte Belehrung ausgeübt werden kann, dass es aber dafür im Hinblick auf das Interesse des Vertragspartners auch zeitliche Grenzen geben muss und dass es dann eben dem nationalen Gesetzgeber gestattet sein muss, diese Grenzen zu konkretisieren.

Eine systematische und rechtsdogmatische Aufarbeitung des Europäischen Zivilrechts stößt somit sowohl auf der Ebene des nationalen Rechts wie auf der Ebene des Europäischen Rechts gegenwärtig auf größte, kaum zu überwindende Schwierigkeiten. In gewissem Umfang ist man sich dieser Probleme mittlerweile auch bewusst geworden. Die Bemühungen der Europäischen Kommission um die Erarbeitung eines ‚gemeinsamen Referenzrahmens', über die Herr Kollege *Lorenz* berichten wird, weisen in diese Richtung. Auf einzelnen Gebieten, etwa im Bereich der Unterlassungsklagen, hat sich auch schon der Europäische Normgeber mit einem gewissen Erfolg um eine zusammenfassende Regelung der in den verschiedenen Einzelrichtlinien vorgesehenen kollektiven Rechtsschutzinstrumente bemüht, und darin liegt durchaus ein Schritt zu einer auf Systematisierung und Abstrahierung bedachten Regelung.

2. Auf dem Weg zu einem Europäischen Zivilgesetzbuch

Man wird wohl für geraume Zeit mit dem geschilderten, in meinen Augen unbefriedigenden Zustand leben müssen. Abhilfe könnte eine Kodifizierung des Zivilrechts auf Europäischer Ebene bringen, die, wenn sie den Namen verdienen will, nur als ein systematisch durchdachtes Gesetzeswerk mit dogmatisch klaren Begriffen und eindeutigen Rechtsgrundsätzen vorstellbar erscheint.

Die Schaffung eines Europäischen Zivilgesetzbuchs als Konsequenz der politischen Einigung Europas hat natürlich etwas Faszinierendes an sich. Für den deutschen Betrachter drängt sich die Parallele zur Entwicklung im 19. Jahrhundert auf. Schon mit dem Wegfall der Zollschranken zwischen den einzelnen Staaten auf dem Gebiet des späteren Deutschen Reiches entstand ein starker Ansporn zur Schaffung einheitlichen Rechts, zunächst auf den wirtschaftsnahen Gebieten wie dem Wechselrecht, dem Handelsrecht und weiterreichend dem Obligationenrecht. Nach der Gründung des Deutschen Reiches schuf man, obgleich dies in der Bismarck'schen Verfassung so noch nicht vorgesehen war, alsbald eine umfassende Gesetzgebungskompetenz des Reichs auf dem Gebiet des Bürgerlichen Rechts und begriff die Schaffung eines einheitlichen Zivilrechts als eine nationale Aufgabe ersten Ranges. Innerhalb der Europäischen Union ist längst der Binnenmarkt verwirklicht und den Grundfreiheiten der Gründungsverträge umfassende Geltung verschafft worden. Es ist kein Wunder, dass damit auch die Forderung nach der Harmonisierung des Rechts der Einzelstaaten immer mehr Unterstützung gewann. Freilich ist die politische Einigung bislang nicht bis zur Gründung eines Bundesstaates Europa weitergeführt worden – die h.M. billigt dem Europäischen Staatenverbund trotz aller Verlagerung von Hoheitsrechten durch die Mitgliedstaaten auf die Europäische Gemeinschaft bislang keine eigene Staatsqualität zu. Auch sind die retardierenden Kräfte aufgrund der Verankerung der jeweils eigenen Kodifikationen in der Rechtstradition und dem Rechtsbewusstsein der einzelnen Nationalstaaten gewiss stärker als dies bei der Gründung des deutschen Reiches im Hinblick auf Gesetzbücher der Länder der Fall gewesen war. Trotzdem dürfte der Trend zu einer Vereinheitlichung des Bürgerlichen Rechts auf die Dauer nicht aufzuhalten sein. Durch das zumindest vorläufige Scheitern der angestrebten Europäischen Verfassung hat zwar das Streben nach politischer Vertiefung einen herben Rückschlag erfahren. Aber die Europäische Union und die Europäische Gemeinschaft sind längst über die Schaffung eines freien Wirtschaftsraums hinausgewachsen und haben wesentliche weitere Felder der Politik besetzt, auch und gerade auf den für das Zivilrecht in Betracht kommenden Gebieten. Dass diese Entwicklung etwa umkehrbar wäre – zurück zu einer bloßen Europäischen Wirtschaftsgemeinschaft – kann sich kaum jemand vorstellen.

Die bereits vorhandenen Ansätze zur Schaffung eines einheitlichen Europäischen Zivilrechts, das diesen Namen wirklich verdient, wird Herr Kollege *Lorenz* im einzelnen schildern. Im Vordergrund steht die Schaffung eines Europäischen Vertragsrechts oder Obligationenrechts. Die traditionellen zivilrechtlichen Kodifikationen wie das BGB bestehen freilich nicht nur aus den in erster Linie am Markt orientierten Rechtsgebieten des Schuldrechts und des Sachenrechts, sondern weisen auch dem Familienrecht und dem Erbrecht einen gleichberechtigten Stellenwert zu. Auf diesen Gebieten sind die Bestrebungen zu einer europäischen Harmonisierung bislang wesentlich schwächer ausgeprägt. Oft wird darauf hingewiesen, die starke Verankerung des Familienrechts und des Erbrechts in der Tradition, der Kultur und dem Rechtsbewusstsein der Einzelstaaten stehe einer Europäisierung entgegen. Persönlich bin ich davon nicht so recht überzeugt. Auch das Familienrecht und das Erbrecht der einzelnen Staaten weisen in vielen Punkten Übereinstimmungen auf, und erst recht sind die grundlegenden Wertungen einheitlicher Europäischer Standard. Auch wenn die Charta der Europäischen Grundrechte bislang keine normative Geltung erlangt hat, gilt doch der Sache nach seit langem eine Europäische Grundrechtsordnung, die aus den Europäischen Verträgen, der Europäischen Menschenrechtskonvention und den Grundrechtskatalogen der Verfassungen der einzelnen Staaten wie etwa dem deutschen Grundgesetz gespeist wird. Gleichheit von Mann und Frau, Gleichstellung von innerhalb und außerhalb einer Ehe geborenen Kindern, Eheschließungsfreiheit, Schutz von Ehe und Familie, aber auch etwa die Garantie des Erbrechts und der Testierfreiheit sind damit längst europäisches Allgemeingut. Von tiefen Gräben, die bei einer Harmonisierung nicht überbrückt werden könnten, dürfte daher auch auf den Gebieten des Familienrechts und des Erbrechts nicht die Rede sein. Aber natürlich handelt es sich dabei um prinzipiell marktferne Gebiete, und darin liegt die simple Erklärung dafür, warum der europäische Gesetzgeber sich bisher auf diesen Sektoren nicht betätigt hat. Nach geltendem Recht dürfte es auch recht eindeutig an einer Kompetenz für den Erlass von Richtlinien oder Verordnungen auf diesen Rechtsgebieten fehlen.

Rascher als zu einer Harmonisierung des materiellen Familien- und Erbrechts wird es wohl zu einer Europäisierung des einschlägigen Kollisionsrechts, also des Internationalen Privatrechts kommen. In Gestalt des Art. 65 Buchstabe b) des EG-Vertrages gibt es dafür eine Kompetenznorm, auch wenn man über deren Reichweite im Einzelnen streiten kann. Die Vereinheitlichung des Internationalen Privatrechts sollte als erste Stufe der Harmonisierung alsbald in Angriff genommen werden, ist es doch ein äußerst misslicher Zustand, wenn etwa die Frage, ob in einem bestimmten Fall deutsches oder französisches Erbrecht anzuwenden ist, von einem französischen oder einem deutschen Gericht aufgrund des jeweils unterschiedlichen Internationalen Privatrechts entgegengesetzt beurteilt wird. Die Europäische Kommission hat hierzu in jüngster Zeit (2005) bereits ein sog. Grünbuch zum Erb- und Testamentsrecht[39] vorgelegt, das einen Fragenkatalog zur Vorbereitung einer einheitlichen Regelung des Kollisionsrechts auf dem Gebiet des Erbrechts darstellt.

Auf dem Gebiet des Vertragsrechts bzw. des Obligationenrechts, dem ich mich nun wieder zuwenden möchte, bietet die Schaffung einheitlichen Europäischen Rechts natürlich die große Chance, den gegenwärtigen antisystematischen Zuschnitt des Europäischen Zivilrechts zu überwinden. Wenn sich allerdings die einheitlichen europäischen Regeln als bloßer Kompromiss zwischen den nationalen Rechten in dem Sinne darstellen, dass jeweils Formulierungen gewählt werden, die mit den Rechtssystemen und der Rechtsdogmatik aller nationalen Kodifikationen vereinbar sind, so gelangt man notgedrungen zu so unbestimmten Wendungen, dass von der Schaffung einer europäischen Rechtssystematik und Rechtsdogmatik, die an die Stelle der herkömmlichen nationalen Rechtslehren treten könnte, nicht die Rede sein kann. Wenn die nationalen Rechtsordnungen tiefgreifende rechtsdogmatische Unterschiede aufweisen, wird man bei einer Harmonisierung, die den Namen verdient, auch Entscheidungen für oder gegen die eine oder andere Lösung treffen müssen. Ob also die Unterscheidung zwischen schuldrechtlichem und sachenrechtlichem Geschäft und die Unabhängigkeit der Wirksamkeit des einen von der des anderen Geschäfts – das berühmte deutsche Abstraktionsprinzip – eines Tages in ein europäisches Schuld- und Sachenrecht Eingang findet, wird man entscheiden müssen. Eine europäische Vereinheitlichung des Vertrags- oder Obligationenrechts sollte außerdem darauf bedacht sein, das Verbraucherschutzrecht von vornherein in Form allgemeiner Regeln zu integrieren, soweit dies nur möglich ist. Sonst läuft man Gefahr, einen Kodex zu entwickeln, der sich in Widerspruch zur Rechtswirklichkeit setzt, in dem er so tut als gebe es zwischen allen Vertragsparteien eine gleichberechtigte Gestaltungs-

39 Auszugsweise wiedergegeben in *ZEV* 2005, 138; dazu H. Dörner, ‚Das Grünbuch Erb- und Testamentsrecht der Europäischen Kommission‘ *ZEV* 2005, 137–138, 137; s. auch H. Dörner u.a., ‚Auf dem Weg zu einem europäischen Internationalen Erb- und Erbverfahrensrecht‘ *IPRax* 2005, 1–8, 1; M. Voltz, ‚Mitteilung: Internationales Erbrecht in der EU – Perspektiven einer Harmonisierung – Symposium des Deutschen Notarinstituts in Brüssel‘ *IPRax* 2005, 64–66, 64.

freiheit und als sei die von Anfang an eintretende Bindung an den geschlossenen Vertrag weiterhin der Normalfall. Es fällt auf, dass etwa in den Vorschlägen der sog. Lando-Kommission die Begriffe Verbraucher und Unternehmer nicht vorkommen und die Widerrufs- oder Rücktrittsrechte des Verbrauchers keine Erwähnung finden.

Ob sich bestimmte dogmatische Strukturen des BGB wie eben das Abstraktionsprinzip (das entgegen häufig geäußerter Kritik durchaus seine Vorzüge besitzt[40]), die in anderen Zivilrechtsordnungen so nicht zu finden sind, durchsetzen werden, wird nicht nur vom inneren Wert der Lösungsmodelle, sondern auch vom politischen Kräfteverhältnis abhängen. Insoweit dürften im Zweifel die Chancen für das deutsche BGB nicht allzu gut stehen. Die deutschen Regierungen haben sich innerhalb des geeinigten Europas stets um Zurückhaltung im machtpolitischen Auftreten bemüht, um nur ja nicht den Eindruck einer Vorherrschaft gegenüber den anderen, insbesondere den kleineren europäischen Staaten aufkommen zu lassen. Viele bemängeln, dass der deutsche Einfluss auf die Einzelheiten der europäischen Normsetzung gering sei. Daher ist auch kaum zu erwarten, dass man sich im Konfliktfall für die Dogmatik des deutschen BGB besonders stark machen wird. Aber vielleicht ist mein Blick in die Zukunft hier zu pessimistisch!

Anhang – Europäische Richtlinien auf dem Gebiet des Zivilrechts

1) RL 85/374 EWG (Produkthaftung): Richtlinie des Rates vom 25. Juli 1985 zur Angleichung der Rechts- und Verwaltungsvorschriften der Mitgliedstaaten über die Haftung für fehlerhafte Produkte (ABl.EG 1985, L 210/29; geändert ABl.EG 1999, L 201/20).

40 Ausführlich hierzu A. Stadler, *Gestaltungsfreiheit und Verkehrsschutz durch Abstraktion – Eine rechtsvergleichende Studie zur abstrakten und kausalen Gestaltung rechtsgeschäftlicher Zuwendungen anhand des deutschen, schweizerischen, österreichischen, französischen und US-amerikanischen Rechts* (Tübingen 1996). Stadler äußert sich differenzierend zu den Chancen des Abstraktionsprinzips im europäischen Einigungsprozess und warnt davor, ‚sozusagen in vorauseilendem europäischen Gehorsam den Abstraktionsgrundsatz der Rechtsvereinheitlichung oder -angleichung zu opfern' (a.a.O. S. 742).

2) RL 85/577/EWG (Verträge außerhalb von Geschäftsräumen): Richtlinie des Rates vom 20. Dezember 1985 betreffend den Verbraucherschutz im Falle von außerhalb von Geschäftsräumen geschlossenen Verträgen (ABl.EG 1985, L 372/31).

3) RL 87/102/EWG (Verbraucherkredit): Richtlinie des Rates vom 22. Dezember 1986 zur Angleichung der Rechts- und Verwaltungsvorschriften der Mitgliedsstaaten über den Verbraucherkredit (ABl. EG 1987, L 42/48); geändert durch Richtlinie 90/88/EWG (ABl.EG 1990, L 61/14); geändert durch Richtlinie 98/7/EG (ABl.EG 1998, L 101/17).

4) RL 90/314/EWG (Pauschalreisen): Richtlinie des Rates vom 13. Juni 1990 über Pauschalreisen (ABl.EG 1990, L 158/59).

5) RL 93/13/EWG (Vertragsklauseln): Richtlinie des Rates vom 5. April 1993 über missbräuchliche Klauseln in Verbraucherverträgen (ABl.EG 1993, L 95/29).

6) RL 94/47/EG (Teilzeitwohnrechte): Richtlinie des Europäischen Parlaments und des Rates vom 26. Oktober 1994 zum Schutz der Erwerber im Hinblick auf bestimmte Aspekte von Verträgen über den Erwerb von Teilnutzungsrechten an Immobilien (ABl.EG 1994, L 280/83).

7) RL 97/5/EG (Überweisungen): Richtlinie des Europäischen Parlaments und des Rates vom 27. Januar 1997 über grenzüberschreitende Überweisungen (ABl.EG 1997, L 43/25).

8) RL 97/7/EG (Fernabsatz): Richtlinie des Europäischen Parlaments und des Rates vom 20. Mai 1997 über den Verbraucherschutz bei Vertragsabschlüssen im Fernabsatz (ABl.EG 1997, L 144/19); geändert durch RL 2002/65/EG (ABl.EG 2002, L 271/16).

9) RL 98/27/EG (Verbraucher-Unterlassungsklagen): Richtlinie des Europäischen Parlaments und des Rates vom 19. Mai 1998 über Unterlassungsklagen zum Schutz der Verbraucherinteressen (ABl.EG 1998, L 166/51).

10) RL 1999/44/EG (Kaufmängelgewährleistung): Richtlinie des Europäischen Parlaments und des Rates vom 25. Mai 1999 zu bestimmten Aspekten des Verbrauchsgüterkaufs und der Garantien für Verbrauchsgüter (ABl.EG 1999, L 171/12).

11) RL 2000/31/EG (elektronischer Geschäftsverkehr): Richtlinie des Europäischen Parlaments und des Rates vom 8. Juni 2000 über bestimmte rechtliche Aspekte der Dienste der Informationsgesellschaft, insbesondere des elektronischen Geschäftsverkehrs, im Binnenmarkt („Richtlinie über den elektronischen Geschäftsverkehr") (ABl.EG 2000, L 178/1).

12) RL 2000/35/EG (Zahlungsverzug): Richtlinie des Europäischen Parlaments und des Rates vom 29. Juni 2000 zur Bekämpfung von Zahlungsverzug im Geschäftsverkehr (ABl.EG 2000, L 200/35).

13) RL 2000/43/EG (Anti-Rassismus): Richtlinie des Europäischen Rates vom 29. Juni 2000 zur Anwendung des Gleichbehandlungsgrundsatzes ohne Unterschied der Rasse oder der ethnischen Herkunft (ABl.EG 2000, L 180/22).

14) RL 2000/78/EG (Berufs-Antidiskriminierung): Richtlinie des Rates vom 27. November 2000 zur Festlegung eines allgemeine Rahmens für die Verwirklichung der Gleichbehandlung in Beschäftigung und Beruf (ABl.EG 2000, L 303/16).

15) RL 2002/65/EG (Fernabsatz-Finanzdienstleistungen): Richtlinie des Europäischen Parlaments und des Rates vom 23. September 2002 über den Fernabsatz von Finanzdienstleistungen an Verbraucher und zu Änderung der Richtlinien 90/619/EWG des Rates und der Richtlinien 97/7/EG und 28/27/EG (ABl.EG 2002, L 271/16).

16) RL 2002/73/EG (Berufs-Gleichberechtigung): Richtlinie des Europäischen Parlaments und des Rates vom 23. September 2002 zur Abänderung der Richtlinie 76/207/EWG des Rates zur Verwirklichung des Grundsatzes der Gleichbehandlung von Männern und Frauen hinsichtlich des Zugangs zur Beschäftigung, zur Berufsbildung und zum beruflichen Aufstieg sowie in Bezug auf die Arbeitsbedingungen (ABl.EG 2002, L 269/15).

17) RL 2004/113/EG (Güter- und Dienstleistungs-Gleichberechtigungs-Richtlinie): Richtlinie des Europäischen Rates vom 13. Dezember 2004 zur Verwirklichung des Grundsatzes der Gleichbehandlung von Männern und Frauen beim Zugang zu und bei der Versorgung mit Gütern und Dienstleistungen (ABl.EG 2004, L 337/37).

English Summary

Karl Riesenhuber

Dieter Leipold sketches the scope of EC private law and analyses its interaction with German civil law (I). EC private law is the sum of rules enacted by the EC in the area of private law (II 1 a)). *Leipold* notes, that the harmonisation approach chosen by the Community has until today been merely punctual rather than systematic (II 1 b)). He criticises that the various directives, rather than addressing systematic categories such as the formation of contracts, address individual factual problems such as doorstep-selling. More than that, the directives do not seem to be based on a coherent harmonisation plan and the rules of the various directives often appear to be inconsistent as well. But EC private law, *Leipold* argues, is not only unsystematic in itself. It also tends to have a disruptive effect on the national systems of private law (II 1 d)).

The report continues to discuss the influence of EC private law on German civil law in the context of individual issues (II 2). The first example is that of 'trash-property' (*Schrottimmobilien*) (II 2 a)). The factual background of such cases is that individuals, induced by tax-legislation, had bought houses in order to make use of tax deductions. When the property later turned out to be of substantially lower value than originally assumed, the buyers, searching for ways to get out of the contract as well as the credit agreement concluded to finance it, argued a right of withdrawal based on doorstep-selling. Such case ultimately triggered the *Heininger*-decision of the European Court of Justice (ECJ) which established the relation of the Doorstep-Selling Directive and the Consumer-Credit Directive. *Leipold* criticises the decision on various levels: the Court's reasoning was a decree more than a discussion; the methods of interpretation appeared rather crude, focussing on the wording and giving less weight to teleological aspects. Returning to the interplay of EC law and national law, *Leipold* points out that the *Heininger*-judgement practically overturned the established German jurisprudence. He indicates that the use for the individual consumers was, however, rather questionable, not only in regard of the practical result of the litigation but also with a view to the lengthy proceedings.

In a second example, *Leipold* discusses the effect of EC consumer protection on national legislation in the area of civil law (II 2b)). While consumer protection had long been implemented into German law by way of special legislation, statutes were integrated into the Civil Code (*Bürgerliches Gesetzbuch, BGB*) in the course of the 'Modernisation' of the law of obligations (*Schuldrechtsmodernisierung*). *Leipold* acknowledges that the integration of consumer protection – in particular rights of withdrawal and the control of unfair terms – into the BGB has in many respects led to a systematisation and a higher degree of coherence. Yet, he criticises that such protective regulation will hardly achieve a level of abstraction so as to be open to systematic legislation and scholarly discussion. He further points out that differences in the regulative approach and aims remain in regard of the control of standard terms. As a consequence, the rules still appear to be somewhat disparate and incoherent.

Beyond specific examples, *Leipold* continues to address anti-discrimination legislation as a fundamental issue in contemporary legal discussion in Germany (II 3). The implementation of the EC directives had turned out to be rather difficult and cumbersome. *Leipold* argues that this is to some extent due to the incompatibility of anti-discrimination laws with the fundamental principle of private autonomy. He therefore criticises the approach of the German legislator to enact a comprehensive anti-discrimination law, going beyond the demands of EC legislation.

Leipold concludes with some observations on the future of systematic legal thought in Europe (III). He reaffirms that EC legislation has a disruptive effect on the German system of private law (III 1). In addition to the punctual approach, *Leipold* criticises the policy of allowing the Member States to maintain or enact more favourable rules. This not only disproves the legislative goal of *harmonising* the national laws. It also leads to methodological difficulties as it makes a purposive interpretation inherently difficult. Would a different harmonisation concept avoid such problems (III 2)? Certainly, a European civil code could ensure systematic coherence. Such codification is, however, a long-term project. For the near future, *Leipold* considers harmonisation of the conflict of laws preferable to harmonisation of substantive law. Harmonisation of private law in Europe, faced with a necessity to compromise, cannot ensure that the best concepts will survive. It is doubtful whether various characteristic aspects of the German BGB such as the principle of abstraction will survive in a unification process, irrespective of their merit, *Leipold* argues.

Karl Riesenhuber

Chapter 7: The Present and Future Role of the German Civil Law in Europe

Stephan Lorenz

Contents

I. Preliminary observations

1. European sources of law

The term 'European Private Law' is in certain respects ambiguous. In fact it does not have a well-defined meaning at all. The current debate focuses mainly on sector specific harmonisation measures, primarily on Community directives. These legislative instruments are limited in scope due to the restricted nature of the underlying legal powers. The very fact that the European Institutions prefer directives in the sense of Art 249 (3) EC-Treaty as legislative instruments thus illustrates that we are not dealing here with a complete and coherent set of rules of European Private Law. It will be recalled that the EC does not yet have a comprehensive legal competence to pass private law legislation.

The more limited interventions by means of directives are however doubtless of great practical importance for the law of obligations. The characteristic feature of directives is that they do not have – generally speaking – direct effect, i.e. they cannot be applied in proceedings exclusively between private parties. To have direct effect they require transposition into national law. Accordingly, directives are addressed to the Member States and leave them the choice as to form and method of achieving the end established by the directive. This enables the Member State to preserve to a great extent the traditional features of the national legal system. Directives have nevertheless often caused irritation in the legal systems of the Member States, at least if viewed from the national perspective. The proper, seamless transposition of such directives poses a considerable challenge for the national legislator.

In any event, this very important aspect of Community Law cannot properly be called 'European Private Law'. These are limited legislative interventions with limited impact on the national legal system which according to their very nature will not lead to the emergence of a *European Ius Commune*. The convergence is further diluted by the fact that directives merely prompt the *national* legal system to absorb certain European policy aims. These interventions are in the ultimate analysis rather a source of disruption for the national legal system than a building block for an authentic European Private Law.

A typical example for these difficulties are the efforts to transpose the Antidiscrimination Directives, which hitherto have not been successful and which once more raise the question of whether so-called 'secondary Community legislation' is compatible with the German Constitution. Germany is, however, not the only country in which these negative effects on the coherence of the national private order are regretted.

These introductory comments suffice to show that presently it is not possible to speak of a European Private Law. What has been so far labelled 'European Private Law' is a random collection of directives, which by their very nature do not add up to a coherent whole. One only needs to open one of the books entitled 'European Private Law' to see the truth of this contention: these books contain no more than a more or less systematic annotation of the different EC-directives and their detailed provisions. The rules emanating from these sources are a source of constant irritation for the national legal systems. Professor *Leipold* already alluded to the various further difficulties, such as the requirement to interpret national law in the light of the directive and the spill-over effects of directives into neighbouring areas of the law, in his presentation.

To sum up, the influence of European law in this field is limited and it is limited because the legal powers, the internal Community competence, in these areas is limited.

2. The influence of primary Community legislation

In addition to the limited harmonisation by means of secondary Community legislation one should also mention the impact of the various economic freedoms granted under the EC-Treaty such as free movement of goods, of capital, of workers and freedom of establishment and to provide services, on national private law. These cornerstones of the free internal market are as part of the 'primary' Community law of direct application in the Member States. In particular the requirement of free movement of goods and the freedom of establishment have a considerable influence on national law, especially commercial and company law. However, in this respect also it is the European source of law which affects certain aspects of the national legal system. This removal of obstacles to trade on the national level does not establish a common Private Law on a transnational, European level.

3. European private law – the law of obligations

A uniform and coherent European Private Law does not exist at present though it may be on the horizon. The lack of legal competence of the Community to pass comprehensive private law legislation is of course not necessarily a permanent obstacle to harmonisation. The Member States may change the Treaty and introduce a legal basis for such legislation. Art. 23 of the German Constitution (the 'Basic Law') allows such a transfer of legal power to the Community to take place. Neither the European Commission nor the scientific community however have suspended their efforts in inquiring into the real possibility of a European Private Law until such a legal basis is actually created. These efforts concentrate at present on the law of obligations, dealing with both contractual and extra-contractual obligations. The harmonisation of family law as well as the law of succession is currently not on the agenda. The following remarks will therefore focus on the law of obligations.

II. European rules of conflict of laws

Before I present an overview over the current state of affairs regarding the harmonisation of substantive private law let me first highlight the importance of private international law or conflict of laws rules. This is an aspect which – unfortunately – is often neglected. I suspect this is because we are dealing here with an area of the law only a few specialists are familiar with. Here, however, the Community does have a legal power to implement European legislation. Art. 65 of the EC-Treaty, which was introduced by the Amsterdam Treaty, provides for Community measures aimed at harmonising international private law and to a certain extent also civil procedure.[1] The aim is thus not

1 Namely improving and simplifying the system for cross-border service of judicial and extrajudicial documents; cooperation in the taking of evidence; the

to increase the convergence of substantive law but to establish uniform rules of jurisdiction, the recognition and enforcement of decisions in civil and commercial cases within Europe, and to establish a shared set of rules as to the applicable law in cases with a foreign element. The importance of this task for the economy in a common market is obvious. Such rules ensure at the level of conflict of laws that it is always the same legal order that governs a concrete case regardless where, i.e. in which Member State, the proceedings were commenced. In other words these rules are meant to reduce the frequency of 'forum shopping' that allows parties to manipulate the outcome of a litigation by bringing the case before a particular court. A system of clear rules of jurisdiction and extensive rules of recognition of foreign decisions further increase this beneficial effect. It is obvious that it will be much easier to reach agreement on these aspects of private law, namely concerning the rules of conflict of laws and jurisdiction, than on the substance of a uniform Private Law Code. Moreover the rules of conflict of laws diverge much less than the provisions of substantive private law. International Private Lawyers have as far as the general part of this area of the law is concerned for a long time now spoken 'the same language'. The EU has not hesitated after the adoption of the specific competence in the EC-Treaty to pursue this agenda vigorously.[2] The first measures were passed in the field of jurisdiction and recognition of decisions in civil and commercial cases. Thus, Council Regulation (EC) No 1347/2000 of 29 May 2000 which came into force on 1 March 2001 regulates the jurisdiction and the recognition and enforcement of judgments in matrimonial matters and in matters of parental responsibility for children of both spouses.[3] There followed Council Regulation (EC)

recognition and enforcement of decisions in civil and commercial cases, including decisions in extrajudicial cases; promoting the compatibility of the rules applicable in the Member States concerning jurisdiction; eliminating obstacles to the good functioning of civil proceedings, if necessary by promoting the compatibility of the rules on civil procedure applicable in the Member States.

2 S. Action plan of the Council and the Commission on how best to implement the provisions of the Treaty of Amsterdam on an area of freedom, security and justice – Text adopted by the Justice and Home Affairs Council of 3 December 1998, OJ 1999 C 19/01.

3 Council Regulation (EC) No 1347/2000 of 29 May 2000 on jurisdiction and the recognition and enforcement of judgments in matrimonial matters and in matters of parental responsibility for children of both spouses, OJ 2000 L 160/19.

No 44/2001 of 22 December 2000 which came into force on 1 March 2001 and which governs questions of jurisdiction and the recognition and enforcement of judgments in civil and commercial matters.[4] This Regulation replaced the Brussels Convention on jurisdiction and the enforcement of judgments in civil and commercial matters of 27 September 1968.[5] The Convention served as a model for the legislative measures of the Community. It is customary to speak of the 'Brussels' conventions in this context. There is a parallel development taking place in relation to private international law. In relation to the law applicable to contractual obligations the Member States ratified the important Convention on the law applicable to contractual obligations ('Rome Convention' of 19 June 1980).[6] The Commission intends to replace the international treaty by a Community Regulation. The legislative procedures are well advanced and on 15 December 2005 the Commission published a Draft Regulation on the law applicable to contractual obligations called 'Rome I' Regulation.[7] On 22 July 2003 the Commission had already presented a proposal for a Regulation on the law applicable to non-contractual obligations (called 'Rome II' Regulation).[8] There exist further so-called 'Green Papers' prepared by the Commission on succession and wills, on the applicable law in divorce proceedings and on maintenance.[9]

It is significant that the Community regularly resorts in this area of the law to the legislative instrument of regulations instead of directives. Regulations, as explained, do not need any further action at

4 Council Regulation (EC) No 44/2001 of 22 December 2000 on jurisdiction and the recognition and enforcement of judgments in civil and commercial matters, OJ 2001 L 12/1.

5 Convention on jurisdiction and the enforcement of judgements in civil and commercial matters (Consolidated version) – 1968 Brussels Convention, OJ 1990 C 189/2.

6 1980 Rome Convention on the law applicable to contractual obligations (consolidated version), OJ 1998 C 27/34.

7 Proposal for a Regulation of the European Parliament and the Council on the law applicable to contractual obligations (Rome I), COM(2005) 650 final.

8 Proposal for a Regulation of the European Parliament and the Council on the law applicable to non-contractual obligations (Rome II), COM(2003) 427 final.

9 Green Paper, Succession and wills, COM(2005) 65 final; Green Paper on applicable law and jurisdiction in divorce matters, COM(2005) 82 final; Green Paper – Maintenance Obligations, COM(2004) 254 final.

national level to have direct effect. As a result the European conflict of laws rules converge to a much higher extent than the rules of substantive private law. Harmonisation progresses faster in this field not only in terms of the legislative process but also as far as the scope of the measures is concerned. For the already existing and the envisaged legislation concerns in addition to the law of obligations the law of wills and family law. This is noteworthy since the substantive law in these fields is not and will not be in the near future at any rate subject to scrutiny with a view to harmonisation.

If there is a lesson to be learnt from this dynamic development it is that the harmonisation of private international law is a stepping stone for the harmonisation of substantive law and should initially be preferred to a somewhat hasty unification of substantive law: Convergence of conflict of laws rules ensures just as much as the harmonisation of substantive law the predictability of outcomes of court decisions. Yet, it leaves the identity of the national legal system intact.

III. Initiatives for the creation a European Contract Law and Law of Obligations

1. Research projects

a) The UNIDROIT-Principles

One of the first initiatives for the creation of a transnational contract law was the research undertaken by the International Institute for the Unification of Private Law (UNIDROIT). After a period of almost 15 years of consultations the Institute published the so-called 'Principles of International Commercial Contracts' (or in short UNIDROIT-Principles, PICC) in 1994 and a revised version in 2004.[10] Their approach can be likened to the Restatements of Law edited by the American Law Institute. They contain a summary and a coherent reproduction of the basic principles of international contract law. The UNIDROIT-Principles do not have any binding effect; they are

10 S. UNIDROIT Principles of International Commercial Contracts 2004 at www.unidroit.org/english/principles/contracts/principles2004/blackletter2004.pdf.

so-called 'soft law'. However they are a reliable indicator of the *lex mercatoria* and as such may be a useful guideline in arbitration proceedings.

b) The Commission on European Contract Law

The Commission on European Contract Law who pursued a parallel agenda similarly produced a set of principles of contract law. The Commission is also known under the name of its chairmen as the 'Lando-Commission'.[11] It consists of a group of acknowledged academics drawn from all Member States who since 1982 have undertaken comparative research into the possibility of formulating common principles of contract law. They were aided financially by the European Commission. The Lando-Commission publishes since the year 1995 the so-called Principles of European Contract Law (PECL). As with the UNIDROIT Principles these Principles are non-binding 'soft law' only. Their main objective is to become part of or at least influence the drafting of a contract law part of a future European Civil Code. In preparing the final draft the Commission took account of the various national systems of contract law as well as the United Nations Convention on Contracts for the International Sale of Goods of 1980 (CISG) and the American Restatement on the Law of Contracts. The aim was to identify the best solution to the problem at hand. The PECL were prepared in three stages. The first Commission worked from 1982 until 1990 and published its report in 1995, the Principles of European Contract Law Part I. The second Commission took over in 1992 and held meetings until 1996 which resulted in the publication of PECL Parts I and II in 1999. These covered the conclusion of the contract, its interpretation and the content of the contract, and the law of irregularities of performance, i.e. liability for breach of contract. The third and final Commission was active between 1997 and 2001. Its results were published as PECL Part III in 2003. This final part concerns rules as to plurality of parties, assignment of claims, the transfer of a contract, set-off, and prescription. The work of the Commission has now with the publication of Part III come to an end. Its work will be continued (in part) by the *Study*

[11] Commission on European Contract Law at http://frontpage.cbs.dk/law/commission_on_european_contract_law/index.html.

Group on a European Civil Code within a new institutional framework.

c) The Study Group on a European Civil Code

The so-called 'Study Group on a European Civil Code'[12] continues the research of the Lando-Commission on a broader basis with a similar method, namely scholarly comparative law research. The Group is composed of 'Working Teams' consisting of experts drawn from the different Member States. They operate with responsibility for research and proposals within the particular fields of private law assigned to them (and which are comparable in style to the PECL). The aim of the draft proposals is not merely to give an account of the various approaches to a specific problem in the MS but to choose the best solution among them. A so-called 'Coordinating Group' is charged with reviewing the content of submissions made by the Working Teams. The Coordinating Group consists of almost fifty professors from nearly all EU Member States and meets biannually. This Group will eventually decide on the shape and content of the principles that are published. Their primary purpose is to serve as possible drafts of a future European Civil Code.

There are presently eight Working Teams:[13] The Dutch Working Team (which consists of various smaller groups) concentrates on sales, services and long-term contracts[14] and published among other documents 'Principles of European Sales Law' in December 2004.[15] Another Working Team works on insurance contracts and its coordinating office is located in Austria, namely the 'Project Group on a Restatement of European Insurance Contract Law'. There is also a Working Team on Trust and a Working Team on Extra-Contractual Obligations (the so-called 'von Bar Group'). This Group has published draft articles in all fields assigned to it, namely tort law, *negotiorum gestio*, and unjustified enrichment.[16] The Working Team on

[12] Study Group on a European Civil Code at: www.sgecc.net.
[13] S. for details www.sgecc.net/index.php?subsite=subsite_3&id=4.
[14] S. www.sgecc.net/index.php?subsite=subsite_3&id=18.
[15] Principles of European Law: Sales, at: http://www.sgecc.net/pages/downloads/sales04_12.pdf.
[16] Principles of European Law on Benevolent Intervention in Another's Affairs – Negotiorum Gestio, at www.sgecc.net/media/download/goanr7vd3_artikel.pdf;

Credit Securities published a first version of draft articles on personal and proprietary securities.[17] There are further Working Teams on Financial Services, E-commerce, Transfer of Moveable Property,[18] and on Rental of Movable Property.[19]

d) European Group on Tort Law (Tilburg Group)

The European Group on Tort Law, the 'Tilburg Group' was founded in 1993. Its members are experts on tort law from the various EU Member States.[20] The Group published its Principles of European Tort Law in February 2005.[21] As far their aim is concerned they can be likened to the Lando-Principles and in relation to their purpose and structure they are similar to the Principles prepared by the 'Study Group'.

e) Academy of European Private Lawyers (Gandolfi Group)

The Academy of European Private Lawyers was founded in 1992 by Professor *Guiseppe Gandolfi* in Pavia. *Alberto Trabucchi, André Tunc*, and *José Luis de los Mozos* acted as presidents. The Group published after ten years of intensive research coordinated by Professor *Gandolfi* in 2001 a first draft for the first part of a future European Civil Code (Code Européen Des Contrats, Avant-projet, Livre Premier). The purpose of the proposal is to serve as a basis for the drafting of a general part of a possible European Contract Law. Unlike the Principles published by the Lando-Commission, Study Group on a European Civil Code or the Tilburg Group this proposal is not merely meant as a preparatory step for the adoption of a future

Principles of European Unjustified Enrichment Law, at http://www.sgecc.net/media/download/unjustified_enrichment.pdf, Principles of European Tort Law, at http://www.sgecc.net/media/download/tort_law.pdf.

17 The Hamburg Working Team on Credit Securities, at www.sgecc.net/index.php?subsite=subsite_3&id=20.

18 The Salzburg Working Team on Transfer of Movable Property, at www.sgecc.net/index.php?subsite=subsite 3&id=31.

19 The Working Team on Rental of Movable Property, at www.sgecc.net/index.php?subsite=subsite_3&id=71.

20 European Group on Tort Law, at http://civil.udg.es/tort/.

21 Principles of European Tort Law, at www.egtl.org/Principles/index.htm.

Code but as a first formulation of the very provisions of that future Code.

f) European Research Group on Existing EC Private Law (Acquis Group)

The so-called 'Acquis Group'[22] was founded in 2002 as a reaction to activities of EU institutions in the field of European contract law (in particular the European Parliament resolution on the approximation of the civil and commercial law of the Member States of 15 November 2001, the conclusions of the Tampere European Council (15 and 16 October 1999), and in particular the Commission communication to the Council and the European Parliament on European Contract Law (COM(2001) 398)). The Group currently consists of more than 40 legal scholars from nearly all EU Member States. Its aim is to create a network of researchers from the Member States of the EU and to analyse the already existing EC contract law. The proposals of the Group are thus harvested from the existing Community law and directed at its further improvement and refinement. This sets them apart from the other research groups who seek to identify solutions independently from the present Acquis Communautaire and which are mainly derived from or inspired by the various national legal orders. Since May 2005 the Acquis Group is part of the Joint Network on European Private Law. By the end of 2008 this network aims to deliver a proposal for the so-called 'Common Frame of Reference' containing the 'Common Principles of European Contract Law'.

g) The Common Core of European Private Law Project (Trento Group)

The so-called Common Core Project was initiated in the mid-nineties.[23] Its origins go back to the comparative methodology of the Cornell project founded by the US-American *Rudolf Schlesinger* and continued and adapted by *Rudolfo Sacco*. The aim of the programme is to explore the common core of the European national private law

22 Acquis Group, European Research Group on Existing EC Private Law, at www.acquis-group.org/.

23 The Common Core of European Private Law, at www.jus.unitn.it/dsg/common-core/home.html.

systems. The Group consists of more than 100 researchers drawn from the Member States of the EU, as well as the USA, Israel, Switzerland, and South Africa. The project covers contract, tort, and property. Unlike the research undertaken by the Lando-Group the aim of the Trento-Project is not to aid the adoption of a unitary Civil Code but to analyse the existing body of private law in Europe. The long-term objective is to facilitate the emergence of a common legal culture in Europe. The method of analysis is inspired by *Rudolf Schlesinger*'s approach and consists of questionnaires prepared specifically for each topic and which contain short problem questions and well designed questions. The answer to the questionnaires ought to reveal the existing legal rules and their implications. This approach has been met with enthusiasm in particular in the U.S.

h) Commission on European Family Law

The Commission on European Family Law (CEFL) was founded on 1 September 2001 in Utrecht.[24] The main aim of the Family Law Commission is the 'launch of a pioneering theoretical and practical exercise in relation to the harmonisation of family law in Europe'. In order to achieve this purpose the Commission will survey the current state of comparative research on the harmonisation of family law in the European countries. On this basis the Commission hopes to find a common core of solutions of several legal problems on the basis of comparing the different solutions provided by the family laws of the various European jurisdictions. The Commission will also analyse the role of EU Member States in the process of the harmonisation of family law. The research is directed at the creation of a set of Principles of European Family Law that are thought to be most suitable for the harmonisation of family law within Europe.

2. The legislative activities at Community level

a) Resolutions of the European Parliament

Except for the Acquis Group the research initiatives were launched irrespectively of the activities at Community level. The first Commu-

24 Commission on European Family Law, at www.law.uu.nl/priv/cefl.

nity institution to promote a more extended approach to harmonisation of private law was the European Parliament. In 1989 and 1994 the European Parliament called for work to be started on the possibility of drawing up a common European Code of Private Law.[25] The Parliament stated that harmonisation of certain sectors of private law was essential to the completion of the internal market. The Parliament further stated that unification of major branches of private law in the form of a European Civil Code would be necessary in order to achieve a single market without frontiers. The Parliament also advocated further support for UNIDROIT and the Lando-Commission in particular. The Commission did not react to these initiatives first. However, the conclusions of the European Council held in Tampere requested, in paragraph 39, 'as regards substantive law an overall study on the need to approximate Member State's legislation in civil matters in order to eliminate obstacles to the good functioning of civil proceedings'.[26] In its resolution of 16 March 2000 concerning the Commission's work program 2000, thus the European Parliament stated in view of these developments 'that greater harmonisation of civil law has become essential in the internal market' and called on the Commission to draw up a study in this area.[27]

b) Communications of the Commission: Actionplan and Common Frame of Reference

(1) Commission Communication on European contract law of July 2001

In July 2001 the Commission published its first Communication on European contract law.[28] In this Communication the European Commission questioned for the first time the extent that the sector

[25] Resolution of the European Parliament on action to bring into line the private law of the Member States, OJ 1989 C 158/400; Resolution of the European Parliament on the harmonization of certain sectors of the private law of the Member States, OJ 1994 C 205/518.
[26] Presidency Conclusions, Tampere European Council 15 and 16 October 1999, SI (1999) 800.
[27] European Parliament resolution on the Commission's annual legislative programme for 2000, OJ 2000 C 377/323 (p. 326 at point 28).
[28] Communication from the Commission to the Council and the European Parliament on European Contract Law, COM (2001) 398 final, OJ 2001 C 255/1.

specific, case-by-case approach might not be able to solve all the problems which might arise in the internal market. At this stage of the discussion, however, the Commission was merely gathering information on the need for further-reaching EC action in the area of contract law. The Commission submitted four options for discussion:

- No EC action is needed since the effectiveness of the market in responding to different social values and to public opinion should not be underestimated. In many cases the market creates problems of public concern, but it also develops its own solutions.
- To promote the development of common contract law principles leading to more convergence of national laws. In order to achieve more convergence of national contract laws, one solution would be for the Commission to promote comparative law research and co-operation between academics and legal practitioners. This co-operation could aim to find common principles in relevant areas of national contract law. This was in fact the status quo at the time.
- To improve the quality of legislation already in place. This approach proceeded on the essentially sound assumption that it is better to adapt the substance of existing legal instruments where necessary before adopting new ones. For instance, the scope of application of various directives should be extended if necessary and if appropriate to those contracts or transactions which have many similar features with those covered by the directive but, for various reasons, were in not included in the scope of application of the directive at the moment of its adoption. This would ensure greater coherence within a well-defined sector of activities or type of transactions.
- To adopt new comprehensive legislation at EC level, comprising provisions on general questions of contract law as well as specific contracts. For this option, the choice of instrument and the binding nature of the measures needed to be discussed. This option would in principle replace existing national law, though a purely optional model could be set up which has to be chosen by the parties, i.e. which applies only when the parties agree that their contract was to be governed by it ('opt-in').

The Parliament welcomed the activities of the Commission in a Resolution of 15 October 2001.[29] However, it regretted the fact that the Commission restricted its communication to private contract law, although under the terms of the mandate of the European Council of Tampere it should have broadened its scope. It further proposed the adoption of an action plan and outlined in detail a possible time schedule for harmonisation.

(2) Action Plan for a more coherent contract law 2003

In February 2003 the Commission presented in a further Communication an 'Action Plan' for a more coherent contract law.[30] The Commission Communication on European contract law of July 2001 launched a process of consultation and discussion about the way in which problems resulting from divergences between national contract laws in the EU should be dealt with at the European level. The 2003 Action Plan presented the Commission's conclusions in this regard. In addition to appropriate sector-specific interventions the Commission suggested three types of additional measures. They included:

- To increase the coherence of the EC acquis in the area of contract law. This was to be achieved by adopting a so-called 'Common Frame of Reference (CFR)'. A common frame of reference, establishing common principles and terminology in the area of European contract law was seen by the Commission as an important step towards the improvement of the contract law acquis. This common frame of reference was described as a publicly accessible document which should help the Community institutions in ensuring greater coherence of existing and future acquis in the area of European contract law. The objectives of the CFR are threefold: First, the Commission intends to use it in the area of contract law when the existing acquis is reviewed and new measures proposed. It should provide for best solutions in terms of common termi-

[29] European Parliament resolution on the approximation of the civil and commercial law of the Member States, COM(2001) 398.

[30] Communication from the Commission to the European Parliament and the Council – A more coherent European contract law – An action plan, COM (2003) 68 final. All documents referred to can be obtained at http://europa.eu.int/comm/consumers/cons_int/safe_shop/fair_bus_pract/cont_law/index_en.htm.

nology and rules, i.e. the definition of fundamental concepts and abstract terms such as 'contract' or 'damage' and of the rules which apply, for example, in the case of the non-performance of contracts. In this context, the Commission emphasised, contractual freedom should be the guiding principle; restrictions should only be allowed where this could be justified with good reasons. The second objective is that it could become an instrument in achieving a higher degree of convergence between the contract laws of the EU Member States. Thirdly, the Commission indicated that it would base its reflections on whether non-sector-specific measures such as an optional instrument may be required to solve problems in the area of European contract law on the common frame of reference. The Commission stressed that the CFR was needed in order to ensure coherence and consistency of the existing and future acquis. This was a priority that needed to be tackled rapidly. Consolidation, codification and recasting of existing instruments, focussed on transparency and clarity, would have to be considered where appropriate.

- To promote the elaboration of EU-wide general contract terms, a project which has in the meantime been abandoned.
- To examine further whether problems in the European contract law area may require non-sector-specific solutions such as an optional instrument. As to its form the Commission suggested EU wide contract law rules in the form of a regulation or a recommendation, which would exist in parallel with, rather than instead of national contract laws. In any event, the content of the CFR was to serve as a basis for the development of the new optional instrument.

There were many reactions to the Action Plan[31] most of which welcomed that the Commission abandoned the idea of establishing a comprehensive Contract Law Code or even a European Civil Code. However, some expressed the concern that the Commission's hesitation was of merely tactical nature. There was thus some uncertainty as to the aims and objectives of the Commission. This was due to the

31 S. the references in S. Vogenauer & S. Weatherhill, 'Eine empirische Untersuchung zur Angleichung des Vertragsrechts in der EG' *JZ* 2005 870, 872.

fact that the Commission intended to continue the consultation process with the Action Plan rather than suggest final solutions.

(3) Communication: European Contract Law and the revision of the acquis: the way forward 2004

In the light of the reactions from EU institutions, Member States and stakeholders to the Action Plan 2003 the Commission finally published a further Communication in October 2004 entitled: European Contract Law and the revision of the acquis: the way forward.[32] The Communication reveals the Commission's intended course of action in relation to the three objectives identified in the Action Plan.

Regarding the first measure (improve the quality and consistency of the acquis in the area of contract law) the Commission gave a more detailed account of its approach to the envisaged CFR. The research preparing the CFR should aim to identify best solutions, taking into account national contract laws, the EC acquis and relevant international instruments, particularly the UN Convention on Contracts for the International Sale of Goods of 1980. The structure envisaged for the CFR is that it would first set out common fundamental principles of contract law. Secondly, those fundamental principles would be supported by definitions of key concepts. Thirdly, these principles and definitions would be completed by model rules, forming the bulk of the CFR. The adoption of the CFR following extensive consultations is planned for 2009.

The Commission indicated that it would use the CFR as a toolbox when presenting proposals to improve the quality and coherence of the existing acquis and future legal instruments in the area of contract law; hence, one of the main (short-term) objectives of the CFR would be to simplify and improve the existing acquis. Even though the CFR is currently not designed as a binding set of rules it is obviously intended to influence and guide the drafting and interpretation of existing and future Community legislation by Community and national institutions. The Commission further suggested that national

[32] Communication from the Commission to the European Parliament and the Council: European Contract Law and the revision of the acquis: the way forward, COM(2004) 651 final, at http://europa.eu.int/comm/consumers/cons_int/safe_shop/fair_bus_pract/cont_law/communication2004_en.htm.

legislators could use the CFR when transposing EU directives in the area of contract law into national legislation. They could also draw on the CFR when enacting legislation on areas of contract law which are not regulated at Community level. Another role suggested is the possible use of the CFR in arbitration.

The CFR is presently prepared by a pan-European group of researchers set up in May 2005.[33] This 'Joint Network on European Private Law, a Network of Excellence' is funded by the European Commission under the Sixth Framework Programme for Research. It includes researchers from over 60 universities. Members are *inter alia* the Study Group, the Acquis-Group and the Common Core-Group. It is planned that a first complete preliminary draft of the CFR is submitted by 2007. Preliminary drafts have already been produced and discussed by experts. The Joint Network is intending to submit the CFR under the label Common Principles of European Contract Law (CoPECL). The final version of the CFR is planned for 2008. Since the participants in the consultation and drafting process may pursue one-sided interests the Commission announced that it would after a further round of consultations assume the overall responsibility for the content and structure of the CFR. The intended date for the adoption of the final text is 2009.

In the 2003 Action Plan, the Commission agreed to examine whether it could promote the development by private parties of EU-wide Standard Terms and Conditions ('STCs') in particular by hosting a website on which market participants could exchange relevant information (the second measure). In the 2004 Communication the Commission had adhered to this plan but has in the meantime, in its first annual progress report, abandoned it: the Commission considers that it is not appropriate to host such a website.[34]

Measure three of the Action Plan was to launch a process of consultation in relation to a non-sector specific measure – an optional instrument in European contract law. The Commission identified a number of parameters for the reflections on the need for an instrument. These

33 Common Frame of Reference, at europa.eu.int/comm/consumers/cons_int/safe_shop/fair_bus_pract/cont_law/common_frame_ref_en.htm.

34 First Annual Progress Report on European Contract Law and the Acquis Review, COM(2005) 456 final.

included the need to take into account differences between transactions with consumers and those between businesses or with public authorities, the degree to which other solutions, including EU-wide STC already offer satisfactory solutions and the need to respect different legal and administrative cultures in the Member States. The Commission indicated that the vast majority of responses favoured an 'opt-in' model, an instrument which would have to be chosen by the parties through a choice of law clause, and concluded that within this group there was significant support for a regulation. The Commission further identified a number of other issues that needed still to be clarified mainly in relation to the scope of the envisaged instrument, such as for instance whether it should cover solely business-to-business transactions. While the Commission does not express a final view on these controversial issues it is at pains to emphasise that the optional instrument will have to be consistent with the CFR.

At first glance the Commission seems to have abandoned the idea of a European Civil Code, since in the 2004 Communication it expressly remarks that it does not intend to establish a 'European Contract Code' that would in a sweeping fashion replace the national contract law rules. However, this restriction is limited to the third measure of the Action Plan, namely in relation to the envisaged optional instrument. In the light of the extremely broad scope of the CFR some academics have expressed doubts, whether the main purpose of the CFR is to merely improve the existing acquis. Some observers fear that the CFR is the nucleus of a future Civil Code and that its very purpose is to facilitate such a Contract Code which of course would endanger the present plurality of national approaches and traditions. Some commentators stress that the focus of the CFR should include social aspects.[35]

In my view measure three of the action plan is a mere tactical diversion. *Nothing* relevant will happen in relation to measure three, because the CFR obviously *already* fulfils *all* possible functions of an optional instrument.[36] So while giving the impression that the Com-

35 S. the references in Vogenauer & Weatherhill, n 31 *supra*, 873.

36 See Annex I to the Communication 2004, and see also Rome I Draft Regulation which, a novelty, allows the parties to choose a non-binding – recognised set of principles.

mission is still consulting the Member States experts on an optional instrument, such a Model Code is already commissioned and under construction. In my view this way of proceeding is at least questionable. At the very least the transparency of the process is seriously prejudiced.

(4) Lehne-Report to the European Parliament

The German MEP *Klaus-Heiner Lehne* on 14 September 2005 gave a report on European Contract Law and the revision of the acquis: the way forward to the European Parliament. He supported the effort at harmonisation of the substantive contract law, yet he demanded a clarification as to the legal nature of the CFR, a clearer demarcation of b-to-b and b-to-c contracts and more weight for the principle of freedom of contract.

(5) First Annual Progress Report of the Commission

In its 2004 Communication the Commission had announced annual progress reports. The first such report was issued on 23 September 2005.[37] It appears that the Commission regards the CFR, which is currently prepared, as a model Code which is aimed to ensure the quality and coherence of the existing Community legislation.

The Commission intends to strengthen the consultation with practitioners. Following a call for expression of interest, the network of stakeholder experts on the CFR ('CFR-net') was established. Its participation is meant to ensure that the research takes into account the practical context in which the rules are to be applied and the needs of users.

A further concern of the Commission at this stage is to emphasise the need for the overall coherence of a draft CFR. Furthermore, the Commission highlights that the principle of freedom of contract needs to be emphasised as crucial for the process. Should rules be mandatory, this should be clarified and justified in the drafts. The Commission maintains that the main aim of the CFR is to improve the quality of existing Community legislation.

37 N 34 *supra*.

In addition to and alongside the CFR project the Commission launched a review process of the consumer acquis which is intended to simplify and complete the regulatory framework. The review process is outlined in the 2004 Communication and draws on the example of the consumer acquis because of its relevance to contract law. The Commission is still in the diagnostic phase which involves an analysis of the transposition and application of the consumer directives by the Member States. The Commission intends to issue a comprehensive document reporting on the review of the consumer acquis. This document is expected for publication in the first half of 2006. If, during the diagnostic phase, the Commission finds evidence that the acquis needs to be revised the Commission suggests that it will consider two options:

- a vertical approach consisting of the individual revision of existing directives (eg revision of the Timeshare Directive) or the regulation of specific sectors (eg a directive on tourism, including provisions of the Package Travel and Timeshare Directives);
- a more horizontal approach, adopting one or more framework instruments to regulate common features of the acquis. This framework instrument(s) would provide common definitions and regulate the main consumer contractual rights and remedies.

Under the horizontal approach, the Commission could, for example, prepare a directive on b-to-c contracts of sale of goods. It would regulate consistently the contractual aspects of sale, which are currently scattered in several directives (eg Directives on the Sale of Consumer Goods, Unfair Contract Terms, Distance Selling and Doorstep Selling). The Commission takes the view that this instrument would rationalise the regulatory framework since all the relevant provisions of the relevant existing directives would be 'systematised' into the new directive. The parts of existing Directives covering marketing techniques (eg restrictions on the use of certain means of distance communication) and services would remain in force. These, if possible and necessary, could be regulated by a separate framework instrument(s) in the future.

These statements as to the Commission's future plans make it quite clear that the CFR will prepare the way to a partial Codification of contract law. The first annual progress report confirms in certain respects those critics who objected that the CFR will after all serve as a European Contract Law despite the fact that the Commission repeatedly stated that it does not pursue the project of a European Civil Code.[38]

(6) Outlook: What is the CFR?

The purpose and the eventual importance of the CFR remain thus uncertain and in need of clarification. The relevant statements, communications etc. of the Community institutions, which quite often are somewhat opaque, ambiguous, and involved, are at pains to emphasise that the CFR is merely meant to consolidate and harmonise the existing and future Community legislation in those fields in which the Community can resort to a clear legal basis such as consumer protection. At the same time this contention is meant to reassure those who fear that the Community is intending to establish a comprehensive European Contract Code, the legal basis of which would be doubtful.

However, if one analyses the actual research done by the different Working Groups on the CFR one is bound to conclude that – so far as the aims and methods can be discerned at this stage – the research is directed at the adoption of an all-encompassing Contract Code. For the researches do not confine themselves to developing definitions of certain legal concepts as a background for the interpretation of the existing laws but devise new and comprehensive rules of contract law. In the light of this finding the Commission's statement that the CFR is merely meant to consolidate the existing acquis is not to be taken seriously. The true political agenda of the Commission seems to be the preparation of a European Civil respectively Contract Code.

38 S. the report on the 'Workshop of the network of Member State Experts on European Contract Law' of 31.5.2005, at http://www.eu.int/comm/consumers/cons_int/safe_shop/fair_bus_pract/cont_law/experts_membstates3105_en.pdf: 'The Commission clarified that it is not intending to produce a European civil code, for such project would be unrealistic and would have no legal basis. Although the Communication on European Contract Law sets some parameters for reflection on a possible future optional instrument, this is not at the moment on the Commission's agenda.'.

IV. The role of German Private Law

If one considers the virtues of German law, one must first and foremost mention its strive towards abstraction. The most typical feature of the BGB and at the same it most valuable asset is the generation of 'general parts'. The BGB seeks to identify far-reaching general principles rather than establishing casuistic rules with a limited scope of application. It is also this aspect of the law of obligations, namely the creation of a general part that rationalised all conceivable irregularities of performance as impossibility of performance, delay or malperformance, which ensured the survival of the Code for more than 100 years. This structure of the Code prevented that the BGB suffered the fate of the French Code Civil (CC) which has been gradually superseded by innumerable statutes of special application and statutory instruments. As a result the CC can no longer, at least less so than the BGB, be regarded as a self-contained Code that lives up to the demands of modern society.[39]

However, the legal powers of the European Community in the field of private law have so far been of limited scope. As a consequence, the characteristic element of German legal culture, namely the prevalence of general principles, could not have any influence on European private law. As explained, the preferred instrument of harmonisation has been the directive. The normative aims of Community law could on the whole be integrated into the German legal system without disruption. The question in this respect, however, is not whether German law had any effect on European law but to the contrary: to what extent did Community law shape German law?

The influence of Community law appears at first blush to have been immense. For the latest sweeping reform of the law of obligations of the year 2002 was triggered by the need to implement the Consumer Sales Directive. In relation to b-to-c sales the Directives made a number of significant changes necessary. However, the aims of the

39 This is why also in France in 2003 a project of a revision of the Law of Obligation of the Code Civil has been lanced. A group of researchers presented in 2005 a first draft of a revised law of obligations in the Code Civil ('Avant-projet de réforme du droit des obligations'), at http://www.henricapitant.org/article.php3?id_article=47.

Directive could have easily been transposed in a much more limited fashion even outside the text of the BGB (the so-called 'small solution') and in any event without comprehensive reform of the law of obligation. There were other and important reasons for the German legislator to reform the BGB more profoundly. In fact the reform had long been in the making. The need for a wholesale revision of the general and special parts of the law of obligations as well as the rules of prescription had been discussed for a long time. The First Commission for the reform of the BGB presented its recommendations already in 1992.

On closer examination, however, the new system of rules relating to irregularities of performance as in force since 1 January 2002 does not involve a change of paradigms. The new rules represent merely an improved and streamlined version of the rules as they were originally intended. It is true, of course, that the wording of the reformed rules appears to a certain extent to be influenced by concepts developed by those research initiatives that aim to establish a European law of obligations, such as for instance the PECL of the Lando-Commission, the PICC of the UNIDROIT Institute and the provisions of the CISG. However, one gets the impression from the preparatory works that they refer to these European principles only where there is a more or less random coincidence between the European principle and the reformed provision of the BGB. One cannot deny that the essential features of the reformed rules of irregularities of performance are identical to the traditional German doctrines which embody more than 100 years of experience with the law of obligations of the BGB.

It is to be expected that sooner or later the European Law of Obligations respectively a European Contract Code will be on the political agenda of the European Community. It is too early to assess the role that German private law can play in this process. The speed with which the Community institutions pursue the creation of common European principles of contract law gives cause for concern. It will not be to Europe's advantage to abandon century old traditions and to abolish well working systems for the sake of the 'CFR' or vague European principles of whatever origin. This uncalled proceeding would diminish the rich European legal culture. Needless to say, this is true not only from the German perspective. In France for instance Professor *Lequette* – a comparative lawyer – has voiced strong objections to this process that have been met with considerable approval.[40] The success of the project of a European Code will to a great extent depend on whether those responsible for its content are able to develop convincing general rules and a coherent structure of contract law in particular in relation to irregularities of performance.

The demands of business are even more complex. It is all the more important to ensure that the solutions adopted can be explained on the basis of transparent general principles. Otherwise the number of casuistic and limited solutions – which have been the mark of the approach of Community law in the past – will increase dramatically and endanger legal certainty and commercial convenience. German law has always been a model approach for a well-ordered abstract system of rules and principles and for this reason has always been worth copying. Since this preference for creating 'general parts' is not shared by all legal systems in the Community, the role of German legal science must be that of stressing the need for general principle. However, given the breathtaking speed with which the European Commission pursues the aim of a European Contract Code, it is uncertain whether this endeavour will be successful.

40 S. Lequette, 'Quelques remarques à propos du projet de code civil européen de M. von Bar' *D.* 2002 *Chr.* 2202 et seq; s. also the criticism of Initiale . Cornu, 'Un code civil n'est pas un instrument communautaire' *D.* 2002 *Chr.* 351 et seq; s. also B. Fages, 'Einige neuere Entwicklungen des französischen allgemeinen Vertragsrechts im Lichte der Grundregeln der Lando-Kommission' *ZEuP* 2003 514–524.

Chapter 8: On the Identity of Japanese Civil Law from a European Perspective

Karl Riesenhuber

Contents

I. Introduction: The Identity of a Legal System

When Professor *Kitagawa* asked me to participate in the present conference, I gladly accepted. It is a great honour and privilege for a young German scholar to present a paper here today. I was, I must confess, somewhat taken aback, though, when he asked me to talk about the identity of *Japanese* Civil Law, given the fact that I do not speak any Japanese and thus do not have access to Japanese Law, jurisprudence or scholarship in its original language. I was reminded of a scene in a book I once read where a teacher, standing in front of the Cologne Dome, describes the building: while the teacher looks up to the Dome, the students watch the teacher looking at the building and describing it: the observation of the observed. I am in the role of these students today and can only talk about the impressions I receive from others who have actually looked at the dome. I can, in many respects, offer no more than observations on the observed. Professor *Kitagawa* was, of course, well aware of this problem. When he asked me to talk about the identity of Japanese Civil Law, it was presumably not so much Japanese law he was interested in, but the European View, the outsider's perspective. That is all I can attempt to give today. Indeed, I would like to anticipate criticism and admit at the beginning that I will be more concerned with evading the question than answering it, and I will do so by turning towards methodological aspects. Professor *Smith's* paper will afterwards offer a common lawyer's view with a profound knowledge of the Japanese law.[1]

Identity is a colourful term. What does it mean? Webster's Dictionary gives various definitions.[2] The core aspect seems to be that of *being and remaining oneself or itself.* And there is, certainly in Germany (or any other EC Member State), ample reason for a reassurance of the state of the identity of the legal system.[3] Numerous influences

1 Smith, ch 9 *infra.*

2 Webster's *Encyclopedic Unabridged Dictionary of the English Language* (New York 1989): Identity is '1. state or fact of remaining the same one, as under varying aspects or conditions (…); 2. the condition of being oneself or itself, and not another …); 3. condition or character as to who a person or what a thing is (…); 4. state or fact of being the same one; 5. exact likeness in nature or qualities (…); 6. an instance or point of sameness or likeness …'. On the roots of the German word *Identität* cf E. Seebold (ed), *Friedrich Kluge – Ethymologisches Wörterbuch der deutschen Sprache* (22nd ed. Berlin, New York 1989) (from the Latin *idem,* the same); G. Schmidt, 'Identität – Gebrauch und Geschichte eines modernen Begriffs' *Muttersprache* 86 (1976) 333-354 (who, incidentally, demonstrates that the German word had originally been established in technical psychology-language and achieved broader recognition when the EC published a declaration on 'The European Identity').

3 Cf S. Doing, T. Meyer, C. Winkler (eds), *Europäische Identitäten – Eine europäische Identität?* (Baden-Baden 2005) (from the viewpoint of historians and political scientists). The cultural or national identity of a people or an ethnic group is frequently an issue of parliamentary discussion; cf O.J. C 2003 C 155 E/1; O.J. 2002 C 40 E/75; O.J. 2000 C 280 E/121; O.J. 1995 C 42/51; O.J. 1989 C 323/29; O.J. 1987 C 324/40; O.J. 1987 C 156/50; O.J. 1982 C 156/30.

affect the legal system and cause substantial changes. For the legal systems of the EC Member States the most fundamental changes come from Community legislation ('Europeanisation').[4] While it had long been assumed that these changes would merely affect administrative law, consumer protection and other special areas of the law, but not civil law as such, recent years have proved the contrary. Consumer protection has been turned into a core aspect of civil law and, in Germany, has been integrated into the BGB.[5] Notably the Consumer Sales Directive[6] has caused a fundamental reform of substantial parts of the German law of obligations in 2002 (*Schuldrechtsmodernisierung*).[7] Is the new regime governing breach of contract still 'German' in its content, structure, language and style? Professor *Leipold* and Professor *Lorenz* have addressed these questions in their papers.[8]

But there are other influences as well. There are, perhaps, 'creeping' changes as caused by a changing legal education and practice.[9] Not few German lawyers end up in foreign law firms and quickly adapt to an Anglo-American style of legal practice, e.g. of drafting contracts. Systems of rules drafted by non-governmental (private) bodies such as the *Principles of European Contract Law* or the *Unidroit Principles of International Commercial Contracts* increasingly gain influence. The EC Commission's plans to allow private parties to choose such rules as the applicable law[10] will reinforce this development.

4 For a brief survey cf Shiomi, ch 3 *supra*.

5 Cf Shiomi, ch 3 *supra*. For an older, but still interesting German-Japanese comparison of consumer law, see Z. Kitagawa & M. Rehbinder (eds), *Gegenwartsprobleme des Verbraucherschutzes* (Cologne, Berlin, Bonn, Munich 1978).

6 Directive 1999/44/EC of the European Parliament and of the Council of 25 May 1999 on certain aspects of the sale of consumer goods and associated guarantees, OJ 1999 L 171/12.

7 Cf Shiomi, ch 3 *supra*.

8 Leipold, ch 6 *supra*; Lorenz, ch 7 *supra*.

9 K.P. Berger, *The Creeping Codification of the Lex Mercatoria* (The Hague 1999); K.P. Berger, *Formalisierte oder „schleichende" Kodifizierung des transnationalen Wirtschaftsrechts* (Berlin, New York 1996).

10 Cf Art. 2(2) of the Proposal for a Regulation of the European Parliament and the Council on the law applicable to contractual obligations (Rome I), COM (2005) 650 final. On the reform, see the contributions in Stefan Leible (ed), *Das Grünbuch zum Internationalen Vertragsrecht* (Munich 2004).

More generally, it is perhaps fair to say that the development of globalisation has resulted in increased international exchange.[11] It has caused mutual influences of the legal systems and often a harmonisation of the law. But if the various legal systems converge,[12] can they remain 'themselves'; can they maintain their diversity and individuality?[13]

In order to comment on the identity of Japanese Civil Law, I will proceed in three steps. I will first give a brief – and, alas!, only second hand – summary of the development of Japanese Civil Law and try to locate its position in the various 'legal families' (II). I will then turn to the issue of identity of mixed legal systems (III). And I will conclude with some observations on methodological aspects (IV).

II. The Comparatists' View of Japanese Civil Law

1. A Sketch of the Development

The fascinating development of Japanese Civil Law over the last century has often been described.[14] It will briefly be sketched in the fol-

11 On 'Globalisation and the Law', see the contributions to the 2005 German-Japanese Conference in Tokyo: J. Murakami, H.-P. Marutschke, K. Riesenhuber (eds), *Globalisierung und Recht – Beiträge Japans und Deutschlands zu einer internationalen Rechtsordnung im 21. Jahrhundert* (Berlin 2007) (forthcoming) (see already http://www.tokyo-jura-kongress2005.de/de_index.php). On the discussion see only the survey of R. Michaels, 'Welche Globalisierung für das Recht? Welches Recht für die Globalisierung?' *RabelsZ* 69 (2005) 525–544. See further K. Riesenhuber & K. Takayama (eds), *Rechtsangleichung: Grundlagen, Methoden und Inhalte – Deutsch-japanische Perspektiven* (Berlin 2006).

12 Whether they converge is, of course, a matter of debate; for some references see below, IV.1.

13 On the latter issue, cf the rich volume of H.P. Glenn, *Legal Traditions of the World – Sustainable Diversity in Law* (Oxford 2000).

14 See in particular Z. Kitagawa, *Rezeption und Fortbildung des europäischen Zivilrechts in Japan* (Frankfurt a.M., Berlin 1970); Kitagawa, ch 2 *supra* sub III 1 with footnote 23; Z. Kitagawa, 'Ein Jahrhundert deutsch-japanische Rechtswissenschaft', in Hans G. Leser (ed), *Ein Jahrhundert deutsch-japanische Rechtswissenschaft* (Marburg 1990) 13, 21–35; Z. Kitagawa, 'Drei Entwicklungsphasen im japanischen Zivilrecht', in H. Coing et al (eds), *Die Japanisierung westlichen Rechts* (Tübingen 1990) 125–141; G. Rahn, *Rechtsdenken und Rechtsauffassung in Japan – Dargestellt an der Entwicklung der modernen japanischen Zivilrechtsdogmatik* (Munich 1990) 23–306; H. Baum, 'Rechtsdenken, Rechtssystem

lowing to give us a basis for further consideration. Following the structure of the conference, the focus will be on civil law or even narrower the law of obligations (leaving family law and succession aside). Other aspects of private law as well as other aspects of the legal system at large – procedure (dispute resolution and settlement!), legal practice, modes of thought, customs etc. –, though equally important, must thus be left aside.[15]

a) The Development of the Japanese Civil Code

The drafting process of the Japanese Civil Code seems to follow the old wisdom *Wenn zwei sich streiten, freut sich der Dritte!* (When two quarrel, a third will be lucky.)[16] The end of the Shogunate in the 19th

und Rechtswirklichkeit in Japan – Rechtsvergleichung mit Japan' *RabelsZ* 59 (1995) 258, 266-269; P. Eubel, 'Bürgerliches Recht', in P. Eubel (ed), *Das japanische Rechtssystem* (Frankfurt a.M. 1979) 99–102; K. Igarashi, *Einführung in das japanische Recht* (Darmstadt 1990) 1–17; H.P. Marutschke, *Einführung in das japanische Recht* (Munich 1999) §§ 4, 5, 8 (33–58, 87–102); H. Oda, *Japanese Law* (2nd ed. Oxford 1999) 12–33, 127–131; W. Röhl, *Fremde Einflüsse im modernen japanischen Recht* (Frankfurt a.M., Berlin 1959) 1–3, 39–41 *et passim*; K. Zweigert & H. Kötz, *An introduction to Comparative Law* (3rd ed. Oxford 1998) 297 et seq; P. Koschacker, *Europa und das römische Recht* (Munich, Berlin 1947) 131 sq with n 1. For the earlier development cf D.F. Henderson & P.M. Torbert, *Contract in the Far East – China and Japan* (Tübingen, Dordrecht, Boston, Lancaster 1992).

15 This does, of course, not express the author's disregard of the law in action. To the contrary, it has to be acknowledged that, in particular with regard to Japanese law, the importance of traditions and of procedural aspects is often emphasized; see eg: Z. Kitagawa, 'Use and Non-Use of Contracts in Japanese Business Relations: A Comparative Analysis', in H. Baum (ed), *Japan: Economic Success and Legal System* (Berlin 1997) 145–165 (on comparative contract law and practice); Z. Kitagawa, 'Resonance Theory – A Tentative Approach to the Dispute Settlement Mechanism', in G. Lüke, G. Ress, M.R. Will (eds), *Rechtsvergleichung, Europarecht und Staatenintegration: Gedächtnisschrift für Léontin-Jean Constantinesco* (Cologne, Berlin, Bonn, Munich 1983) 393–408; M. Oki, 'Schlichtung als Institution des Rechts – Ein Vergleich von europäischem und japanischem Rechtsdenken' *Rechtstheorie* 16 (1985) 151–162; J. Llompart, 'Japanisches und europäisches Rechtsdenken' *Rechtstheorie* 16 (1985) 131–149; Glenn, n 13 *supra*, 279–317; Rahn, n 14 *supra*; H. Stoll, 'Zur neueren Entwicklung des japanischen Zivilrechts in rechtsvergleichender Sicht', in H. Coing et al (eds), *Die Japanisierung westlichen Rechts* (Tübingen 1990) 156 sq.

16 A rough equivalent is the allegedly fourteenth century proverb 'When two dogs are fighting for a bone, a third runs away with it.' (kind reference of Tony Weir).

century marks the beginning of a period of openness and increased interest in the technological and cultural developments of other countries. Japanese scholars studied law in European countries and in the United States and as a consequence, a 'French' and an 'Anglo-Saxon School' of legal thought developed in Japan,[17] the former, not surprisingly, with a tendency towards natural law theory, the latter with a tendency towards a common law tradition. In the area of civil law, the French school seemed to carry the victory when *Gustav-Emil Boissonade*[18] was charged with the task of drafting a civil code. *Boissonade's* draft (also referred to as the 'old Civil Code')[19] closely followed the model of the French *Code Civil* with some signs of Italian, Belgian and Dutch influence.[20] When, however, the code was brought before the Parliament in 1890, it was faced with strong opposition, – the so-called *Codification Dispute.*[21] It was the 'Anglo-Saxon school' of legal thought in particular that objected the code was too strongly biased towards the French system and had not sufficiently taken other comparative sources and Japanese customs into account.[22] The systematic order, inspired by the system of the *Institutions* of Roman law, was criticized.

It was then the 'Anglo-Saxon school' which appeared to turn out as the winner when, as a consequence of the Codification Dispute, the parliamentary proceedings were stalled and a resolution on the draft postponed. A new Commission was charged with a revision of the draft in 1893.[23] It mandated the work to a group of three professors among whom one was a member of the 'Anglo-Saxon school', two

17 On these Rahn, n 14 *supra*, 98–104.

18 On *Boissonade* see Rahn, n 14 *supra*, 91 sq.

19 As no parliament existed at the time, *Boissonade's* code came into force by a mere act of the senate; Marutschke, n 14 *supra*, 89. In 1892, the Imperial Diet decided to postpone the implementation of the code and amend it, *de facto*, however, it installed a new commission with a view of drafting a new code; Oda, n 14 *supra*, 129.

20 Marutschke, n 14 *supra*, 89 sq; Oda, n 14 *supra*, 128.

21 Z. Kitagawa, 'Das Methodenproblem in der Dogmatik des japanischen bürgerlichen Rechts' *AcP* 166 (1966) 330, 331 sq; Rahn, n 14 *supra*, 91–97; Marutschke, n 14 *supra*, 90–92; Oda, n 14 *supra*, 8, 128 sq.

22 Marutschke, n 14 *supra*, 90 sq, points out that matters of rules and system were, perhaps, only the superficial reasons for the dispute while cultural and political issues were really at stake; Oda, n 14 *supra*, 128.

23 Rahn, n 14 *supra*, 106–113.

were members of the 'French school'. The revised draft prepared by this group and completed (already!) in 1896, however, turned out to be strongly influenced[24] by German *pandectist* legal thought and the First and Second Drafts of the German Civil Code,[25] even though the French influence was still remarkable.[26] The drafting technique and the systematic organisation of the German Draft Civil Code seem to have exerted a strong influence on the Japanese draftsmen.[27]

Thus, somewhat surprisingly, German law had in the end gained substantial influence on the Japanese Civil Code, even though French and Anglo-Saxon legal thought had dominated previously and even in the first phase of the drafting process. The Japanese Civil Code, however, was not a mere translation or transposition of the German draft,[28] but rather stood for an 'eclectic and mixed type of reception of foreign law'[29]. Elements of English, French and German law are intertwined to a new product in this codification.[30]

24 For a more detailed account cf Kitagawa (1970: 'Rezeption'), n 14 *supra*, 33–43; Oda, n 14 *supra*, 129 sq ('while maintaining the façade of being strongly influenced by German law, the legislature at that time kept certain parts of the previous Code which were influenced by the French Code').

25 T. Oka, 'Einige Bemerkungen über den Einfluss des deutschen Rechts bei der Entstehung des Entwurfs zum japanischen BGB und bei seiner Beratung', in I. Schwenzer & G. Hager (eds), *Festschrift für Peter Schlechtriem zum 70. Geburtstag* (Tübingen 2003) 141–152. See already Kitagawa (1970: 'Rezeption'), *n* 14 *supra*, 32; Kitagawa, n 21 *supra*, 330, 331 sq; Eubel, n 14 *supra*, 100 sq.

26 Kogayu, ch 4 *supra* sub II 1 (on the 1965 'Hoshino paper'); *Kogayu* also points out that the genealogical linkage is often rather controversial; eg sub III 1 (2).

27 It is still debated why the group of Japanese draftsmen in the end in many ways preferred the German model over the French or the Anglo-Saxon they were familiar with; cf Kitagawa (1970: 'Rezeption'), n 14 *supra*, 32 sq and (on the reception of theories) 94–97; Marutschke, n 14 *supra*, 94 sq; Zweigert & Kötz, n 14 *supra*, 298; see also Leipold, ch 6 *supra* sub I 2.

28 Already the number of sections (§§) demonstrates the differences: While the German BGB contains some 2300 sections the Japanese Civil Code counts a mere 1000 sections; see also Marutschke, n 14 *supra*, 95.

29 Kitagawa (1970: 'Rezeption'), n 14 *supra*, 43 (trans. by the author). See also Marutschke, n 14 *supra*, 95; Oda, n 14 *supra*, 130.

30 Stoll, n 15 *supra*, 152.

b) *The Development of Scholarship and Jurisprudence under the new Civil Code*

'After the process of reception of foreign civil codes, German legal theories sweepingly invaded into Japan and immediately dominated over Japanese jurisprudence.'[31] This statement sums up the development which Professor *Kitagawa* has examined in some detail and describes a phenomenon that he has aptly called the *reception of theories* (Theorienrezeption).[32] *Claus-Wilhelm Canaris points* out that *Kitagawa* deserves the credit of having discovered the issue of reception of theories as a unique legal problem.[33]

Reception of foreign law is a process that every German law student is familiar with. It is, of course, the reception of Roman law that the European peoples have experienced in a long process.[34] The (sweeping) reception of legal theories *after* the completion of a process of reception of foreign law appears to be quite unusual and unique. The sources of the phenomenon perhaps lie in the special features of the rather hasty legislation process. Arguably, an isolated reception of rules is quite impossible. Arguably, rules, methods, theories – the whole of legal culture are indivisible and thus an isolated reception of rules necessarily has to be followed by a process of consolidation.[35] Indeed, *Kitagawa* argues that the process of reception of theories has smoothened the assimilation of the new law.[36] The reception

31 Kitagawa, ch 2 *supra* sub III 3.
32 See in particular the seminal work Kitagawa (1970: 'Rezeption'), n 14 *supra*. Further Rahn, n 14 *supra*, 114–128; Shiomi, ch 3 *supra passim*; Kogayu, ch 4 *supra passim*.
33 C.-W. Canaris, 'Theorienrezeption und Theorienstruktur', in: H.G. Leser & T. Isomura (eds), *Wege zum japanischen Recht – Festschrift für Zentaro Kitagawa zum 60. Geburtstag* (Berlin 1992) 59.
34 See only F. Wieacker, *A History of Private Law in Europe*, trans. T. Weir (Oxford 1995) 71–195.
35 Cf also H. Kötz, 'Gemeineuropäisches Zivilrecht', in H. Bernstein, U. Drobnig, H. Kötz (eds), *Festschrift für Konrad Zweigert zum 70. Geburtstag* (Tübingen 1981) 481–500 (common legal culture and infra-structure as a pre-requisite for successful harmonisation). On legal transplants, see below, IV 1.
36 Kitagawa, n 21 *supra*, 330, 332; Kitagawa (1970: 'Rezeption'), n 14 *supra*, 21 sq, 54, 97 sq; Kitagawa (1990: 'Ein Jahrhundert'), n 14 *supra*, 21.

of theories has, in some instances, helped to discover the *principles* underlying the received rules.[37]

It may be mentioned that the civil laws of the EC Member States are today confronted with similar issues. The harmonisation of private law experienced since the 1990s could not be based on a common legal culture. The national laws were confronted with new legal concepts. The introduction of the principle of good faith into English Common Law through (in particular) the Unfair Contract Terms Directive[38] is but one example.[39] Here as well, the rules asked for a theoretical foundation and triggered a process of assimilation in the Member States.

It was again an influence of German law or rather German legal theory that dominated in this period of reception of theories which covers approximately the first two decades of the twentieth century.[40] The well-defined and well-thought-through system of terms, rules and principles devised by the German *pandectist* school offered an appealing method. However, German jurisprudence was not taken over wholesale.[41] It could only serve as a model where the framework of the code so allowed. This was, in particular, the case with respect to legal terminology and system-building.[42] Still, German legal theory applied to a Civil Code that was substantially different from

37 Kitagawa (1970: 'Rezeption'), n 14 *supra*, 97 sq.

38 Council Directive 93/13/EEC of 5 April 1993 on unfair terms in consumer contracts, OJ 1993 L 95/29.

39 For an English view of the process, see H. Collins, 'Good Faith in European Contract Law' *Oxf. J. Leg. Stud.* 14 (1994) 229–254 ('The criterion of good faith is mysterious and exciting to an English lawyer.'; 249); see also K. Riesenhuber, *System und Prinzipien des Europäischen Vertragsrechts* (Berlin 2003) 58–61.

40 Here as well, the reasons for the German influence seem diverse and debated; cf Kitagawa, n 21 *supra*, 330, 332 sq; Marutschke, n 14 *supra*, 96; Oda, n 14 *supra*, 129 sq (who ascribes the influence of German theory to 'the belief [!] that the new Code was based on German law').

41 Kitagawa (1990: 'Drei Entwicklungsphasen'), n 14 *supra*, 127 sq: eg the principle of protection of good faith (*Gutglaubensschutz*) was not applied with regard to the land register and only favoured *de lege ferenda*. In other cases, however, where the code so allowed, a creative adaptation was successfully completed, for example with regard to the doctrine of *culpa in contrahendo;* this development duplicates the German development where the doctrine was also applied although it found but little ground in the code and had arguably been rejected by the legislator.

42 Kitagawa (1970: 'Rezeption'), n 14 *supra*, 99.

the BGB and under unique and in many ways different social and cultural circumstances was bound to be lead to tensions.[43]

Not surprisingly, the period of reception of theories was thus followed by a period of *assimilation*[44] or *acculturation*[45]. After the Second World War,[46] German *Begriffsjurisprudenz* (legal formalism)[47] found opposition in a sociological jurisprudence and an *Interessenjurisprudenz* focussing on the law in action, the case law and the social issues the law is designed to resolve.[48] The interest of Japanese scholarship to some extent shifted to other jurisdictions including, in particular, France[49] and the United States[50].[51] It is noteworthy, though, that the ensuing period of foreign influence or comparison with other legal systems did not lead to a new period of reception of theories.[52] Rather, the contact to other legal systems was reduced to singular instances of transfer or adoption. The reception of theories seems to have been a unique phenomenon of the early years of the Japanese Civil Code. In regard of legal theory, Japanese jurisprudence and scholarship now shifted from a relatively coherent theory *more Germanico* to a pluralism of legal theories[53] experienced in other countries as well.[54]

43 Kitagawa (1990: 'Drei Entwicklungsphasen'), n 14 *supra*, 126.
44 Kitagawa (1970: 'Rezeption'), n 14 *supra*, 21 sq, 54.
45 Rahn, n 14 *supra*, 130.
46 The period between 1921–1945 is left aside in this brief account, its impact and importance are controversial; for a detailed discussion, see Rahn, n 14 *supra*, 130-168; Kitagawa (1990: 'Ein Jahrhundert'), n 14 *supra*, 34 sq.
47 German-style jurisprudence was not so well respected since the 1920s and often discredited as *Begriffsjurisprudenz*. It is, however, still debated whether the term adequately describes the methods employed by Japanese scholars; Rahn, n 14 *supra*, 128 sq.
48 Kitagawa n 21 *supra*, 330, 337–340; Kitagawa, ch 2 *supra* sub III 4.
49 See in particular Kogayu, ch 4 *supra passim*, drawing particular attention to the seminal paper of E. Hoshino on 'Influence of French Civil Law on the Japanese Civil Code' of 1965.
50 Matsumoto, ch 5 *supra* sub II 1 (1) *et passim*.
51 Kitagawa (1990: 'Drei Entwicklungsphasen'), n 14 *supra*, 130–132; Rahn, n 14 *supra*, 183–201; 202–306.
52 Kitagawa (1990: 'Drei Entwicklungsphasen'), n 14 *supra*, 131.
53 Ibid 132 sq.
54 For Germany S. Grundmann, 'Methodenpluralismus als Aufgabe – Zur Legalität von ökonomischen und rechtsethischen Argumenten in Auslegung und Rechtsanwendung' *RabelsZ* 61 (1997) 423–453.

This latter period of assimilation or acculturation is perhaps the decisive part for our purposes. It is this process which predominantly established (and still establishes) the identity of Japanese Civil Law today. Indeed, Professor *Kitagawa* has also used the term *Japanisation* to describe the process of assimilation.[55] The extraordinary process of legal development in the phase of the reception gradually gave way for the resurgence of the 'normal' way of legal development.[56] The judicial application and development in particular reinforced a distinctly Japanese tradition.[57]

2. Japan and the Theory of Legal Families

The previous sketch of the development can only give us a faint impression of the much richer picture. Still, it will be useful as a background for an attempt to define the family-ties of Japanese Law: Where can we locate Japanese Law in the whole of legal families of the world?

a) The Theory of Legal Families

The theory of legal families (*Rechtskreislehre*)[58] is, of course, in itself rather debated. Taking into account a number of factors such as history, characteristic institutions,[59] the role of lawyers (judges, academics) or the 'style', the theory of legal families attempts to place

55 Kitagawa (1990: 'Drei Entwicklungsphasen'), n 14 *supra*, 125–141 (in particular at 140).

56 Kitagawa (1970: 'Rezeption'), n 14 *supra*, 101-104, who "distinguishes two phases of development in contemporary Japanese law".

57 Ibid 86–104.

58 On the *Rechtskreislehre* Zweigert & Kötz, n 14 *supra*, 63–73; H. Kötz, 'Abschied von der Rechtskreislehre?' *ZEuP* 1998 493–505. The history of legal families in comparative law finds a correlation in the *Stadtrechtsfamilien* (families of laws of the free cities); K. Kroeschell, *Deutsche Rechtsgeschichte Band 1: bis 1250* (12th ed. Stuttgart 2005) 258–261; A. Laufs, *Rechtsentwicklungen in Deutschland* (6th ed. Berlin, New York 2006) 40 sq.

59 Our previous *caveat* has to be repeated here: The sketch of the history of Japanese law given above II 1 a) has been no more than rudimentary and many aspects of the law, such as issues of dispute resolution or legal institutions, have been left aside here. Consequently, a discussion of the classifications of Japanese law can only be superficial.

the vast number of legal systems of the world into an order that makes the plurality comprehensible and that may make access to individual legal systems easier.[60] It is not our purpose to question the *Rechtskreislehre* here.[61] Our interest rather is to explore where comparatists locate Japanese (Civil) Law within the legal families of the world. The answers vary considerably.

b) Classifications of Japanese Law[62]

Zweigert & Kötz deal with Japanese Law under the heading of 'Law in the Far East'.[63] However, it cannot be assumed that the authors would have overlooked that indeed there are great differences between the legal systems of this region.[64] In fact, already the phrasing of the subtitles of the book discloses that this chapter on 'Law in the Far East' is not used to identify a *legal family* in the same sense as *Zweigert* and *Kötz* speak of the Romanistic, the Germanic, the Anglo-American and the Nordic Legal Families. 'Far East' is but a useful and rather loose *geographical reference*.[65] The title certainly does express a euro-centrism of the authors.[66] And, to some degree, it perhaps does express a lack of attention for the various legal systems of the region.[67] With regard to the classification of Japanese law, *Zwei-*

60 Zweigert & Kötz, n 14 *supra*, 63 sq.

61 For a recent defence see Kötz, n 58 *supra*, 493–505 (confining its application narrowly).

62 For a more detailed survey cf Oda, n 14 *supra*, 3–6: A. Schnitzer, 'law of the Asian countries' (along with Turkish, Persian, Hindu, Mongolian and Afghan law); P. Arminjon, B. Nolde & M. Wolf: 'German law in the Far East'; R. David: 'Laws of the Far East' (together with Chinese law, acknowledging Romano-Germanic elements); K. H. Ebert: 'Far Eastern Law' (together with Chinese law); Hozumi: 'family of Roman law'.

63 Zweigert & Kötz, n 14 *supra*, 286. Glenn, n 13 *supra*, 279–317, similarly considers 'an Asian legal tradition'. His aim is different, though. He acknowledges that 'Asia is a big place' and concedes that 'since we are now dealing with more than half the worlds population, we may have to climb rather high to see common features'. He does, however, find common features, mainly in a Confucian tradition.

64 Kötz, n 58 *supra*, 493 sq.

65 Critical against the localisation of Japanese law in such 'residual category' Baum, n 14 *supra*, 258, 263.

66 Ibid 258, 259–261, 262.

67 The focus of Zweigert and Kötz is certainly justifiable with a view to their pedagogic aims. Similarly, euro-centrism must not be understood as a criticism.

gert and *Kötz* merely discuss the issue, ultimately without taking a definite position. They end their discussion saying that 'the doctrine of legal families should not be taken too seriously, for it can often lead to simplifications which do violence to the facts'.[68] 'Law in the Far East' is not a category of legal families and presumably was never meant to be one.

Hiroshi Oda does not take the theory of legal families too seriously either. He extensively surveys the various approaches and carefully weighs the arguments and factors discussed. *Oda* convincingly dismisses any geographic classification as inconclusive for the purposes of comparative law.[69] He rejects the contention that extra-legal ways of dispute resolution are a characteristic of Japanese law and rightly points out that an analysis of family ties among the various countries has to differentiate between the various areas of the law (civil law, commercial law, public law etc.). Mainly with a view to civil law, *Oda* considers Japanese law as 'part of the Romano-Germanic family of law, with some elements of US law'.[70]

Kitagawa in his paper comes to a similar classification. He considers Japanese law to be a member of the Germano-American legal family.[71] This certainly is not meant to deny the Roman influence highlighted by *Oda*. It rather seems that *Kitagawa* finds these influences incorporated in the German influences.

III. Identity of a Mixed Legal System

Thinking of family relations in the *Mozart Year*, the year of *Mozarts* 250th birthday, one is reminded of the fact that Wolfgang Amadeus

E. H. Gombrich, for instance, had reservations against translating his wonderful book *Kleine Weltgeschichte für junge Leser* into English. One of his concerns was that he would have to choose a different perspective for an English readership. A translation has recently been published – posthumous; E. H. Gombrich, *A little history of the world*, trans. C. Mustill (New Haven, London 2005).

68 Zweigert & Kötz, n 14 *supra*, 299.

69 Oda, n 14 *supra*, 5 (*contra* a classification of Japanese and Chinese law as 'Far Eastern', noting that China turned to socialism in 1949).

70 Ibid 9.

71 Kitagawa, ch 2 *supra* sub III 1 with note 25.

was the son of Leopold. What does this tell us about *Mozart*? Wolfgang Amadeus was the son of Leopold, but he was also the son of Anna Maria. He grew up in a different environment than his parents had. He was the brother of Maria Anna ('Nannerl'). He travelled a lot and met many important people of his time at a young age. Certainly, Wolfgang Amadeus was different from Leopold in a number of ways.[72] – Let me try to translate these considerations into terms of legal families.

1. Family relations: Roots and Character

The example of *Mozart* demonstrates both, the merits and the limits of family-classifications.[73] Certainly, the theory of legal families leads us to a result that can count on a wide degree of acceptance: Japanese law as part of the Germano-Roman-American legal family. But at the same time, this categorisation seems to disprove the usefulness of categorisation altogether and even ridicule it.[74] Had legal families originally been construed so as to draw rough distinctions between, in particular, the French and German legal systems and the Common Law tradition, we now find that in the instance of Japanese law (and perhaps other legal systems) the distinction is blurred.[75] A clear-cut classification seems impossible. And the categorization with regard to a family proves of little help in cases of inter-family marriages: While the double or triple name(s)[76] give us some hints as to the parents, they do not express the degree of influence flowing from one parent or another. Indeed, the whole family picture seems to be rather irritating. The Roman wisdom '*Mater semper certa est; pater*

72 On Mozart, see eg M. Geck, *Mozart – Eine Biographie* (Hamburg 2005); P. Gay, *Mozart – Biographie* (Paperback edition Berlin 2005).
73 See already Zweigert & Kötz, n 14 *supra*, 65 sq.
74 This should not be misunderstood as a general rejection of the theory of legal families. The 'modest usefulness' ascribed to it by Kötz, n 58 *supra*, 493, 505, can hardly be denied, neither its ordering and didactic function.
75 A similar point is made by Smith, ch 9 *infra* sub IV, hinting at a convergence of common law and civil law.
76 German family law used to accept multiple last names, and there are prominent examples illustrating the fact. § 1355 BGB now limits the possibilities of "adding" names for spouses.

est, quem nuptia demonstrat'[77] does not apply, and there seems a possibility of a plurality of fathers (or mothers).

The case of Japanese law certainly drives the family-classification to its boundaries. It demonstrates that the strength of family-categorisation lies in its function to discover the *roots* of a legal system. At the same time, it becomes obvious that the family-categorisation tells us but little about the *character* of a legal system. Highlighting the roots, we disregard the fact that a mixture of two ingredients might lead to an entirely new product. Again, the example of *Mozart* is revealing: Who would deny that the children, while formed by the genes of their parents, have their own identity. We can discern elements of Leopold in the work of Wolfgang Amadeus, elements of *Thomas Mann* in the work of *Klaus Mann*, but the family relation expressed in the last name tells us but little about the son. It is not only the old dispute whether a person is formed by the genes or his environment: Even if one were to emphasise the formative influence of the genes one would have to acknowledge that the combination of different genes leads to a unique and original result. In other words, mixed legal systems, while related to other legal systems, gain an identity by the simple fact of the 'mixture'.

Therefore, one certainly should neither deny nor neglect the roots of any legal system, be that the Roman roots of European civil laws or the (mainly) German, French and English roots of Japanese law. At the same time, a differentiated view will probably acknowledge that the European and Anglo-American ingredients of Japanese law, as continuously applied and amended over the years, have led to a unique new legal system.

It may be noted that it is a matter of perspective whether we emphasize the 'Western' or the Japanese element. Laying the path for his theory of the 'law model of the near future', *Kitagawa* distinguishes this model from two other models of law, the Western model and the pluralist model. While the former takes European legal systems as a measure to analyse legal systems, the latter embraces other legal systems as well.[78] Whether and to what extent we ac-

77 Dig. 2, 4, 5: *Paulus libro quarto ad edictum:* quia semper certa est, etiam si volgo conceperit: pater vero is est, quem nuptiae demonstrant.

78 Z. Kitagawa, 'A Reflection on the Three Law Models', in J. Becker et al. (eds), *Recht im Wandel seines sozialen und technologischen Umfeldes – Festschrift für Manfred Rehbinder* (Munich, Bern 2002) 559–562.

knowledge the independence and originality of a legal system certainly also is a matter of perspective.

2. Illustrations[79]

Japanese Law offers many examples for its unique and original position within the world's legal families, and I can draw on other publications as well as on the papers submitted by the Japanese colleagues to illustrate the point.

a) Transfer of Property

A well-known characteristic of German law is the distinction of the obligation from the transfer of title, the 'principle of distinction' (*Trennungsprinzip*) and the 'principle of abstractness' (*Abstraktionsprinzip*). This contrasts with the principle of causal transfer of title as practised in other countries. The Japanese Civil Code does not contain a clear decision for either model but seems to be based on the French system of causal transfer. Indeed, that was the prevailing view after the codification. The phase of reception of theories, however, triggered a different development. In a first step, the transfer of title was separated from the causal obligation. And in a second step, the abstractness of the transfer of title was recognised.[80] The theory could, however, never really establish in Japanese jurisprudence and was never accepted by the courts. It has thus not survived long.[81]

Incidentally, *Konrad Zweigert*, advocating comparative law as a method of interpretation, considered the principle of distinction and the principle of abstractness, deficient as they were from his perspective, as insurmountable by comparative guidance.[82]

[79] For further examples cf eg Z. Kitagawa, 'Rechtssoziologisches zum Problem- und Systemdenken im japanischen Recht', in G. Paulus, U. Diederichsen & C.-W. Canaris (eds), *Festschrift für Karl Larenz zum 70. Geburtstag* (Munich 1973) 310–320.

[80] Marutschke, n 14 *supra*, 97–99.

[81] Kitagawa (1970: 'Rezeption'), n 14 *supra*, 90 sq; Kitagawa (1990: 'Drei Entwicklungsphasen'), n 14 *supra*, 127.

[82] K. Zweigert, 'Rechtsvergleichung als universale Auslegungsmethode' *RabelsZ* 15 (1949/50) 5, 17.

The example demonstrates how the Japanese Code, a mixture of French and German influences, was a unique piece of legislation from the outset. It also illustrates the ongoing influence of German legal theory during the period of reception of theories. The final step, however, seems decisive: that the process of acculturation and practical application decided over the development in the long run.

b) Breach of Contract

Professor *Kitagawa* in his paper offers what may be called a 'subtraction method' for examining the unique structure of Japanese law. 'In order to examine the original form of Japanese civil law jurisprudence and to create legal theories for achieving independence from it, it was necessary to study German civil law jurisprudence and its predecessor, the *Pandektenwissenschaft* in the 19th century'.[83] In order to reveal the unique Japanese elements, we have to determine the *Pandectist* elements and subtract them from current Japanese civil law.

Incidentally, it may be noted that the *Pandektenwissenschaft* seems to have lived on in other countries such as Japan and Greece after German jurisprudence, captured by the Code of 1900, had largely abandoned it.[84]

Kitagawa illustrates the point with the example of contractual liability. In the German BGB of 1900, contractual liability was based on the distinction between impossibility (further differentiated into initial and subsequent impossibility), default (in the sense of *Verzug*) and warranty. The system was later supplemented by the categories of *culpa in contrahendo* and 'positive breach of contract' (*positive Vertragsverletzung*), both developed by scholarship and jurisprudence in order to fill *lacunae* experienced in legal practice. The differentiated system, though theoretically fascinating, had often been criticised. And indeed, *Kitagawa* reminds us that, working on Japanese law,[85] he had pointed out its defects and proposed a unified system

83 Kitagawa, ch 2 *supra in fine*.

84 On this point, see also Kitagawa, n 21 *supra*, 330, 341 with note 29. F. Regelsberger's *Pandekten* (Leipzig 1893) have been translated into Greece in 1935!

85 On the Japanese law on breach of contract, see eg Marutschke, n 14 *supra*, 155–163. The rules on breach of contract bear some resemblance of the French system but have, in the course of the reception of theories, been construed in a German fashion.

of contractual liability.[86] With the Reform of the Law of Obligations (*Schuldrechtsmodernisierung*) of 2002, German law has now moved in a similar direction (see in particular §§ 280, 437 BGB).[87]

c) The Law of Damages

A well-known example of a 'mixed reception' is the law of damages.[88] The Japanese Civil Code has followed the Common Law model and adopted the rationale of *Hadley* v. *Baxendale*[89] with its distinction of normal damages as would usually occur and exceptional damages due to the specific circumstances (§ 416 Civil Code). This contrasts with the German model that employs a uniform definition of damages, based on the 'difference theory' (*Differenztheorie*) that provides for full compensation, § 249 BGB. The damages recoverable are limited by a number of counteracting principles, one of which remains the 'adequance-theory' (*Adäquanztheorie*) pursuant to which only such consequences which were reasonably foreseeable ('adequate') are recoverable.

In the phase of the reception of theories, two schools of thought offered different approaches.[90] The 'pure German school of thought' argued that the German concept of damages should be applied wholesale, irrespective of the wording of the code. The 'modified German school of thought' advocated a limited reception, based on the structure of § 416 of the Civil Code. The latter seems to have carried the day.

Civil law and Common Law have thus been successfully melted (even though it has been questioned whether this can be regarded as an instance of successful *reception*!).[91] Today, the Japanese law

86 Kitagawa, ch 3 *supra* sub IV 2; Kitagawa (1990: 'Ein Jahrhundert'), n 14 *supra*, 15–17 (with note 9!).

87 Whether and to what extent the reform constitutes a shift of paradigm is, however, debated. Lorenz, ch 7 *supra* sub IV, argues that the *Schuldrechtsmodernisierung* largely follows the established tradition and merely refines it.

88 Kitagawa (1990: 'Ein Jahrhundert'), n 14 *supra*, 31 sq.

89 *Hadley* v. *Baxendale* (1854) 9 Ex. 341.

90 Kitagawa (1970: 'Rezeption'), n 14 *supra*, 92; Kitagawa (1990: 'Drei Entwicklungsphasen'), n 14 *supra*, 128 sq.

91 Kitagawa (1990: 'Drei Entwicklungsphasen'), n 14 *supra*, 128 sq; see also Kitagawa (1970: 'Rezeption'), n 14 *supra*, 93.

seems to be quite unique. The Common Law-starting point of *Hadley* v. *Baxendale* which concerns liability for breach of contract only has been generalised so as to build a uniform fundament which also applies for damages in tort.[92] And German doctrine seems to influence jurisprudence in a subtle way.

d) The Protection of Good Faith in the Land Register

Professor *Kitagawa* has pointed out that the Japanese Civil Code does not provide for a protection of good faith (*Gutglaubensschutz*) in the land register. The courts have, however, been able to help the aggrieved parties in adequate cases by means of a general protection of good faith (*Vertrauensschutz*), i.e. a different theoretical construction.[93]

The mixed reception of foreign laws has led to legal issues which are quite unique, not known to the 'mother-jurisdictions'. Jurisprudence and scholarship were thus confronted with unique issues and forced to develop new solutions.

e) Constant Adaptation

Apart from these examples of individual rules or doctrines, there is one general undercurrent that seems to be characteristic for Japanese law: its *adaptability* over time and the ongoing process of digesting foreign influences.[94, 95] Japanese lawyers seem to have developed (or maintained) such openness for development long before the slogan of life-long learning came up. Perhaps we find here a lesson that the history of Ancient Greece seems to purport as well: It is the constant influx and digestion of new ideas that keeps a culture vital and young.

92 Stoll, n 15 *supra*, 153–155.

93 Kitagawa (1990: 'Drei Entwicklungsphasen'), n 14 *supra*, 133 sq.

94 Smith, ch 9 *infra* sub VI, makes a similar point when he speaks of the Japanese legal system as 'an evolving system; it is not static'.

95 The methodological issues connected with the adaptation of foreign influences cannot be discussed here.

IV. Methodological Aspects

These considerations lead me to a final section that deals with methodological aspects. Constant change has become a challenge for the civil law systems of the EC Member States. The constant influx of new rules (and principles) is a challenge to the legal system as such. In the European Community, the adaptability of the legal system is a separate issue. A discussion of related issues may also shed some light on the question of the identity of Japanese law.

1. Legal Transplants vs. Legal Irritants

Recently, an older debate has gained new attention, it is the question of whether, in how far and under what conditions legal transplants are possible and can be successful. *Alan Watson* had discussed the issue in the 1970s.[96] Inquiring into the use and aims of comparative law, he argues that legal transplants (or 'legal borrowings') are possible even if made from a legal system 'at a much higher level of development and of a different political complexion'. 'Successful borrowing could be achieved even when nothing was known of the political, social or economic context of the foreign law'.[97] *Watson* quotes rich historical evidence including the reception of Roman law in Europe and the reception of French and German law in Japan as examples of successful transplantation.

The issue is, of course, not new,[98] and it is rather debated. The underlying assumption of autonomy of the legal system (autonomous from society) is challenged radically by a culturalist approach as, for example, recently advanced by *Pierre Legrand.*[99] Other critique is not

96 A. Watson, *Legal Transplants – An Approach to Comparative Law* (Charlottesville 1974) 21–30 *et passim*; A. Watson, 'Legal Transplants and Law Reform' *L.Q.R.* 92 (1976) 79-84; A. Watson, *The Evolution of Law* (1985); A. Watson, 'Aspects of Reception of Law' *Am. J. Comp. L.* 44 (1996) 335–351.
97 Watson (1976: 'Legal Transplants'), n 95 *supra*, 79.
98 Montesquieu, *De l'Esprit des Lois,* Book XXIX ch 13.
99 P. Legrand, 'Comparative Legal Studies and Commitment to Theory' *M.L.R.* 48 (1995) 262–273; P. Legrand, 'European Legal Systems are not Converging' *ICLQ* 45 (1996) 52–81; P. Legrand, 'The Impossibility of "Legal Trans-

so radical but still emphasizes that at least some legal rules and institutions are related to other elements or systems of society and thus withstand an isolated transplantation. The publication of *Watson's* book coincided with that of *Otto Kahn-Freund's* Chorley Lecture 1973 who takes the opposite stance.[100] He distinguishes 'mechanical' rules from 'organic' rules. While the former, due to their technical character, can easily be detached from a legal system, the latter are more closely linked with the social and political context. He therefore concludes, 'we cannot take for granted that rules or institutions are transplantable'.[101]

Harmonisation of private law in Europe has triggered new interest in the question and *Gunther Teubner* has reconsidered it recently.[102] Building on *Kahn-Freund's* distinction, *Teubner* examines the effects of the 'implantation' of the good faith principle into English law. He points out how a transplantation of a concept previously unknown to English law can lead to an adverse reaction of the organism of the law. The transplant can end up as an irritant. With regard to harmonisation, *Teubner* demonstrates how such irritation can have adverse effects, leading to disintegration – new divergences.[103]

With regard to our subject, we do not have to decide whether the functionalist approach or the culturalist or contextualist approach is better founded. The various authors agree that legal rules or institutions – if to a different degree – are interrelated with other rules, the legal system at large and extra-legal institutions such as customs,

plants'" *MJ* 4 (1997) 111–124; P. Legrand, 'Against a European Civil Code' *M.L.R.* 60 (1997) 44–63.

100 O. Kahn-Freund, 'On Uses and Misuses of Comparative Law' *M.L.R.* 37 (1974) 1–27.

101 Ibid.

102 G. Teubner, 'Legal Irritants: Good Faith in British Law or How Unifying Law Ends Up in New Divergences' *M.L.R.* 61 (1998) 11–32.

103 Incidentally, *Shiomi* has indicated similar experiences in Japan. He has hinted at 'problems that would occur upon the introduction of foreign laws into domestic legislation'; Shiomi, ch 3 *supra* sub II 2 (2). And he points out: 'Neither should it be overlooked that it was considered difficult to transplant the spirit of German jurisprudence into Japan given a different historical environment.'; loc. cit., sub III 2.

religion, language[104] etc. Following *Watson's* picture, we can well agree that law is a living organism. For that reason, however, transplantation can have diverse effects. The transplantation may work effectively and even heal a suffering legal system. It may, however, lead to adverse reactions of the organism that have to be cured with other medication, or to a rejection of the transplant. 'A successful legal transplant', says *Watson*, '– like that of a human organ – will grow in its new body, and become part of that body just as the rule or institution would have continued to develop in its parent system.'[105]

Returning to Japanese Civil Law, its identity can today hardly be at issue. Even if the Japanese Civil Code had been a mere translation of the *Code civil* or the BGB, it would have been moulded into something new and unique through the process of assimilation ('Japanisation') and through its integration into and interaction with the legal system as a whole. Indeed, the apparent paradox is the outset for *Alan Watson's* discussion of legal transplants: 'Law shows us many paradoxes. Perhaps the strangest of all is that, on the one hand, a people's law can be regarded as being special to it, indeed a sign of that people's identity, and it is in fact remarkable how different in important detail even two closely related systems might be; on the other hand, legal transplants – the moving of a rule or a system of law from one country to another, or from one people to another – have been common since the earliest recorded history.'[106]

An Austro-German example may further illustrate the point. The civil laws of these countries are, of course, rather different with the Austrian *Allgemeines Bürgerliches Gesetzbuch* on the one hand and the German BGB on the other. Still there are convergences in many fields. The theory of contracts with protective effect on third parties (*Vertrag mit Schutzwirkung für Dritte*) is an example. The theory had originally been developed in Germany and was later successfully adopted in Austria. Once part of the Austrian legal system, it be-

104 Indeed, it has been pointed out that the relation of law and language is of particular importance when we compare European legal systems with the Japanese; cf Llompart, n 15 *supra*, 131, 132. On law and language generally B. Großfeld, 'Der Buchstabe des Gesetzes – Zur Rechtsvergleichung mit anderen Schriftkulturen' *JZ* 1997 1–10; T. Weir, 'Die Sprachen des europäischen Rechts – Eine skeptische Betrachtung' *ZEuP* 1995 368–374 (with regard to Europeanisation of civil law). See also Shiomi, ch 3 *supra* sub II 2 (2).

105 Watson (1974: 'Legal Transplants'), n 95 *supra*, 27.

106 Ibid 21.

gan to lead its own life, though. And while the German *Bundesgerichtshof* was unwilling to use the theory as a foundation for products liability, the Austrian *Oberster Gerichtshof* has gone just that way.

2. The Legal System as a Living Organism

This leads me to yet another methodological point, this one concerning the effects of application of the law. *Watson's* work on legal transplants is based on the conception of the legal system as a living organism. Indeed, this picture is widely accepted. The legal system 'lives' and changes constantly, if 'creepingly'. *Larenz* characterises the application of the law as a value-oriented mode of thought.[107] Jurisprudence, including the mere interpretation and application of the law, is not just a mechanical process but includes a value statement. Every interpretation of the law thus has a creative element. Therefore, every application of the law, be it by way of adherence of those subject to it or by way of a court decision, contributes to its life.

Consequently, the same rules will gradually work differently – diverge – in different legal systems. A constant divergence can only be avoided through a common court system.[108] Various examples illustrate the issue. Thus, the harmonisation effects of the Rome Convention[109] were at doubt while there was no recourse to the European Court of Justice as a common court. In German private law, the application of the same law through the various courts of appeal may well lead to disparate results if there is no recourse to the *Bundesgerichtshof*. We have already hinted at such processes in Japanese

[107] K. Larenz, *Methodenlehre der Rechtswissenschaft* (Berlin, Heidelberg, New York 1991) 204–206, 214–224, 312–316, 366–369.
[108] See also T. Weir, 'Divergent Legal Systems in a Single Member State' *ZEuP* 1998 564–585, who illustrates the point with example of England and Scotland; he demonstrates that the same rules can have different meanings in England and Scotland and points out, that 'it can hardly be said that having one [common supreme court] has produced much common law' (569); on the relation of English and Australian law and the consequences of the Australia Act 1986 which ended the recourse to the Priviy Council C. Hofmann, 'Australisches Vertragsrecht: Eine Einführung unter besonderer Berücksichtigung der Rechtsquellenlehre' *ZVglRWiss* 104 (2005) 395–426.
[109] Convention on the law applicable to contractual obligations opened for signature in Rome on 19 June 1980, OJ 1980 L 266/1.

Civil Law by which the transplanted rules have been applied, systemised and thereby, of course, changed. It is the process of assimilation or acculturation ('Japanisation') that followed the reception of the law and the reception of theories (*supra,* II 1 b) and III 2).[110]

V. Conclusion

Let me end our tour around the Cologne Dome at this point. I could not offer you more than some observations on the observed, together with some rather general thoughts about more general aspects of comparative law and methods. All I can hope for, therefore, is that my audience will agree that I have been successful in evading the subject.

The unique development of modern Japanese civil law demonstrates a strong genetic relation to German civil law. And this relation has been intensified by the process of the reception of legal theories. This development and the common roots justify the classification of Japanese law as part of the Germanic legal family (but, of course, also of other legal families). Yet, all we know about legal transplants and the legal system as a living organism confirms that Japanese civil law is unique and has its own identity. The papers of our Japanese colleagues have highlighted this with several examples.

It is therefore not surprising that German-Japanese comparisons are by no means a one-way enterprise. The reception periods have long been passed and Japanese civil law has emancipated[111] from its parents. The economic success, but also original concepts, institutions and theories have triggered increased interest in Japanese law.[112]

110 See again Kitagawa, n 78 *supra*, 307 sq, 310–320.

111 Indeed, Kitagawa (1990: 'Drei Entwicklungsphasen'), n 14 *supra*, 126, indicates that the reception of theories was followed by a process of emancipation (‚befreit').

112 An example is the recent conference volume H. Baum (ed), *Japan: Economic Success and Legal System* (Berlin 1997). See also Baum, n 14 *supra*, 258–292; Igarashi, n 14 *supra*, IX sq; Z. Kitagawa, 'Von der Japanisierung zur Entjapanisierung', in H. Coing et al (eds), *Die Japanisierung westlichen Rechts* (Tübingen 1990) 441, who points out that *Japanisation* is (primarily, but) not

In the light of the German *Schuldrechtsmodernisierung,* the example of Professor *Kitagawa's* contribution to the law of contractual liability (*supra,* III 2b)) is ample proof that such comparative exchange can be mutually beneficial.

exclusively an aspect of the assimilation of Western law to Japanese customs and traditions but also a reception of Japanese legal thought in the West.

Chapter 9: On the Identity of Japanese Civil Law from Common Law Perspectives

Malcolm Smith

Contents

I. Introduction

May I acknowledge at the outset my intellectual debt to Professor *Kitagawa.* A translation of his seminal work on the 'Theory Reception' phase of the construction of the Japanese legal system in the early part of the 20th century became available in English just as I commenced my teaching career in 1974.[1] I have used it ever since with my students in Australia and Canada. I have used it not only with my

1 Z. Kitagawa, 'Theory Reception – One Aspect of the Development of Japanese Civil Law Science' (transl. by R. E. Lee) *Law In Japan: An Annual* 4 (1974) 1–16.

students studying Japanese Law, but also with my Australian students as they have studied the theory of the common law method. It has influenced my publications, and it will influence my discussion today.

I am also grateful to be involved in a seminar that brings together specialists from Germany and Japanese specialists on German and French law, as well as the Anglo-American system of the United States. It has been surprising to me that there are no programs regarding the Japanese legal system in Germany or France, and, I understand, only one permanent teaching position for Japanese Law in Germany. In contrast, there are at least four chairs in the USA, at the University of Washington, Harvard, Michigan, and Columbia; one in Canada at UBC, at least three positions in the United Kingdom, two at London and one at Oxford Brookes; and four positions in Australia at Melbourne, ANU, Sydney and UNSW. On the other hand, it is my observation that the chair, or *koza* system, in Japanese Law Faculties has tied professors into particular fields. Japanese scholars who specialize in German Law, French Law or Anglo-American Law usually are not regarded by their colleagues as experts in Japanese Law. *Kitagawa* is therefore exceptional in being recognized as an expert in both civil law and common law scholarship.

II. What is an 'Identity'?

Today, my topic is 'The Identity of Japanese Civil Law: a View from the Common Law Perspective'. In November 2004, I was invited to speak at another conference on the general identity of Japanese law in the global era. My views have not changed, so I will repeat some of what I said then.[2] However, today's topic challenges me to go beyond discussing a general identity and to explore the identity of the civil law system in Japan. It will emerge that even though I have studied Japanese law for 35 years, my interests have not carried me very deeply into the Japanese civil law system.

2 M. Smith 'The Identity of Japanese Law', in Waseda University Institute of Comparative Law, *Waseda Proceedings of Comparative Law* Vol. 7 503–511 (2005).

The English dictionaries that I have consulted all give meanings for 'identity' that relate to distinguishing characteristics. So what are the characteristics of Japanese civil law that set it apart from others, or which define its nature and essence?

I said in 2004: 'first, I would argue that the concept of the "identity" of Japanese law involves a consideration of two important perspectives: 1) the way in which Japanese view their own legal identity; and 2) the identity that outsiders impose on Japanese law. These views are usually influenced by their own perspectives of the role of law in their own communities. In turn, these perspectives are influenced greatly by the methodologies that are brought to bear on the task of establishing legal identities. There is some evidence that these two perspectives operate independently of each other, at least to the extent that Japanese scholars may not place much store by what foreigners think about their legal system.'[3]

I think a Japanese view on the identity of Japanese civil law will emerge from the papers prepared for this conference by Japanese scholars. I am giving the view of a common law-trained outsider regarding the identity of Japanese law, particularly civil law. May I say at the outset that, unlike many other areas of the Japanese legal system, I have always associated the Japanese Civil Code with continental legal systems, and used it as a contrast to other areas where the influence of common law systems seemed more obvious to my students. This is a matter of historical origins and subsequent interpretation.[4] I also am using the term 'civil law' more broadly in the sense of non-public law, non-criminal law and non-procedural law.

When teaching Japanese law at universities in common law countries, most subjects take the approach of providing a broad overview. Few law schools have the space in their curriculum for multiple subjects

3 See H. Sono, 'The Multiple Worlds of Nihon-ho', in T. Ginsburg, L. Nottage and H. Sono (eds), *The Multiple Worlds of Japanese Law: Disjunctions and Conjunctions* (Victoria 2001) for a discussion of the interaction between outside commentators and Japanese scholars.

4 K. Takayanagi, 'A Century of Innovation: the development of Japanese Law 1868–1961', in A.T. von Mehren, *Law in Japan: the Legal Order in a Changing Society* (Harvard 1963) and Kitagawa, n 1 *supra*.

on Japanese law.[5] The common law approach is to select broad issues that highlight the way in which the Japanese legal system has developed, and the way in which it approaches the resolution of specific social problems. Civil law is not usually taught as an integrated area, as in Japan. Rather bits and pieces of civil law emerge in discussion when they are relevant to broader issues. There is little time, and insufficient references, to undertake the type of close comparison of Japanese doctrines with that of Germany or France that is displayed in many of the papers prepared for this conference. If these papers are published, it may trigger a re-evaluation of how civil law is taught at universities in common law countries.

In discussing the evolution of Japanese law, I have usually focused on principles of common law that clearly were imported into the Japanese civil law system, and have explored their subsequent application. In particular, I have discussed the concept of damages (Civil Code, Art. 416)[6] and the powers of a corporation (Civil Code, Art. 43).[7] Then I might discuss the Securities and Exchange Act and the Antimonopoly Act as examples of legal constructs taken directly from American law that were assimilated into the Japanese legal fabric. Civil law would re-emerge in specific topics on contract law, tort law, environmental law, product liability law, family law and labor law. I have now been teaching about Japanese law in law schools since 1974, in Australia, Canada and the United States as well as in Japan and Thailand. What sort of identity have I been attaching to Japanese civil law? What sort of resources have I been using to teach about Japanese law?

5 Exceptions would be the L.L.M. program in US-Japan transactions at the University of Washington, and my own experience at Melbourne Law School in the period 1988-98 when I taught an introductory subject in the L.L.B. program and multiple subjects on Japanese dispute resolution and joint ventures at the graduate level. In the late 1990s student preferences turned to themed subjects covering a number of countries in Asia.

6 This issue is discussed by virtually all the commentators at this conference, led by *Kitagawa*. See *Kitagawa's* translated paper in *Law In Japan: An Annual*, n 1 *supra*.

7 A. Takeuchi, 'How should We Abolish the *Ultra Vires* Doctrine in Corporate Law?' (1968) 2 *Law In Japan: An Annual* 140.

III. A Basic Selection of English Publications on Japanese Civil Law

I think it is fair to say that during the last fifty years, the great majority of English-language scholarly analysis concerning Japanese law has been produced by scholars from the United States, or by Japanese scholars addressing an American audience. One goal of my own career has been to try to develop an alternative common law interpretation. In my own view, the American System is an 'outlier' among common law systems. It exists at a distance from all other common law countries that have adopted the English approach to law and legal institutions. Many of the analyses have measured Japan against an idealized American model. Many of the conclusions have stressed how different Japan is to the American model. Today, talking to a Japanese and German audience, I would like to suggest that if in many areas of law Japan is distant from the American model, then it should be noted that most other common law systems are also different from the American model.[8] Tomorrow, in my Comment an *Tsuneo Matsumoto's* paper, I plan to introduce the work of the current generation of young Australian scholars of Japanese law who largely dissent from the traditional approaches.[9] Today I will limit myself to asking "does this mean that Japan is dose to those other common law systems, or is it distant from the United States, but in a different direction?"

Another preliminary issue is that many of the commentators have not been comparative lawyers an the American side. Rather, they have been what we might call "foreign law" specialists: scholars who have made a special study of the Japanese System without any explicit comparative intent. However, their assumed (but often not stated) basis of evaluation is the American system. The objective of these

8 I have pursued this point in much of my own writings; see, e.g., my S.J.D. dissertation "Administrative Discretion in Foreign Trade Regulation; Japan, Australia and the United States" (Harvard 1976); Kyushu University Faculty of Law and Japan Society for the Promotion of Science, 2002 Asian Science Seminar "Law and the Open Society in Asia"; Malcolm Smith, "Comparative Law and Legal Culture" in (2003) 15 *Bond Law Review* 12.

9 Veronica Taylor (ed.), *Asian Law through Australian Eyes* (Law Book Co. 1997); Tom Ginsburg, Luke Nottage and Hiroo Sono (eds.) *The Multiple Worlds of Japanese Law: Disjunetions and Conjunctions* (2001).

scholars is usually to explain how the Japanese legal system operates in a particular area, not to make an analysis of the doctrinal basis for specific principles of law. Accordingly, for example, more time is spent an asking why Japanese do not use the civil procedure system than in making an inquiry into the specific civil law rules an warranties.[10] I would suggest that the two topics most discussed by common lawyers have been the rules regarding the practice of foreign lawyers in Japan and Japanese litigation rates.[11]

Alternatively, other key interpretations are found in works of Japanese scholars that are directed to an American audience. Often these scholars are specialists of the Anglo-American legal system in their own universities in Japan, or they are specialists in particular areas of Japanese law who have produced their work while studying in the United States. I note *Matsumoto's* point that many German scholars also introduce American principles into their work on German law, which is then taken up by Japanese scholars of German law. The process of legal development is not a simple matter when dealing with interaction between mature legal systems. Let me give some examples of key publications used by common lawyers for the benefit of our German guests.

1. General Introductory Texts

The seminal English-language text on Japanese law is *Arthur von Mehren's* Law in Japan, an edited set of conference papers published in 1963.[12] All the chapters were prepared by leading Japanese scholars, lawyers, prosecutors and judges with the assistance of bilingual American lawyers. Each chapter introduces an area of Japanese law and serves as the base for any further research in that area. Apart from a section on legal history, there is no chapter on the civil law as

10 Some have evolved into leading comparative law scholars, e.g. John Haley, who now is co-author of Merriman's text an Comparative Law.

11 Richard Rabinowitz, who has practiced law in Tokyo for some 50 years and is a considerable scholar of Japanese law, has lamented the fact that so much effort has been wasted an the foreign lawyer issue.

12 Sadly, von *Mehren* passed away in early 2006. I took his subject at Harvard Law School in 1972. He was not himself a scholar of Japan, but is forever associated with the development of knowledge about Japanese Law.

such. There are specific chapters on family law, labor law, motor vehicle accidents, commercial law, corporation law and tax law. Professor *Michida's* chapter on 'The Legal Structure for Economic Enterprise: Some Aspects of Commercial Law' deals with sales, contracts and warranties in just four pages.[13] All the authors assume Japan in 1963 to still be firmly in the civil law system camp and the chapters touching on civil law largely try to explain German concepts to an American audience.

I refer my students routinely to three contemporary American authors. These books do confer an understanding of the identity of Japanese law. All three see the role of the bureaucracy as crucial in understanding how all areas of Japanese law work in practice. *John O. Haley* has published two general introductory texts on the Japanese legal system during the past 15 years.[14] *Haley* makes a complex argument that links Japan's pre-1867 traditions with its contemporary legal system. Unlike proponents of the legal culture school, he is very conscious of the detailed operation of laws in Japan. He sees the development of Japan's legal system as largely the preserve of the bureaucrats, but he disputes that they have uncontrolled powers. As the title of his first book suggests, he sees authority exercised in Japan without the kind of sanctions that underpin the powers of American civil servants or judges. Accordingly, he thinks the bureaucrats have to negotiate to get their way.

Frank Upham published his major general introductory text in 1987.[15] He starts from an interpretation based on the role of the judiciary in a system dominated by the bureaucracy. Unlike *Haley*, he concludes that civil servants in Japan have so much power conferred on them by the relevant legislation that they don't have to exercise it by using sanctions. The mere threat of sanctions backs their success in negotiating outcomes. He uses four case studies to prove his point. Only one case study concerns civil law as such, and it is in the specific field of environmental law.

13 A.T. v. Mehren, n 4 *supra*, 519–523.
14 J. Haley, *Authority without Power: The Japanese Paradox* (Oxford 1991) and *The Spirit of Japanese Law* (Athens GA 1998); J.H. Merryman, D.S. Clark and J.O. Haley, *The Civil Law Tradition: Europe, Latin America, and East Asia* (Charlottesville 1994).
15 F.K. Upham, *Law and Social Change in Postwar Japan* (Harvard 1987).

More recently, *J. Mark Ramseyer* has written extensively on Japanese law, offering an economic interpretation that essentially denies ascribing any particular identity to Japanese law. His writing challenges a broadly accepted view that Japanese law is identified by its unique cultural and social contexts. His key argument is that Japanese civil law is so clear and predictable that there are few issues that require an interpretation from a judge through litigation. Therefore, he identifies Japanese civil law as extremely rational and predictable compared with a high degree of uncertainty in systems with high litigation rates, especially concerning civil litigation in the 50 states of the United States.[16] He also employs political agency theory to argue that the real principals in the past 20 years have been the legislators, who can control both civil servants and judges. This view has prompted major debates among Anglo-American scholars, particularly in relation to the issue of the independence of judges in Japan.[17]

2. Specific Textbooks on Civil Law

In the realm of textbooks, I can think of no general textbook on the civil law system written by a common lawyer. There are some texts on specific areas, such as *Luke Nottage's* work on product liability law,[18] but no general text.

16 J. M. Ramseyer and M. Nakazato, *Japanese Law: an Economic Approach* (Chicago 1999).

17 See an ongoing series of articles on judicial independence in which John Haley engages in a debate with *Ramseyer*. J. M. Ramseyer and E. B. Rasmusen, 'Why Are Japanese Judges So Conservative in Politically Charged Cases?' 95 *American Political Science Review* (2001) 331–344; J. M. Ramseyer and E. B. Rasmusen, 'Judicial Independence in a Civil Law Regime: The Evidence From Japan' 13 *Journal of Law Economics and Organization* (1997) 259–286. On 28 February 2006, I attended a conference in Australia at which a young legal scholar and an economist comprehensively questioned *Ramseyers's* methodology, as well as his conclusions. He is criticized for using outdated Chicago School methodology without taking into account more recent work by the behavioral economists. This is a new development.

18 L. Nottage, *Product Safety and Liability Law in Japan: from Minamata to Mad Cows* (Oxford 2004).

3. Treatises

There are two English-language treatises in English on Japanese law aimed primarily at practitioners, both of which have sections concerning the civil law system. *Kitagawa*'s monumental seven-volume work 'Doing Business in Japan' was published first in 1982 by *Matthew Bender* and is regularly updated. Many of the chapters were written with the assistance of leading Japanese practitioners. A team of young researchers, including Australians, assisted with the text. However, I think it is fair to say that the identity created for Japanese civil law in that treatise is based on Japanese interpretations, albeit directed primarily at a North American audience. The second practitioners' treatise is published by CCH and is entitled 'Japan Business Law Guide', originally edited by *Mitsuo Matsushita*. He is an expert in international trade law and antimonopoly law. Chapters were commissioned to both Japanese and foreign authors. The Contracts chapter was written by *Kato* of Nagoya University, as were most other areas dealing with civil law principles. I wrote the chapter on Corporations, so a difference in approach may be observable.

4. Casebooks

There are a number of casebooks designed for teaching a general introductory course on Japanese law. I think it is fair to say that they do not have space to deal in any depth with the civil law system. They try to provide points of discussion concerning most areas of law. Most are selections of materials that the editors believe are important in establishing the identity of Japanese law to foreign students. In the civil law area there are usually introductory materials on basic contract law, especially interpretations on the use of contracts by Japanese business, and specific examples of tort law drawn from environmental law, medical negligence cases or product liability. In the tort law area the focus is usually on the Japanese system's provision of alternatives to the tort system, such as no-fault schemes and the use of mediators.

I must mention *Tanaka's* casebook, as I was heavily involved in its production.[19] You will notice it contains a significant amount of case

19 H. Tanaka, *The Japanese Legal System* (Tokyo 1976).

law as he was preparing it for his classes at Harvard Law School in 1974 and believed that American students expected to learn from reported cases. The selected cases do provide insights into the way that judges reason in Japan, as well as introducing key areas of civil law. I will use examples from these materials later to illustrate some of my points, but the cases translated for the book introduce contract law, property law and tort law, as well as the function of the general clauses in the Civil Code and the way in which judges have interpreted specific provisions of the Code.

Notable contemporary casebooks include the materials published and used by Harvard and Columbia Law Schools. These materials are edited by Professors *Young*, *Ramseyer*, and *Milhaupt*, all leading American specialists on Japanese law, and all with close associations with Harvard and Columbia, as either graduates or teachers. The first materials used at Harvard and Columbia were brought together by *Charles Stevens* and Professor *Takahashi Isshu* in the late 1960s. *Stevens* taught as an Adjunct Professor at Columbia and was the first appointee to the Mitsubishi visiting position at Harvard. When *Michael Young* graduated from Harvard and was appointed to Columbia, he produced his own materials for Columbia. *Ramseyer* began his career in the 1980s and *Milhaupt* in the 1990s. Their materials are important as they present the contemporary view of the Japanese legal identity to law students at two of the most important programs in the United States.

More recently, general introductory casebooks have been produced by *Kenneth Port and Gerry McAllin*[20], who are both American law professors, and *Meryl Dean*, who is now Dean of Law at Oxford Brookes University in England, and is aiming at a UK audience in her selection of materials.

The final word must be reserved for the pioneer in this field: the Asian Law program at the University of Washington. Starting in 1964 the Washington program, under the direction of the late Professor *Dan Fenno Henderson*, began compiling casebooks in a variety of areas relevant to the L.L.M. program in U.S.-Japan Business

[20] K. Port and G. Mcallin, *Comparative Law: Law and the Legal Process in Japan* (2nd ed., Durham 2003).

Transactions. The general introductory materials were published as *Henderson and Haley* 'Law and the Legal Process in Japan' in 1978. Other materials include US/Japanese Contract and Sales Problems, edited by *Warren Shattuck* and *Kitagawa*,[21] and Cases and Materials on Japan and U.S. Business Corporation Law by *Richard Kummert* and *Misao Tatsuta*.[22] These are pure gold for those who have access to them.

5. Journals

From 1967 on, the field has been well served by a publication of the Japanese-American Society for Legal Studies, *Law in Japan: An Annual*. It reached 25 issues, but sadly went out of publication in 2002. There are many articles on Civil Law, including both translations of articles from Japanese journals and original works in English by Japanese and western authors. The early editions are particularly rich in material regarding the civil law system by famous Japanese scholars.[23] When I was editing *Law in Japan: An Annual* in the late 1970s and early 1980s, there was no doubt that the translations that were hardest to edit were those regarding the Japanese civil law and administrative law systems, because the concepts involved owed most to German or French law, and both the translators and myself were largely ignorant of the details of German and French legal concepts. To a significant extent, I have studied German and French law through a Japanese filter.

Since *Law in Japan: An Annual* ceased publication, the major source for new English-language material on Japanese law is actually produced in Germany. The bilingual *Zeitschrift für Japanisches Rechts* is

21 W. Shattuck and Z. Kitagawa, *United States & Japanese Contract & Sale Problems* (Seattle 1970, 1973 revised).

22 M. Tatsuta, *Cases and materials on Japanese and U.S. Business Corporation Law* (Seattle 1986). Again, there have been various versions since the 1960s. There was an update in 1988 and I believe *Lawrence Repeta* prepared a subsequent version.

23 Eg Professor *Kitagawa's* work on Damages in Contract Law appeared in Vol. 3 and his Theory Reception work in Vol. 4. Professor *Kato Ichiro's* work on Balancing of Interests was translated in Vol. 2 and his interpretation of Tort Law in Vol. 1. Professor *Kawashima's* work on Contract Consciousness in Japan appeared in Vol. 7.

now in its 20th issue and is making a major contribution. Young American legal scholars in the late 20th and early 21st centuries apparently are more heavily rewarded professionally for contributing articles to in leading American law journals, and so major articles are now circulated through those journals. The Australian *Journal of Asian Law* also publishes many articles on Japan.

So if I have perpetuated the idea that the identity of Japanese civil law lies in the European camp, is that still accurate or useful? I am reminded by reading the Japanese papers at this conference that all of the contributors assert an independent identity for Japanese civil law. How has this come about? How will Japan assimilate new solutions for new social problems?

IV. Methodology

A second major point I have made throughout my career is that the traditional methodologies of comparative law, particularly the 'legal families' approach, are exposed as being insufficient when applied to Japan.

'In this respect it does not seem to me to be very useful to apply the traditional 'tags' of the comparative lawyers to ascertain the identity of Japanese law. I don't think the basic terms "civil law system" or "common law system" help us much any more, at least when the essential difference is seen in terms of legal systems based on legislative action and legal systems based on judicial action. The distinction is no longer valid in comparisons between Europe and the United Kingdom, where the original distinction emerged. Legislation is now far more important as a source of law in England than case law, and this is true in all other common law countries. Indeed this has been true for over half a century. On the other hand, in Europe, the role of case law is increasing. There is a convergence. Rather than constituting an organizing principle by which legal systems can be identified, the distinction is now a limited, technical point about the relative roles of the courts in different national legal systems.'[24]

24 Smith, n 2 *supra*, referring to E. Hondius, 'Precedent in East and West', International Academy of Commercial and Consumer Law, Conference 'Global-

The papers at this conference suggest that there may still be sufficient historical connection between Japanese civil law on the one hand and German and French civil law on the other, to make close doctrinal comparisons valid. However, let me deal with general issues first.

I have asserted that the convergence of legal systems based predominantly on legislation and legal systems that allocate a significant role for judge-made law has rendered the old civil law/common law divide meaningless. How do the methodologies differ? *Kitagawa* gave a lucid explanation in his work in the late 1960s. As one who has taught and published on the common law method for over three decades, let me expand on two issues. One is how judges make judge-made law, based purely on prior cases. The other is the important, but neglected, theory on how common law judges interpret legislation, which is now their primary role.

1. Pure Judge-made law and Case Law Development

In the case of the 'method' followed by Japanese judges in developing the civil law system, as distinct from the 'substance' of the principles they develop, is there a significant difference from the common law judicial approach? Two distinctions are usually asserted: 1) there is no doctrine of precedent and 2) judges do not make law. My understanding, based on my early work with *Tanaka*, is that from the 1920s, following a spirited attack by *Suehiro*, Japanese judges and law reporters have followed a similar pattern to the common law systems.[25]

The Japanese law reporters give a full description of the facts as found by the court, an outline of the arguments of counsel, and each judge sets out the reasons for his or her decision. I understand that the judges seldom, if ever, refer to academics by name, nor do they cite articles or books when adopting new ideas, but it is only recently that English courts began to cite living authors. The *Tanaka* casebook

ization, Regionalization and Transplants in Commercial and Consumer Law', (Riga, Latvia, August 2004) (unpublished manuscript).

25 Tanaka, n 19 *supra*, 146–150. However, a German colleague assures me that the Japanese approach is French, not German or common law.

contains many examples of judgments that cite previous cases. *Kawashima* has argued that a concept of precedent applies at the highest level, since a Full Bench of the Supreme Court must be convened to settle differences in approach by any two of its Petty Benches, or to overturn a principle established by a prior Supreme Court Full Bench.[26] The technical differences in reasoning seem minor to me. The major difference is hierarchical in that a common law judge is bound to follow the decisions of the next highest court, but a Japanese judge seems free to depart from the reasoning of higher courts, thereby throwing the burden of appealing onto those who want to uphold the higher court's view.

In theory, Japanese judges are supposed not to make law. However, there seem to be many examples where judges have in fact made up new principles when there seemed to be no solutions in the existing legislation. Two examples in the *Tanaka* Casebook are the development of protection for women living in relationships that have not been formalized under civil law (*naien* marriages)[27] and the development of a principle allowing heirs to succeed to claims for pain and suffering which might have been asserted by the deceased (the so-called *zannen hanketsu*).[28] Further examples seem to be the development of general principles derived from European law in the 1920s and 1930s, such as 'good faith and trust' and 'abuse of rights', which were later added to the Civil Code in 1948,[29] and the doctrine of 'changed circumstances' (*jijo henkou).*[30] An example from property law would be the 'provisional registration security device' that is now also the subject of new legislation.[31]

In all these instances the Japanese judges have framed new principles without any direct legislative basis. In other cases I will discuss below, the judges have interpreted legislative provisions to cover new

26 T. Kawashima, *Kawashima Takeyoshi Chosakushū* [Takeyoshi Kawashima's collected works] (Tokyo 1982) Vol. 5, 272.
27 Tanaka, n 19 *supra*, 157–162.
28 Ibid, 151–161.
29 Ibid, 114–125.
30 T. Sawada, *Subsequent Conduct and Supervening Events* (Ann Arbour 1968).
31 J.O. Haley, 'The Preliminary Contract for Substitute Performance: A Reflection of Japanese Judicial Approach', *Law in Japan: an Annual* 7 (1974) 133–148. This article was drawn from Haley's LL.M. thesis.

situations arguably not contemplated at the time the legislation was drafted and adopted.

2. Theory Reception and the *Dorset Yacht Case*

The approach of judges was a central element of *Kitagawa's* thesis on theory reception. I understand that his examples were based on judicial interpretation of legislative provisions, and his four-stage theory reception model proceeds from stage 1, the legislative basis. I am very interested in his views on cases where there seemed to be no direct legislative basis. At about the same time an eminent English judge propounded the theory of the common law judicial method in a tort case that involved breaking new ground in the law of negligence, namely, the responsibility of government officials for damage inflicted on private property by the criminal actions of those in their legal care and control.

Lord *Diplock* began by noting the conservative nature of common law judges when extending existing principles to new areas: 'this function, which judges hesitate to acknowledge as law-making, plays at most a minor role in the decision of the great majority of cases, and little conscious thought has been given to analyzing its methodology'. He then analyzed the methodology as follows:

> 'And the judicial development of the law of negligence rightly proceeds by seeking first to identify the relevant characteristics that are common to the kinds of conduct and relationship between the parties which are involved in the case for decision and the kinds of conduct or relationship which have been held in previous decisions of the courts to give rise to a duty of care. The method adopted it this stage of the process is *analytical* and *inductive*. It starts with an analysis of the characteristics of the conduct and relationships involved in each of the decided cases. But the analyst must know what he is looking for. (…) For the second stage, which is *deductive* and *analytical* the conduct and relationship involved in the case for decision is then analyzed to ascertain whether they possess each of these characteristics. If they do, the conclusion follows that a duty of care does arise in the case for decision.'[32]

This process may result in the exposition of a more general principle, which will then be applied to new situations by the deductive and

32 *Dorset Yacht Co. Ltd* v. *Home Office* [1970] AC 1004 per Lord Diplock at 1058–59.

analytical method described. As Professor *Kitagawa* has argued, if you start from a legislated principle, then you may begin with the deductive process.

3. Interpreting Legislation

One part of the identity of the Japanese civil law system remains largely hidden from the common lawyer: what is the theory used by Japanese judges to determine the meaning of the words in a code section? I readily admit that this is my own fault, as I had the chance to press my mentor for more information when he was compiling his English-language casebook on the Japanese legal system.[33] The papers for this conference do in fact take up the issue, but assume the reader understands the difference between the 'legislator's intent' and the 'legislation's intent' theories. When interpreting Art. 415, 416 or 709, where do the judges find the meaning of terms such as 'intent', 'negligence' and 'foreseeable'? Where in the Code are these terms or concepts defined?

When I took my first subject as a law student in 1964 over half of it was devoted to the role of judges in statutory interpretation. The subject was called Introduction to Legal Method. We were told that common law legislation was not usually in the form of a code, which we were told purported to replace all prior law in an area, and set out a complete, scientific framework for dealing with an area of law. Instead, we were told that common law judges jealously protected their judge-made principles from legislative interference, and required very explicit statements in a statute before they would accept that it was intended to override an established common law principle. Second, we were presented with at least four approaches to interpretation: literal, purpose, mischief and the Rule in *Heydon's Case*. We were taught that a particular judge could choose between these approaches, but that the common approach was to give the words of the statute their clear literal meaning, unless this would defeat the purpose of the legislation or impute to the legislators a clearly unjust intention.

33 See Tanaka, n 19 *supra*, 61–98, and the cases referenced therein.

We were then taught some very detailed rules that common law judges had developed to help them achieve consistency in interpreting the words of a statute. They involved both canons of interpretation and rules to exclude what the judges considered to be extraneous information gleaned from the legislative process.[34]

However, all this changed substantially in Australia in the 1970s, when legislatures adopted legislation directing the judges how they were to interpret legislation in the future.[35] Today an Australian judge must seek the 'purpose' of the legislature in adopting a law, and give effect to that purpose. The judges still rely on the words in the statute, and its general structure, but they are directed to a wide range of additional material to ensure that they actually do find the true 'purpose' of the legislation. I understand that the United Kingdom has similar legislation. In the United States, most civil law issues are dealt with at the state level, so there are 50 different legislative processes to examine. The federal United States Supreme Court, unlike those in Australia and Canada, has no over-arching jurisdiction to standardize civil law on a national basis.

This discussion becomes relevant in assessing the identity of Japanese civil law: how do judges settle on the meaning of a law if it is based in legislation? How is its identity determined in a concrete case? This is particularly important in considering the way in which principles from the common law have been re-interpreted along German lines. Here the common lawyer would seek some indication of the identity of Japanese civil law by exploring the fate of principles that clearly were derived from the common law. My mentors always pointed to two examples: damages under Art. 416 of the Civil Code and the powers of corporations under Art. 43 of the Civil Code. In both cases the distinctively English principles were deprived of their identity by a process of interpretation designed to give them a German identity. The cases in the *Tanaka* Casebook at pages 61–98 are further examples of how judges have interpreted legislative pro-

34 See now M. Smith, K. Pose and T. Bryant (eds), *Cases and Materials on the Australian Legal Process* (6th ed., Sydney 1994).

35 Eg Acts Interpretation Act 1974 (Commonwealth) §§ 15A & 15B; Interpretation of Legislation Act 1984 (Vic) §§ 34–35.

visions to logically cover situations that may not have been in the minds of the original drafters.

4. Equity

The simplistic reference to English law as a 'common law system' has to be qualified, as prior to 1873 there were actually two separate bodies of law and two separate court systems in England and the United States, one called common law, exercised by the courts of law and the other equity, administered by the Chancery Courts. In 20th century comparisons with civil law countries the term 'common law' is intended to cover both court systems in England and the United States.

The assertion is frequently made that civil law systems do not have a concept of equity, and so have a very different identity. The search for a body of law for equity in Japan is thought to be useless. However, the legal system of equity is often poorly defined. What are the crucial indicia of equity (what is its identity?). One answer focuses on the 'trust', a uniquely English solution to the problems of both allowing someone to control their property into the future and protecting people who suffer legal disabilities. The device of separating legal ownership from the right to benefit from the use and profits of property was a stroke of genius: a trusted friend held the legal rights but was bound to exercise those rights for the benefit of others. This concept seems to have found its way into specific legislation in Japan in the banking area, but not into the Civil Code. However, the legal system of equity is much more than the trust device.

A second approach to equity would focus on the duties of the trustee. In conferring on a person the rights of a legal owner but then subjecting that person to the duty of exercising those rights for the benefit of other parties, legal principles concerning equity developed a series of onerous duties which now have parallels in other areas of law, particularly agency law, partnership law and company law. These rules cover the obligations of 'fiduciaries'. I would argue that very similar principles are now found in Japanese civil law in the provisions dealing with representatives, partners, company directors and company auditors.

Third, some, including myself, would identify equity primarily by reference to the remedies it offers, remedies that are now administered along with the common law remedies by the same judge. The unique remedies exercised against the person were the basis of the Lord *Chancellor's* authority. He could tell you to do something, or not to do something and you went to jail if you disobeyed, even though you were exercising your common law rights. My understanding is that the key equitable remedies all exist in Japan: specific performance, injunctions, declarations and damages. If common law and civil law remedies are virtually the same in general structure, even if differing in details, can reference to remedies be used to 'identify', or distinguish, the two allegedly different systems of law in Japan and the Anglo-American world?

V. New Theories of Comparative Law

For these reasons, I do not think that Japan can be 'identified' simply as a civil law system, or as a common law system. A detailed analysis would be needed to see if 'civil law' in 21st century civil law systems has any unified identity, apart from their common origins in Roman law, by a close analysis of similar or historically linked provisions in legislation. I think the contemporary legal function of each provision would also need to be explored in each society.

Attempting a close comparison of seemingly similar provisions also may be fraught with danger due to translation problems. For example, many of the papers for this conference refer to the concept of 'warranty'. In the common law of insurance, the word 'warranty' has a meaning similar to guarantee. However, it has its more generally applicable meaning in the common law of contract which is set out in my State's Goods Act[36] as:

> '"Warranty" means an agreement with reference to goods which are the subject of a contract of sale but *collateral to the main purpose* of such contract the breach of which gives rise to claim *of damages but not the right to reject the goods and treat the contract as repudiated.*'[37]

36 Goods Act Victoria 1958.
37 Emphasis added.

A similar meaning is given for English law in Halsbury's Laws of England (4th edition) Vol. 18, § 1299 and for American law in Black's Law Dictionary (8th edition 2004). Lord *Greene* MR once said that 'Warranty is one of the most ill-used expressions in the legal dictionary' before repeating that it referred to a collateral or incidental promise in a contract.[38]

The common law focuses on the right to damages or to repudiate the contract in the case of breach. It sets up a hierarchy of terms in any contract and gives them different weight. If you were examining this issue in the 1960s and 1970s, you would have intersected with a false trail started by the English courts about the 'fundamental breach' of a contract that gave rise to the right to repudiate, and other breaches that did not. However, I don't recall any real focus on the nature of performance, relating to the nature of the thing to be delivered. Until reading *Kitagawa's* paper I was blissfully unaware of the significance of the term 'warranty' (liability for defect in things) in Japanese law. I had simply understood it to be one aspect of product liability law sounding in contract.

Are there any other useful comparative law devices to confer an 'identity' on a system? Let me refer briefly to two recent attempts at creating new classifications for legal identities.

'The European legal systems were built on a Judeo-Christian culture, though they have become increasingly secular over the last century. The claim of universality for laws has been with us since the enactment of the Napoleonic Codes. Some Europeans and Americans have attempted to divorce law from the underlying culture, and a very recent manifestation of this is seen in the works of the law and economics scholars.[39] However, other contemporary thinkers such as *Mark van Hoecke*[40] have made culture the key distinguishing feature of legal systems. I think *van Hoecke's* system of identities based on

38 *Finney* v. *Allen* [1943] 1 KB 405 at 430.

39 For an evaluation of Japan from the Law and Economics perspective see M. Ramseyer and M. Nakazato, *Japanese Law: An Economic Appraisal* (Chicago 1999).

40 M. van Hoecke and M. Warrington, 'Legal Cultures, Legal Paradigms and Legal Doctrine: Towards a New Model for Comparative Law' (1998) 47 ICLQ 495.

underlying cultural families is a step forward. He would identify legal cultures as "western" or "non-western" by their approach to three issues: the society's concept of law; the role of law in the society; and the way conflicts are handled in the society. He argues that western societies and non-western societies, divided into Asian, Islamic and African societies, deal with these issues in very distinctive ways. However, his starting point is to define the "western legal culture" and then distinguish other systems from that western culture. In my view his treatment of other systems is very superficial. For example he equates "Asian legal culture" only with Confucian societies.'[41] His classifications are made all the more important by his assertion that it may be impossible to compare legal systems from two different legal cultures.

Note that *van Hoecke* does not single out the nature of civil law in conferring a western or Asian identify on a legal system. His three criteria would involve an analysis of civil law principles in order to understand the Japanese concept of law and the role of law, and the Japanese approach to dispute resolution, but it is not central to the theory. In particular, does Japan see a key role for civil law in its legal structure, or is it still part of a 'Confucian Asia' in associating law with public order and criminal sanctions? Again, do the Japanese consciously use civil law principles in the day-to-day ordering of their affairs and in resolving disputes? It is hard for me to escape the conclusion that Japan is more 'western' than 'Asian' on the basis of the application of the first two criteria to its civil law system, and the whole thrust of *Kawashima's* argument as far ago as 1963 was to argue that the Japanese were increasingly resorting to the civil law rules in resolving their disputes.

Let me repeat my earlier conclusion: 'based on my three decades of work on Japan, I think that these three issues in fact have been constantly used by foreign commentators to identify distinguishing characteristics of the Japanese legal system. In most cases the aim has been to differentiate Japan from the United States. The English-language literature on Japanese law goes much deeper than any of the general comparative studies outlined above. For my detailed views on these issues, I would like to simply refer you to arguments

41 Smith, n 2 *supra*.

that I have been pondering since a previous international symposium at Kyushu University in November 2002[42], and which I have subsequently revised and published in 2004 in the Bond University Law Review.[43, 44]

Interestingly, *von Hoecke* asserts that it is impossible to compare legal systems from two different legal cultures. If Japan's legal culture is indeed non-western, he seems to be saying that it is pointless comparing Japan to western legal systems. However, even if Japan was a non-western culture, in the close doctrinal context of the Civil Code some scope for comparison does seem to exist, due to the clear historical links. However, these rules would also need to be examined in the context of each society.

There has been a third typology offered by a scholar versed in both the civil law and American law systems. However, I think that this recent sophisticated attempt to establish a system for classifying legal systems also breaks down when it is applied to Asia by its author, and more particularly when he applies it to Japan.[45]

I refer particularly to the work of *Ugo Mattei* in 1997. He attempted a different approach to the taxonomy (or identification) of legal systems, based on a different set of identifying criteria. He identified legal systems as falling into one of three groups:

(1) Systems that follow the rule of law in the European sense of allocating law an autonomous zone, separate from politics, religion and morality and allowing law to control the rulers.

(2) Systems in which law and politics are not separate, and where law does not control the rulers, rather, the rulers control law and use it as an instrument of control.

(3) Systems where law is subsumed in a prevailing traditional religious or social philosophical system.

42 Kyushu University Faculty of Law and Japan Society for the Promotion of Science, 2002 Asian Science Seminar 'Law and the Open Society in Asia'.
43 M. Smith, 'Comparative Law and Legal Culture' (2003) 15 *Bond Law Review* 12.
44 Smith, n 2 *supra.*
45 U. Mattei, 'Three Patterns of Law' (1997) 45 Am. J. Comp. L. 5.

I find this system of identification attractive in theory, but disagree with his application of the theory to countries in practice, especially to Japan. He insists on identifying Japan with the third group, over the objections of *Frank Upham*, a leading specialist on Japan, who, like me, would identify 21st Century Japan among the rule of law group.[46]

In general terms, civil society in Japan has been ruled since 1947 by a Constitution that proclaims the primacy of law. In the civil law area, we would need more detailed studies in English to establish the extent to which civil law principles set out in the legislation actually are autonomous from traditional morality and religion, or from modern politics. Certainly, the only major modifications to the Civil Code in the immediate post-war period did remove provisions from the family law area that upheld Confucian concepts. The scope for interpretation allowed to judges is very relevant here, as in interpreting very general words or concepts they are in a position to assert what they see as 'Japanese' values.

VI. My View of the Identity of Japanese Civil Law

If I do not find any clear civil law or common law 'identity' for the Japanese civil law system, what are the characteristics of the system in my view? In my Waseda university paper I set out ten characteristics of the Japanese legal system in general that I believe are essential to its identity. I will restate them here and add some comments on those aspects that relate most directly to civil law.

(1) It is a long-standing, *mature* system in its current form. The constitutional and public law systems have followed western models for over 100 years and in its present forms have been operating for almost 60 years. *The private law system is at least 100 years old and has undergone little legislative change with the exception of family law.* The court system and the civil and criminal procedure codes that are used in the courts also have a settled history of continuity, with only one major period of

46 Smith, n 2 *supra*.

change in the 1940s. Indeed, Japan is one of the oldest of the 'modern' civil law systems.

(2) The Japanese legal system is an *evolving* system; it is not static. This is clearly true of the civil law. While the Civil Code has not been amended, apart from the family law provisions, civil law has developed through judicial interpretation and the adoption of new laws, like the Consumer Protection Contracts Law of 2001 and the Product Liability Law of 1994 (effective July 1, 1995).

(3) Japan has been adept at *assimilating* new laws into a long-established society, so much so that this is part of its legal identity. All of the papers at this seminar refer to the process of assimilating foreign civil law principles in Japan, whether they are from Germany, France or the common law sphere.

(4) Japan has successfully *adapted western laws to a non-western* (non-Christian) *society*, and both the processes and the results are part of its legal identity. This is clearly evident in the civil law system.

(5) Compared with most nations of the world, Japan's legal system operates successfully in the context of a *highly developed economy*.

(6) The Japanese legal identity is based on a *highly literate people* who, on any measure, are highly legally literate. This is reflected in the number of law graduates, the ease of access to the written laws (if not to the case law), and the quality of news reports about law, including international legal issues.

(7) The high level of *cultural homogeneity*, in language/religions/aesthetic culture, is a key part of Japan's legal identity. This has many manifestations in the operation of the civil law system.

(8) The Japanese legal identity involves a *complex interplay of factors* that cannot be reduced to any simple formula. I personally do not subscribe to any overarching explanations of the system, or how it works.[47]

47 Cf eg Haley, n 10 *supra*.

(9) Using the so-called Mattei classification, Japan's legal identity clearly involves a commitment to the *rule of law*, although this may be stronger in the public law sphere than in private law.

(10) Following the *van Hoecke* analysis, I think we also usefully can focus the Japanese legal identity around his three issues:

- The modern Japanese *concept of law* is probably not uniform across the community. Those educated in the law faculties of universities probably have a quite western concept, and allocate to law its own autonomous sphere. However, the continuity of traditional thought after over 100 years of the current system, and more than sixty years since the concepts of *kokutai* were discredited, is still asserted. If there is still a Confucian, or *Tokugawa*, concept of law prevailing, then this would indeed be an important characteristic of Japan's legal identity. Many commentators still assert that the traditional social concepts prevail over the adopted laws, but where is the contemporary evidence for this?

- The *role of law* in modern Japan seems to me to be constantly expanding into new fields. While the argument 30 years ago was that Japanese law was unimportant and that people avoided the legal system and equated law with punishments, today, my daily newspapers are full of examples of contemporary Japanese people using the legal system to achieve a wide range of results.

- *Dispute resolution* has been a central issue in my research on Japanese law, *and in most analyses of Japanese law*. The identity of Japanese Law in many articles is built around supposedly characteristic approaches to dispute resolution, ranging from the traditional use of *wakai* or *chotei*, in preference to litigation, to economic analyses showing that the court system demonstrates a degree of certainty that eliminates the need for litigation. Along the way, the Japanese legal identity has been framed around the number of (or lack of) lawyers, the lack of judges, the lack of litigation in general and the absence of litigation in areas of interest to western lawyers, such as administrative litigation, tax litigation and corporate

> litigation.[48] All of these analyses have been challenged, and the challenges help to clarify the identity of Japanese law.[49] One crucial issue that needs further study is the tendency for North American lawyers to equate the rule of law with the use of courts to resolve disputes. A broader investigation of the rule of law would cover the use of law to resolve disputes through the negotiating process or the mediation/conciliation process. Is dispute resolution outside the courts in Japan based on the application of relevant law, or does it really occur without resorting to law?'

In summary, Japan's civil law system is identified by its maturity, its evolutionary nature, its assimilation of western legal principles into a highly literate, culturally homogeneous non-western industrial society, and by its consistency with the principles of the rule of law in private affairs.

VII. Outlook: Japanese Law in the 21st Century

As a common lawyer, I am naturally interested in how Japanese civil law will develop in the future. The other papers under discussion at this conference have suggested that while German or French influence may be waning as those systems develop along their own 21st century trajectories, Japan is increasingly assessing EU law and U.S. law for the purposes of developing its own system to meet new social challenges. Examples are doctrinal developments in tort law, bankruptcy law, and corporation law. While Japan may identify with certain sources of certain laws, it is difficult to say that the Japanese system is ever identical to any of those systems. Looking ahead, when Japan does adopt a new law, will it follow subsequent doctrinal developments at the source, will it re-interpret doctrines according to a

48 There is a huge amount of English literature in this area, sparked by Professor *Kawashima* in the 1960s and taken up by Professor *Haley*, among others, in the 1970s. A representative sample extracted for US law students is in K. Milhaupt, J.M. Ramseyer and M. Young, *Japanese Law in Context: Readings in Society, the Economy and Politics* (Cambridge MA 2001) 107–141.

49 For example the extensive work in English by *John Haley* and *Mark Ramseyer*.

third country system, or will it apply its own approaches, taking into account its own social needs, rather that following the demands of academic and judicial logic, as has been traditionally applied to the evolution of legislation?

Japan was a model in the 20th century for emerging nation-states in Asia to follow in terms of legal transplantations and transformations. However, as a mature legal system I doubt if it will follow the path it followed for the first 50 years of the Civil Code, as sketched out by *Kitagawa*, and simply follow one foreign national model in developing legislative interpretations.

Bei Fragen zur Produktsicherheit wenden Sie sich bitte an:
If you have any questions regarding product safety,
please contact:

Walter de Gruyter GmbH
Genthiner Straße 13
10785 Berlin
productsafety@degruyterbrill.com